2-21

THE ORIENTAL INSTITUTE OF THE UNIVERSITY OF CHICAGO

ASSYRIOLOGICAL STUDIES • NO. 19

THE AKKADIAN INFLUENCES ON ARAMAIC

By
STEPHEN A. KAUFMAN

THE ORIENTAL INSTITUTE OF THE UNIVERSITY OF CHICAGO
ASSYRIOLOGICAL STUDIES • NO. 19
THE UNIVERSITY OF CHICAGO PRESS • CHICAGO AND LONDON

International Standard Book Number: 0-226-62281-9
Library of Congress Catalog Card Number: 74-16674

The University of Chicago Press, Chicago 60637
The University of Chicago Press, Ltd., London

Published 1974. Printed in the United States of America.

In Memory of
Eduard Yechezkel Kutscher

ACKNOWLEDGMENTS

This book represents a substantial revision of my doctoral dissertation presented to the faculty of the Graduate School of Yale University in candidacy for the degree of Doctor of Philosophy in 1970. Its subject was suggested by Professor Franz Rosenthal, who also served as my major advisor. Other readers, all of whom gave freely of their time and valuable counsel, were professors J. J. Finkelstein, W. W. Hallo, and Marvin H. Pope. I take this opportunity to offer them once again my appreciation and gratitude and to express the hope that this study does no disservice to the consistently high quality of their instruction and scholarship.

The decision to prepare this work for publication, and to do so as soon as possible, was taken at the urging of many teachers and colleagues, chief among them the late Professor E.Y. Kutscher. His enthusiasm and assurances as the quality of its contents far outweighed my own dissatisfactions with its less than ideal dissertation style. During my year in Jerusalem and later, during his last trip to America, we discussed together almost every substantive issue treated herein, often disagreeing, to be sure. It is with deep sadness and sincere gratitude that I dedicate this book to the memory of this great scholar, teacher, and friend.

I am grateful to Yale University, whose Sterling Fellowship enabled me to devote full time to the researching of the material collected herein, and to the Hebrew University, for granting me the Warburg Prize and a post-doctoral fellowship which allowed me to spend a year in Jerusalem doing additional research.

Stephen A. Kaufman

Chicago
April 1974

CONTENTS

ABBREVIATIONS

AANL	Rome. Accademia Nazionale dei Lincei. Atti. . . (Rome, 1847—).
AbKM	Leipzig. Deutsche morgenlandische gesellschaft. Abhandlungen fur die Kunde des Morgenlandes (Leipzig, etc., 1859—).
AD	G. R. Driver. Aramaic Documents of the Fifth Century B.C. (Oxford, 1954; abridged edition, Oxford, 1957).
Additamenta	S. Krauss, B. Geiger, *et al.* Additamenta ad librum Aruch Completum (reprint, New York, 1955).
Adon	*KAI*, No. 266.
AF	Franz Rosenthal. Die aramaistische Forschung seit Theodor Nöldeke's Veröffentlichungen (Leiden, 1939).
AfO	Archiv für Orientforschung (Berlin, etc., 1938—).
AG	N. Aime-Giron. Textes araméens d'Egypte (Cairo, 1931).
AHw.	W. von Soden. Akkadisches Handwörterbuch (Wiesbaden, 1959—).
AJSL	American Journal of Semitic Languages and Literatures (Chicago, etc., 1884-1941).
Akk.	Akkadian.
ANET	James B. Pritchard, ed. Ancient Near Eastern Texts Relating to the Old Testament (2d ed., Princeton, 1955; 3d ed., 1969).
An.Or.	Rome. Pontifico instituto biblico. Analecta Orientalia (Rome, 1931—).
AOAT	Alter Orient und altes Testament (Neukirchen-Vluyn, 1969—).
AP	A. Cowley. Aramaic Papyri of the Fifth Century B.C. (Oxford, 1923).
Ar.	Aramaic.
Arab.	Arabic.
ARMT	André Parrot and Georges Dossin. Archives royales de Mari (Paris, 1950—).

Ar.Or.	Archiv Orientální (Prague, 1929——).
Aruch	The Talmudic dictionary of Nathan ben Jeḥiel, in the edition of A. Kohut. Aruch Completum (8 vols.; reprint, New York, 1955).
AS	Chicago. University. Oriental Institute. Assyriological Studies (Chicago, 1931——).
AS, No. 16	Studies in Honor of Benno Landsberger (1965)
Ass.	Assyrian.
Aššur Ostracon	*KAI*, No. 233.
Aššur	M. Lidzbarski. Altaramäische Urkunden aus Assur (Leipzig, 1921).
BA	Biblical Aramaic.
BA	The Biblical Archaeologist (New Haven, etc., 1938——).
Bab.	Babylonian.
BASOR	Bulletin of the American Schools of Oriental Research (South Hadley, etc., 1919——).
BDB	F. Brown, S. R. Driver and C. O. Briggs. A Hebrew and English Lexicon of the Old Testament (Oxford, 1962).
Behistun	The Aramaic version of the Behistun inscription. *AP*, pp. 248 ff.
BH	Biblical Hebrew.
Bi.Or.	Bibliotheca Orientalis (Leiden, 1943——).
BSOAS	Bulletin of the School of Oriental and African Studies (London, 1917——).
BT	Babylonian Talmud(ic).
BWL	W. G. Lambert. Babylonian Wisdom Literature (Oxford, 1960).
BZAW	Zeitschrift für die alttestamentliche Wissenschaft. Beiheft (Geissen, etc., 1896——).
CAD	I. J. Gelb, *et al.*, eds. The Assyrian Dictionary of the Oriental Institute of the University of Chicago (Chicago and Gluckstadt, 1956——).
CAH	The Cambridge Ancient History (rev. ed. Vos. I and II; Cambridge, 1961——).
Caquot, "Inscription"	André Caquot. "Une inscription araméenne d'époque assyrienne," Hommages a André Dupont-Sommer (Paris, 1971). Pp. 9-16.
CIWA	H. C. Rawlinson. The Cuneiform Inscriptions of Western Asia (5 vols.; London, 1861-1884).

CPA	Christian Palestinian Aramaic.
CT	London. British Museum. Cuneiform Texts from Babylonian Tablets (London, 1896—).
DEA	L. Delaporte. Épigraphes araméens (Paris, 1912).
DISO	Charles-F. Jean and Jacob Hoftijzer. Dictionnaire des inscriptions sémitiques de l'ouest (Leiden, 1965).
DJD	Discoveries in the Judaean Desert (Oxford, 1955-62).
EA	J. A. Knudtzon. Die El-Amarna Tafeln (Leipzig, 1908-15).
ESA	Epigraphic South Arabian.
GAG	W. von Soden. Grundriss der akkadischen Grammatik (Rome, 1952).
GAG Erganz.	W. von Soden. Ergänzungsheft zum Grundriss der akkadischen Grammatik (Rome, 1969).
HABL	R. F. Harper. Assyrian and Babylonian Letters Belonging to the Kouyonjik Collection of the British Museum (14 vos.; London and Chicago, 1892-1914).
Hat.	Hatran.
Heb.	Hebrew.
Hh.	Lexical series HAR.ra = *hubullu* (Hh. I-IV, Landsberger, *MSL* V; Hh V-VII, Landsberger, *MSL* VI; Hh VIII-XII, Landsberger, *MSL* VII; Hh XIII-XIV, XVIII, Landsberger, *MSL* VIII; Hh XXIII, Oppenheim-Hartman, *JAOS* Suppl. X 22-29).
HM	R. Macuch. Handbook of Classical and Modern Mandaic (Berlin, 1965).
HUCA	Hebrew Union College. Annual (Cincinnati, 1914—).
IEJ	Israel Exploration Journal (Jerusalem, 1950—).
Imp. Ar.	Imperial Aramaic.
IOS	Jerusalem. Israel Oriental Society. Oriental notes and studies (Jerusalem, 1951—).
JA	Journal Asiatique (Paris, 1822—).
JAr.	Jewish Aramaic.
JAOS	Journal of the American Oriental Society (New Haven, 1849—).

JBL	Journal of Biblical Literature (Middletown, Conn., 1881—).
JCS	Journal of Cuneiform Studies (New Haven, 1947—).
JEOL	Leiden. Societe Orientate Ex Oriente Lux. Vooraziatisch-Egyptische genootschap Ex Oriente Lux. Jaarbericht (Leiden, 1933—).
JESHO	Journal of Economic and Social History of the Orient (Leiden, 1957—).
JNES	Journal of Near Eastern Studies (Chicago, 1942—).
JNWSL	Journal of Northwest Semitic Languages (Leiden, 1971—).
JPA	Jewish Palestinian Aramaic.
JRAS	London. Royal Asiatic Society of Great Britain and Ireland. Journal (London, 1834—).
JSS	Journal of Semitic Studies (Manchester, 1956—).
KAI	H. Donner and W. Röllig. Kanaanäische und aramäische Inschriften (3 vols.; Wiesbaden, 1962-68).
KBL	L. Koehler and W. Baumgartner. Lexicon in Veteris Testamenti Libros, with Supplementum ad L. . . (2d ed., Leiden, 1958; 3d ed., revised by W. Baumgartner, *et al.*, Lieferung 1, ʾ-tbh, Leiden, 1967).
KBo	Berlin. Deutsche Orient-gesellschaft. Keilschrifttexte aus Boghazköi, Vol. I—. Wissenschaftliche veröffentlichungen (Leipzig, 1923—).
KUB	Berlin. Deutsche Orient-gesellschaft. Keilschrifturkunden aus Boghazköi (Berlin, 1921—).
LB	Late Babylonian.
Leš.	Academy of the Hebrew Language. Lešonénu (Jerusalem, 1929—).
lex.	for Akkadian words: attested only in lexical texts; for Syriac: attested only in the native Syriac lexicographers.
LS	C. Brockelmann. Lexicon Syriacum (2d ed., Halle, 1928).
MA	Middle Assyrian.
MAD	Chicago. University. Oriental Institute.

	Materials for the Assyrian Dictionary (Chicago, 1952—).
Mand.	Mandaic.
MAOG	Berlin. Altorientalische gesellschaft. Mitteilungen (Leipzig, 1925-43).
MB	Middle Babylonian.
MCT	O. Neugebauer and A. Sachs. Mathematical Cuneiform Texts (New Haven, 1945).
MD	E. S. Drower and R. Macuch. A Mandaic Dictionary (Oxford, 1963).
MDP	France. Memoires de la Délégation en Perse (Paris, 1900—).
MG	T. Nöldeke. Mandäische Grammatik (Halle, 1875).
MGWJ	Monatschrift für Geschichte und Wissenschaft des Judenthums (Frankfort, etc., 1851—).
MH	Mishnaic Hebrew.
MRS	C. Schaeffer, ed. Mission de Ras Shamra (Paris, 1936—).
MSL	Benno Landsberger, ed. Materials for the Sumerian Lexicon (Rome, 1937—).
MVAG	Berlin. Vorderasiatisch-Aegyptische Gesellschaft. Mitteilungen (Berlin, etc., 1896—).
NA	Neo-Assyrian.
Nab.	Nabatean.
NB	Neo-Babylonian.
OA	Old Assyian.
OAkk.	Old Akkadian.
OB	Old Babylonian.
OIP	Chicago. University. Oriental Institute. Oriental Institute Publications (Chicago, 1924—).
OLZ	Orientalistische Literaturzeitung (Berlin, etc., 1898—).
Onk.	Targum Onkelos.
Or.	Rome. Pontificio instituto biblico. Orientalia (Rome, 1920—).
OT	Old Testament.
Paik.	E. Herzfeld. Paikuli (Berlin, 1924).
Palm.	Palmyran.
PBS	Philadelphia. University. University Museum. Publications of the Babylonian Section (Philadelphia, 1911—).
PEQ	Palestine Exploration Quarterly (London, 1869—).

Persepolis	R. A. Bowman. Aramaic Ritual Texts from Persepolis. *OIP* XCI (Chicago, 1970).
Phoen.	Phoenician.
Phrah.	E. Ebeling. Das aramäisch-mittelpersische Glossar Frahang-i-Pahlavik. . . (Leipzig, 1941).
Proceedings	Proceedings of the International Conference on Semitic Studies held in Jerusalem, 19-23 July 1965 (Jerusalem, 1969).
PRT	E. Klauber. Politisch-religiöse Texte aus der Sargonidenzeit (Leipzig, 1913).
PRU	C. Schaeffer, ed. Le Palais royal d'Ugarit, Vols. II-VI. *MRS* VI— (Paris, 1955—).
RA	Revue d'assyriologie et d'archéologie orientale (Paris, 1884—).
RB	Revue biblique (Paris, 1892—).
REJ	Revue des études juives et historia Judaica (Nos. 101-17, n.s. 1-17; Nos. 118—, 3. ser.; Paris, 1880—).
RES	Revue des études sémitiques et Babyloniaca (Paris, 1934-45).
RH	Rabbinic Hebrew.
RHA	Revue hittite et asianique (Paris, 1930—).
RQ	Revue de Qumrân (Paris, 1958—).
RSO	Revista degli Studi orientali (Rome, 1907—).
Sam.	Samaritan.
SB	Standard Babylonian.
St.Or.	Studia Orientalia Edidit Societas Orientalis Fennica (Helsinki, 1925—).
Sum.	Sumerian.
Suppl. *VT*	Vestus Testamentum. Supplement (1959—).
Syr.	Syriac.
Targ.	Targum.
TCL	Paris. Musée national du Louvre. Textes cunéiformes (Paris, 1910—).
Ugaritica V	J. Nougayrol, *et al*. Ugaritica V. *MRS* XV (Paris, 1968).
UF	Ugarit-Forschungen (Bonn, 1969—).
Ug.	Ugaritic.
UT	C. Gordon. Ugaritic Textbook. *An.Or*. XXXVIII (Rome, 1965 with Supplement, 1967).
Uruk	The cuneiform Aramaic incantation from Uruk-Warka.
VAS	Berlin. Staatliche Museen. Vorderasiatische Schriftdenkmäler der Königlichen museen (Leipzig, 1907—).
VT	Vestus Testamentum (Leiden, 1951—).

Wagner	Max Wagner. Die lexikalischen und grammatikalischen Aramaismen in alttestamentlichen Hebräisch. *BZAW* XCVI (Berlin, 1966).
Wb.KAS	M. Ullman, *et al*. Wörterbuch der klassischen arabischen Sprache, in fascicles (Wiesbaden, 1960—).
WZKM	Wiener Zeitschrift für die Kunde des Morgenlandes (Wien, 1887—).
YBT	New Haven. University. Yale Oriental Series. Babylonian Texts (New Haven, 1915—).
YOS	New Haven. University. Yale Oriental Series. Researches (New Haven, 1912—).
YT	Jerusalem Talmud.
Z	H. Zimmern. Akkadische Fremdwörter als Beweis für babylonischen Kultureinfluss (2d ed., Leipzig, 1917).
ZA	Zeitschrift für Assyriologie und verwandte Gebiete (Leipzig, etc., 1886—).
ZAW	Zeitschrift für die alttestamentliche Wissenschaft (Giessen, etc., 1881—).
ZDMG	Leipzig. Deutschen Morgenländischen Gesellschaft. Zeitschrift (Leipzig, etc., 1847—).
ZNW	Zeitschrift für die neutestamentliche Wissenschaft (Geissen, etc., 1923—).

NOTE

Sheer oversight is responsible for the omission of any reference in the body of this work to the important review-article by M. Dietrich, "Zum mandäischen Wortschatz," *Bi.Or.* XXV (1967) 290-305. (Thanks are due Dr. M. Sokoloff of Bar Ilan University for bringing it to my attention.) Regrettably, space prohibits a detailed consideration of all the etymological suggestions presented therein. For the present, suffice it to note his independent (and indeed prior) recognition of the Akkadian origin of *marula* and *šara*. Of the new Akkadian etymologies offered by Dietrich, the following merit serious consideration:

hipa: "violence" (apparently not actually attested in Mandaic, but found in Syriac *ḥʾpʾ* [and in JAr. *ḥyph*, but only in Targum Proverbs, i.e., from Syriac])—Hardly from *hīpu*, "break," but perhaps from the expression *hip(i) libbi*, "panic."

HUṢ, HṢṢ: "to construct with reeds"—*haṣāṣu*, etc.

kalia, kiliata, "dike"—*kālû, kilâtu*.

riuana, "merciful(?)"—*rēmē/ānu*.

INTRODUCTION

The Aramaic language is unique among the Semitic languages in that its development as a living language is well documented for a period of almost three thousand years, from the earliest inscriptions in the first centuries of the first millennium B.C. until the present day. Owing to various factors of geography and history, during the course of these three millennia various Aramaic dialects came in contact with other languages of the Near East, leaving a discernible mark on many of them and, in turn, becoming subject to the influence of these languages as well. Thus, the study of Aramaic is an excellent choice for the linguist who seeks to learn about the problems of languages in contact.[1]

This fact has by no means escaped the attention of earlier scholars. Comprehensive, though mostly out-of-date studies of borrowing, mostly of loanwords, are available for Greek and Latin in Aramaic,[2] Old Persian in Aramaic,[3]

1. The nature and characteristics of languages in contact and bilingualism have received much attention from linguists in recent years, especially after the publication of Uriel Weinreich's important book, *Languages in Contact* (New York, 1953). See, for example, James E. Alatis, ed., *Report of the Twenty-First Annual Round Table Meeting on Linguistics and Language Studies, Bilingualism and Language Contact* (Washington, D.C., 1970) and Els Oksaar, "Bilingualism," in *Current Trends in Linguistics IX* (The Hague, 1972) 476-511. Nevertheless, little if anything has been presented in the way of general conclusions that might help scholars investigating similar phenomena in ancient and imperfectly known literary languages.

2. S. Krauss, *Griechische und lateinische Lehnwörter im Talmud, Midrasch und Targum* (Berlin, 1898-99); A. Schall, *Studien über griechische Fremdwörter im Syrischen* (Darmstadt, 1960). The latter is limited to the Greek words in the earliest Syriac texts. For the reverse see H. Lewy, *Die semitischen Fremdwörter im Griechischen* (Berlin, 1895) and the recent work by Émilia Masson, *Recherches sur les plus anciens emprunts sémitiques en Grec* (Paris, 1967).

3. See the bibliography in *AF*, pp. 119 f. More recent work on Achaemenid and Biblical Aramaic is to be found scattered in many articles and reviews, notable by W. Eilers and E. Benveniste. For Middle Persian in Aramaic see G. Widengren, *Iranisch-semitische Kulturbegenung in parthischer Zeit* (Cologne and Opladen, 1960) pp. 25 ff., 89 ff., and S. Telegdi, "Essai sur la phonétique des emprunts Iraniens en Araméen talmudique," *JA* CCXXVI (1935) 177-256. A study of the influence of Aramaic on the early Iranian dialects is well-nigh impossible because of the borrowed writing system with all of its logograms.

Aramaic in Biblical Hebrew,[4] Aramaic in Mishnaic Hebrew, and Aramaic in Arabic and in Ethiopic.[5] Notably missing from this list, however, is a study of the Akkadian influences on Aramaic and the reverse, the Aramaic influences on Akkadian (though Akkadian loanwords in general were treated by Zimmern in the work discussed below).[6] The importance of Akkadian for Aramaic studies stems from its position as the first foreign language to leave its imprint on Aramaic as a whole and from the fact that it was Akkadian that Aramaic replaced both as the native language of Mesopotamia and as the lingua franca of the ancient Near East. Accordingly, the subject under study here will be the Akkadian influences on Aramaic. To be sure, the influences of Aramaic upon the declining Akkadian dialects were quite substantial as well, but it is my belief that the study of this second group of influences, although of great importance, can be undertaken only after the results of the current study are known, though the hoped-for final synthesis must ultimately consider both processes together.

The entire spectrum of Akkadian loanwords in all languages including Aramaic was studied over fifty years ago by Heinrich Zimmern in his important work *Akkadische fremdwörter als Beweis für babylonischen Kultureinfluss*.[7] Although Zimmern's compendium remains essential for all work in this area (for example, the great majority of words discussed herein are already to be found in it), his work suffers from several major flaws: It was produced at the height of the Pan-Babylonian period of ancient Near Eastern scholarship when Akkadian was assumed to be the origin of almost everything. Furthermore, since, as indicated by its title, the work had other than

4. Most recently Max Wagner, *Die lexikalischen und grammatikalischen Aramaismen im alttestamentlichen Hebräisch* (*BZAW*, Vol. XCVI [Berlin, 1966]). On loan-translations see E. Y. Kutscher, "Aramaic Calque in Hebrew," *Tarbiz* XXIII (1963) 118 ff. (Heb.).

5. S. Mannes, *Über den Einfluss des Aramäischen auf den Wortschatz der Mišnah an Nominal- und Verbalstämmen* (Berlin, 1899); S. Fraenkel, *Die aramäischen Fremdwörter im Arabischen* (Leiden, 1886; reprint, Hildesheim, 1962); T. Nöldeke, "Lehnwörter in und aus dem Äthiopischen," in his *Neue Beiträge zur semitischen Sprachwissenschaft* (Strassburg, 1910) pp. 32 ff. See also H. J. Polotsky, "Aramaic, Syriac, and Geʾez," *JSS* IX (1964) 1-10.

6. First steps toward a modern compilation of Aramaisms have been taken by W. von Soden, "Aramäische Wörter in neuassyrischen und neu- und spätbabylonischen Texten. Ein Vorbericht," *Or*. n.s. XXXV (1966) 1 ff., XXXVII (1968) 261 ff. See also E. S. Rimalt, "Wechselbeziehungen zwischen dem Aramäischen und dem Neubabylonischen," *WZKM* XXXIX (1932) 100 ff.

7. The first edition was published in Leipzig, 1915. The second edition, with a valuable index, appeared in 1917.

linguistic motivations,[8] it is almost completely lacking in documentation. Nevertheless, as the only work of its kind, it has remained standard, and a great many of Zimmern's overzealously suggested "Fremdwörter" have achieved an almost canonical status among Assyriologists as well as among students of West Semitic, notably Biblical Hebrew.

The other invaluable source for Akkadian etymologies of Aramaic words is to be found in the etymological notes in the second edition of C. Brockelmann's *Lexicon Syriacum* (Halle, 1928), the Akkadian material of which was prepared by P. Jensen. Unfortunately, however, many of the new suggestions proposed there by Jensen, as opposed to his earlier suggestions published in various studies (and already included in Zimmern's work), are of very dubious value.

Both of these works suffered from the ultimate and inescapable flaw of being products of their own time. Both men were truly great scholars, but Assyriology was still a new discipline, and Akkadian lexicography was just beginning to establish itself on a firm footing. In the early stages of Assyriology, each new word was more often than not assigned a meaning on the basis of its presumed Semitic cognates rather than on the accumulated evidence of usage, which was often very limited. Thus, many false correspondences were proposed, and, since Akkadian was the older language, it was usually viewed as the origin of the term in question. By Zimmern's time many of the more blatant errors had been eliminated, but many remained; nor are we free of some of them today, as the continuing stream of Akkadian lexicographic studies indicates.

Since the 1920's, a great deal of significant new evidence has come to light which alters the nature of the material that must be considered when making judgments on etymological matters. The discovery and study of Ugaritic have shed important new light on the comparativist's view of the North West Semitic languages while expanding our knowledge of West Semitic lexicography and pushing back its chronology. The archives of Ras Shamra and particularly of Mari have given us a new, if as yet uncertain, picture of the relationship between speakers of Akkadian and West Semitic during the second millennium. Aside from these, new Akkadian texts in great numbers and analyses of them have and are constantly being published. In the field of lexicography, great advances have been made, most notably in the area of material

8. And, as shown by his concluding remarks, other than scholarly motivations as well.

culture. Important here have been the works of Benno Landsberger and A. Salonen, and the works of R. Campbell-Thompson are also significant. Certainly most crucial for our immediate purposes are the two modern dictionary projects, the Chicago *Assyrian Dictionary* and W. von Soden's *Akkadisches Handwörterbuch*, which already make available an analysis of the majority of the vocabulary of Akkadian. The study of Akkadian grammar was greatly advanced by the publication of von Soden's *Grundriss der akkadischen Grammatik*. Our knowledge of Sumerian, also important for the proper understanding of Akkadian, though still far from perfect, has progressed immensely in the last generation.

Nor have Aramaic studies remained static, though perhaps their progress has not been quantitatively as large as the recent achievements of cuneiform studies. Many important new groups of texts have been published, even new dialects discovered. New lexicographical works have very recently appeared, notably dealing with the older stages of Aramaic[9] and with Mandaic.[10] Significant new studies of Aramaic dialects have been made, new issues raised and old ones re-examined. Thus, the time now seems ripe for studies of the type undertaken here.

9. C.-F. Jean and Jacob Hoftijzer, *Dictionnaire des inscriptions sémitiques de l'ouest* (Leiden, 1965); I. N. Vinnikov, "Slovar' aramejskich nadpisj," *Palestinskij Sbornik* III-XIII (1958-68).

10. *MD*.

I

PRELIMINARY CONSIDERATIONS

GOALS OF THIS STUDY

Any etymological study of Aramaic should have at least three immediate results of interest to the philologist. It should improve his knowledge of the meaning of the Aramaic words studied; it should enable him to choose from a group of variants the form that is most probably correct (a problem especially frequent in Jewish Aramaic texts); and it should permit him to derive some rules to guide further etymological inquiries. Because of the special role that Aramaic played in the ancient Near East, however, a properly oriented study of the Akkadian influences on Aramaic should shed light on some other important issues as well. Accordingly, an attempt has been made here to concentrate on the evidence for Akkadian-Aramaic contact during the major period of that contact, roughly the first half of the first millennium B.C., which witnessed the decline of Akkadian as a spoken language, its replacement by Aramaic as the language of Mesopotamia, and the use of Aramaic as the lingua franca of the entire Near East. As a basic outcome of such a study, we might expect an improvement in our knowledge of the relationships which existed between the two languages and between the groups of people that spoke them.[1] More specifically our study should help to illuminate the two languages themselves, or rather the various dialects of the two languages, and their interrelationships.

Like all long-lived and widespread languages, Akkadian developed many dialects. Modern scholars generally divide them into two major groups—Babylonian and Assyrian—which can be traced as far back as the beginning of the second millennium.[2] Unfortunately, because of the important position

1. The historian will note that I have chosen to draw few historical conclusions in this work. Problems of intercultural contact in the ancient Near East are of major importance, to be sure, but also of a nature such that the evidence of language can play only a small part in their elucidation. (For some of the problems involved in such a procedure see T. E. Hope, "Loan-Words as Cultural and Lexical Symbols," *Archivum Linguisticum* XIV [1962] 111 f., especially p. 115, and XV [1963] 29 ff.) Accordingly I leave the proper use of such evidence as this work may represent to others.

2. This is not to say that Neo-Assyrian is necessarily a direct lineal descendant of Middle Assyrian, though it almost certainly is, or

of writing in Mesopotamian society and its long history, the cuneiform sources do not present a complete picture of these dialects in the period with which we are concerned. For literary purposes, in almost all cases a special dialect was employed, termed by many scholars Standard Babylonian, which functioned similarly to modern Literary Arabic,[3] and only brief glimpses of colloquial forms appear. Even in letters and economic documents, which are generally couched in dialectal Akkadian, conservative orthography is predominant, masking the actual pronunciation. Especially in matters of phonetics and phonology, though significant amounts of evidence can be accumulated from the available texts, scholars have been extremely hesitant to propose analyses that seem to contradict so much of the written evidence. At best they speak only of free variation and, in so doing often ignore some of the evidence as well as the first principle of the historical linguist, the regular nature of phonetic change. Fortunately, the study of the Neo-Assyrian and Neo-Babylonian dialects themselves has aroused some renewed interest in recent years.[4] It is hoped that this study can provide some further information on the nature of these dialects for the benefit of Assyriologists.

Similarly, one might expect some help on matters of early Aramaic phonology. To be sure, the problems there are rather different, since the alphabetic system of writing was used, and our interest centers on the bivalent nature of some letters used for phonemes which were beginning to merge with others, notably the spirants, and on evidence for the status of vowel reduction in that early period.

that either of them is a direct lineal descendant of Old Assyrian, which may in fact not be the case. But it is beyond doubt that in all these periods there was a group of mutually intelligible dialects spoken in the geographical area of Assyria which differed from that group spoken in southern Mesopotamia. The extent to which members of the two dialect groups were intelligible to each other at any given moment cannot be determined, but intermittent contact between the two groups no doubt kept the two from increasing their differences to an extreme degree.

3. Inasmuch as this dialect functioned as the language of the official cult and was thus well known orally and aurally, it could well have been spoken on a wide scale among certain classes in some periods. Nevertheless, one can be certain that the traditional orthography masks the current pronunciation even in liturgical use. As with Modern Literary Arabic, different readers of the same text might be expected to produce renditions quite mutually distinctive, each tending toward the phonetics of his own native dialect.

4. See notably for Neo-Assyrian the works of K. Deller. Manfried Dietrich has made an auspicious start on the Neo-Babylonian material.

Not all of the speakers of early Aramaic were in close contact with speakers of Akkadian. Thus, any Akkadian features found in the descendants of such dialects must have spread to them by various means through Aramaic itself. An analysis of these Akkadian features which takes into account the quantity and nature of their distribution in the various Aramaic dialects might be an important new tool in the study of the development of Aramaic, its spread throughout the Near East, and the classification and analysis of the various Aramaic dialects.

In dealing with the Aramaic dialects, however, one is immediately confronted by the problem of terminology on which, except for the broadest outlines, no great agreement is to be found in the literature. A system of terminology based mostly on chronology is now fashionable, using the terms Old Aramaic, Official or Imperial Aramaic, Middle Aramaic, and Late Aramaic, though here, too, there is disagreement, and classificatory presuppositions must be made, especially for those dialects on the boundaries of the various divisions.[5] Although I accept this terminology as adequate in most cases and support its use as an aid to scholarly communication and mutual understanding, it is clearly inadequate for our purposes here. For our terminology must not presuppose solutions to the problems we are trying to solve, nor should it mask some of the differences we are trying to discover. It should by no means be classificatory, but merely descriptive. Accordingly, the terminology to be used herein is given below together with a summary of some of the problems that each dialect or group presents to scholars.

Old Aramaic.—By Old Aramaic is meant that Aramaic represented by the earliest known Aramaic texts from Syria up until the end of the eighth century B.C.[6] This is a convenient terminal date because there is a gap of perhaps as much as a century before the next Syrian Aramaic inscriptions known to us. One of the important issues of Old Aramaic studies is whether or not to consider the unique dialect represented by the Hadad and Panammuwa inscriptions from

5. Cf. J. A. Fitzmyer, *The Genesis Apocryphon of Qumran Cave I*, (2d ed., rev.; Rome, 1971) p. 22n. Many scholars would reserve the term Late Aramaic for the modern dialects and use "middle" for Fitzmyer's "late"; see Jonas C. Greenfield, "Dialect Traits in Early Aramaic," *Leš*. XXXII (1968) 359, n. 1 (Heb.)

6. For the texts and grammar see Rainer Degen, *Altaramäische Grammatik* (*AbKM*, Vol. XXXVIII, 3 [Wiesbaden, 1969]), who omits the Samalian material, however.

Zinjirli as a dialect of Aramaic.[7] In terming this dialect Samalian Aramaic and including it in this study, I concur with the majority of scholars.[8] But what of the origin and nature of the remainder of Old Aramaic which can be called Standard Old Aramaic? There are two basic theories. One views Standard Old Aramaic as originally the dialect of the empire of Damascus, adopted by the Assyrian conquerors as they annexed the areas in the West.[9] The other sees its origins in the Aramaic spoken by the Aramaic tribes of the East and used for administrative purposes in Assyria itself.[10] Both positions take into account the fact that Aramaic inscriptions are found in places where a previous different native language (or dialect) is known or can be supposed to have existed. But there can be no doubt that by the end of the eighth century and probably earlier, Aramaic was in widespread use as the colloquial language of all of Syria. Was this all one standard dialect or were there old dialect divisions? Is Standard Old Aramaic itself really a literary dialect which masks dialectal differences or are there differences in it which accurately reflect the colloquial speech? Some of these problems have received attention,[11] but much remains unclear.

Mesopotamian Aramaic.—By the term Mesopotamian Aramaic I refer to all of the Aramaic texts known from Mesopotamia

7. *KAI,* Nos. 214-15. The short inscription of Kilammuwa, *KAI,* No. 25, is taken by many to be Phoenician like Kilammuwa's long inscription (cf. Benno Landsberger, *Samᵓal* [Ankara, 1948] p. 42, n. 102, and Donner and Röllig in *KAI*). I include it in Samalian, however (as in *DISO* and J. J. Koopmans, *Aramäische Chrestomathie* [Leiden, 1962]). There is no adequate explanation for the forms *lh* (cf. W. Röllig, *Bi.Or.* XXVII [1970] 378, n. 2) and *ḥy* in Phoenician, whereas they are quite correct in Samalian.

8. Johannes Friedrich is the main proponent of a separate classification for "Yaudic" (Samalian). See most recently "Zur Stellung des Jaudischen in der nordwestsemitischen Sprachgeschichte," *AS,* No. 16, pp. 425-29. The alternative position has been argued effectively by H. L. Ginsberg, most recently in "The North-West Semitic Languages," in B. Mazar, ed., *World History of the Jewish People* II (Tel Aviv, 1967) 62 ff. (Heb.).

9. W. F. Albright, *CAH,* fasc. 51, p. 47; B. Mazar, "The Aramean Empire and Its Relations with Israel," *BA* XXV (1962) 109 ff.; A. Dupont-Somer, *Les Araméens* (Paris, 1949) pp. 84 ff.

10. H. L. Ginsberg, "Aramaic Dialect Problems," *AJSL* L (1933) 3, LII (1936) 95-103; G. Garbini, *L'Aramaico antico* (*AANL,* "Memorie," Scienze Morali, Series VIII, Vol. VII [Rome, 1956]) pp. 282 ff. J. C. Greenfield, in *Leš.* XXXII (1968) 359, describes it only as the Aramaic used by the Assyrian governmental scribes without committing himself as to its geographic origin.

11. Notably by J. C. Greenfield, in *Leš.* XXXII 362 f. Cf. also G. Garbini, *L'Aramaico antico,* p. 275.

up until the cuneiform Aramaic incantation from Uruk, probably of the early Seleucid period.[12] Most scholars class this group with Imperial Aramaic, and in fact several of the Imperial Aramaic texts may have their origin in Mesopotamia. Aside from the important Aššur Ostracon,[13] written from Babylonia to Assyria, and the Uruk Incantation, most of these texts are short Aramaic endorsements or dockets on cuneiform tablets. On some tablets the complete text is in Aramaic without any cuneiform.[14] It is most unfortunate that our sources are so limited for this group, for it is precisely here that the contact we wish to study was taking place.

Though the differences that separated later Eastern and Western Aramaic had not yet developed, it is extremely important to realize that there must have been dialectal differences between the Aramaic of the western Syrian kingdoms, the Aramaic of the upper and middle Euphrates and its tributaries, and the Aramaic of the Arameans living on the immediate boundaries of or actually in Assyria and Babylonia themselves. The Aramaic speakers of the second and third groups had been in contact with Akkadian-speaking peoples in Assyria and Babylonia ever since the appearance of the Arameans on the stage of history,[15] and there was certainly sufficient separation for many differences with the West to develop. As we shall see, the difficulties caused by the uncertain linguistic history of this region will prove to be most problematic.

Imperial Aramaic.—Imperial Aramaic, which is also known as Official Aramaic or *Reichsaramäisch*, was the dialect used for administrative purposes in ruling the great Near Eastern empires. The texts from the Neo-Assyrian period are included in the previous two groups, and thus are not included here,[16]

12. *ANET* (3d ed.) p. 658.

13. *KAI*, No. 233.

14. The tablets from Halaf (Gozan), *ca.* 650 B.C. (J. Friedrich, "Die aramäischen Tonurkunden," in *Die Inschriften von Tell Halaf* [*AfO* Beiheft VI (Berlin, 1940)] pp. 70 ff.) are included in this group.

15. On the area of Aram Naharaim and Assyrian contacts, see primarily A. Malamat, *The Arameans in Aram Naharaim and the Rise of Their States* (Jerusalem, 1952; Heb.). For the Babylonian Arameans see J. A. Brinkman, *A Political History of Post-Kassite Babylonia*, *An. Or.*, Vol. XLIII [Rome, 1968]) pp. 267-85, and the more specialized study by M. Dietrich, *Die Aramäer Südbabyloniens in der Sargonidenzeit* (*AOAT*, Vol. VII [Neukirchen-Vluyn, 1970]).

16. Classification of the Nerab stelae (*KAI*, Nos. 225-26) is difficult. Since they come from an Aramaic-speaking area of Syria during the last years of the Assyrian period, they will be treated separately from either Old Aramaic or Imperial Aramaic, but in the final analysis they

nor are the native Mesopotamian texts from the Neo-Babylonian period. All other texts of the Neo-Babylonian and Achaemenid empires will be considered under this rubric. So, too, will the various inscriptions from peripheral areas dating well into the Christian era.[17]

With the publication of every new text, scholars are becoming increasingly aware that there is no uniform dialect of Imperial Aramaic, that at the very least localisms make themselves apparent, and that in different genres of texts different dialects are used. What can be determined about these dialects, and can the features of a general Imperial dialect be isolated? If so, can the origin of Imperial Aramaic be determined? If it is a direct development of the administrative language of the Neo-Assyrian period, as most scholars seem to agree, then Imperial Aramaic should merely be a development of Old Aramaic, if either of the theories about Old Aramaic is correct. But perhaps Old Aramaic is western, while Imperial Aramaic has its origin in the eastern colloquial dialects of Mesopotamia.

In light of these difficulties, forms will be cited as occurring in Imperial Aramaic only when no finer distinction would be productive. Normally citations will be more specific, referring to specific texts or groups of texts. The most important groups of Imperial Aramaic texts are those from Egypt and Biblical Aramaic. In the former, geographical, chronological, and dialectal differences indicate that at least three sub-groups must be distinguished: the main bulk of papyri and ostraca, primarily from Elephantine,[18] the personal letters on papyri from Hermopolis West,[19] and the official

will be shown to be Imperial Aramaic. The Nerab tablets (F. Vattioni, "Epigrafia aramaica," *Augustinianum* X [1970] Nos. 137-41), slightly later—already in the Neo-Babylonian period—must be considered under Imperial Aramaic, though the Aramaic of those tablets, like the cuneiform, is similar to that found on Babylonian tablets. The new inscription from Syria published by Caquot (Caquot, "Inscription") is also to be dated to the Neo-Babylonian period (see Chap. II, s.v. *bēl piqitti*). In this case its orthography (*ʾḥd*, "seize") clearly places it under the broad rubric of Imperial Aramaic.

17. It should be noted that in at least some of the texts of this late group from Iranian areas it is difficult to determine whether the texts are really Aramaic or merely Iranian written with many logograms; cf. W. B. Henning, "Mitteliranisch," in *Handbuch der Orientalistik*, Vol. IV: *Iranistik*, Part 1 (Leiden, 1958), pp. 27 ff.

18. Of course here further refinement is necessary as well, most notably between the letters and legal documents. Even the letters must be divided into personal and official correspondence, though the private letters, mostly on ostraca, are usually fragmentary.

19. E. Bresciani and M. Kamil, *Le lettere aramaiche di Hermopoli* (*AANL*, "Memorie," Scienze Morali, Series VIII, Vol. XII [Rome, 1966]).

letters on leather, probably sent from Babylonia, published by Driver.[20] In Biblical Aramaic, the Aramaic of Ezra and that of Daniel can be separated. The great bulk of the Aramaic in the book of Ezra is probably nearly contemporary with the events it describes and is unquestionably to be considered Imperial Aramaic, though some of the spelling may be modernized. Daniel, which most scholars now date well into the Seleucid period, is the only literary work left to us from that time, but it is still best considered to come under the broad rubric of Imperial Aramaic. Late Biblical Hebrew is also an important secondary source for Imperial Aramaic lexical material.

Monumental Dialects.—The designation Monumental Dialects is merely a convenient way to refer to Palmyran, Nabatean, and the ever increasing corpus of Hatran Aramaic. These are by no means to be considered members of the same dialect, but they are roughly contemporary, and their inscriptions are similar in nature and type. Hatran almost certainly represents a colloquial dialect with strong Eastern Aramaic traits. The nature of Palmyran and Nabatean, their relationship to a spoken Aramaic dialect and to literary Imperial Aramaic have not yet been adequately resolved.[21]

Eastern Aramaic and Western Aramaic.—The main Aramaic dialects of the first millennium of the Christian era are usually divided into Eastern and Western Aramaic—a division which is not to be confused with the earlier but as yet not fully elucidated differences between the Aramaic of Syria and that of Mesopotamia referred to above.[22] While Western Aramaic retains the corresponding features known from Old Aramaic and Imperial Aramaic, Eastern Aramaic is generally distinguished by at least four major characteristic features: *l-* or *n-* as the third person imperfect prefix, *-ê* as the ending of the masculine plural determined noun, the loss of the determining force of final *-â*, and the loss of the *n-*bearing pronominal suffixes of the imperfect.[23] The dialects of Eastern Aramaic are Syriac, Mandaic, and Babylonian Talmudic. (The latter two may be termed together Babylonian Aramaic.) In Western Aramaic are included Jewish Palestinian Aramaic,

20. G. R. Driver, *Aramaic Documents of the Fifth Century B.C.*

21. Cf. Franz Rosenthal, *Die Sprache der palmyrenischen Inschriften und ihre Stellung innerhalb des Aramäischen* (*MVAG*, Vol. XLI [Leipzig, 1936]) and *AF*, pp. 89 ff., 100 ff.; H. L. Ginsberg, "Aramaic Studies Today," *JAOS* LXII (1942) 237.

22. Rosenthal's term "Jungaramäisch" for Western Aramaic (*AF*, pp. 104 f.) has not been generally accepted.

23. For other distinguishing features see E. Y. Kutscher, "Aramaic," *Encyclopedia Judaica* III 275.

Samaritan Aramaic, and Christian Palestinian Aramaic.

Jewish Aramaic.—While there is no single dialect meant by the term Jewish Aramaic, it is often used to refer to all of the Aramaic dialects (except Biblical Aramaic) attested in Jewish literature. One of the great difficulties of Aramaic lexicography is that the existing dictionaries treat all or large portions of the corpus of Jewish Aramaic together, and it is often difficult, and sometimes impossible, to get an accurate lexical picture of any of the individual dialects. it is to be hoped that future lexicographers will see fit to prepare comparative dictionaries of related dialects, such as Babylonian Talmudic and Mandaic or the various Palestinian dialects.

For a long while the influence of Biblical Aramaic (and without a doubt, at least in the early periods, other Imperial Aramaic texts no longer preserved) made itself felt in Jewish circles; and for religious use, perhaps to provide intelligibility to speakers of various dialects, written works were composed in a literary dialect similar to Imperial Aramaic. As usual, however, dialectal traits always make themselves known. In this group we find the Targums and the still limited published material from Qumran.[24]

The Targums present us with some of the oldest problems in Aramaic studies, and debate remains lively today, largely propelled by the new impetus of Qumran studies and the discovery of a complete manuscript of a Palestinian Targum, the Codex Neofiti I.[25] The main problem is to determine the date and place of origin of the several Targums now available. Everyone seems agreed that the presently known Targums to the various books of Hagiographa are late and, though probably not all of Babylonian origin, are frequently influenced by Talmudic Aramaic.[26] While early scholars proposed a Babylonian origin

24. Of the published texts, the most important are the so-called Genesis Apocryphon (see Fitzmyer, *Genesis Apocryphon*) and the Job Targum (J. P. M. van der Ploeg, *Le Targum de Job de la grotte XI de Qumrân* [Leiden, 1971]). Megillat Ta^canit (H. Lichtenstein, in *HUCA* VIII [1931-32] 318-51) and the Antiochus Scroll (cf. G. Dalman, *Grammatik des jüdisch-palästinischen Aramäisch* [reprint; Darmstadt, 1960] p. 7) are also important representatives of this type of literature, though their dating is still subject to dispute.

25. A facsimile edition of Neofiti I was published by "Makor" Publishing, Ltd., in Jerusalem, 1970. A scholarly edition with extensive introductions is being published by Alejandro Diez Macho, *Neophyti I* (Madrid and Barcelona, 1968-71). The text of Genesis, Exodus, and Leviticus has appeared so far.

26. On the targums to the Hagiographa see R. le Déaut, *Introduction à la littérature targumique* (Rome, 1966) pp. 131 ff.; M. McNamara, *Targum and Testament* (Shannon, 1972) pp. 209 ff. That early Palestinian targums of the Hagiographa existed is shown by the fragmentary Job Targum found

for Targum Onkelos and Targum Jonathan to the Prophets and most still agree that at the very least the vocalization of these two Targums is of Babylonian origin, lively discussion still ensues over the place of origin of the consonantal text as we know it, whether Babylonian or Palestinian, and its date. For the Palestinian Targum, the diversity among the four main representatives of this group known today—Pseudo-Jonathan, the Fragment Targum (or Yerushalmi), the Geniza fragments, and the Neofiti—clearly shows that no early standardization of the text took place; but while earlier scholars believed they could prove that all of the Palestinian Targums relied upon Onkelos, this is no longer universally the case, and some now attempt to date the basic, though uncanonized Palestinian text very early while assigning Onkelos a later, Babylonian origin.[27]

Other important Jewish Aramaic texts are the inscriptions and documents from various Palestinian sites. Significant in the latter group are the Murabba^{c}at documents and the Aramaic Bar Kochba letters.[28] Also known from inscriptions but preserved primarily in the Aramaic portions of the Palestinian Talmud (Yerushalmi) and the Palestinian Midrashim is Galilean Aramaic. From Babylonia come the Jewish magic bowl texts.[29]

at Qumran as well as by the well known passage in the Babylonian Talmud (Sabb. 115*a*) telling of Gamaliel I's ban on the Targum of Job.

27. On early targumic scholarship see *AF*, pp. 127 ff. More up-to-date summaries can be found in the works cited in the previous note. The position of the Kahle school is enunciated in Matthew Black, "Aramaic Studies and the Language of Jesus," *In Memoriam Paul Kahle*, ed. Matthew Black and Georg Fohrer (*BZAW*, Vol. CIII [Berlin, 1968]) pp. 17 ff., as well as in the companion articles by M. C. Doubles ("Indications of Antiquity in the Orthography and Morphology of the Fragment Targum," pp. 79-89) and G. J. Kuiper ("A Study of the Relationship between *A Genesis Apocryphon* and the Pentateuchal Targumim in Genesis 14_{1-12}," pp. 149-61); all three show a propensity toward misstating the position of their chief antagonist, E. Y. Kutscher. Cf. also the bibliographies in Fitzmyer, *Genesis Apocryphon*, p. 24, n. 61, and p. 30, n. 71. On Targum Jonathan cf. S. H. Levey, "The Date of Targum Jonathan to the Prophets," *VT* XXI (1971) 186-96. An important article on Onkelos is M. Z. Kaddari, "Studies in the Syntax of Targum Onkelos," *Tarbiz* XXXII (1963) 232 ff. (Hebrew with English summary), which is significant for its attempt to analyze only those portions without a Biblical *Vorlage*, thus avoiding one of the most difficult aspects of targumic studies, the translation nature of the targums.

28. P. Benoit, J. Milik, and R. de Vaux, *Discoveries in the Judaean Desert*, Vol. II: *Les grottes de Murabba^{c}at* (Oxford, 1961); for the Bar Kochba letters see E. Y. Kutscher, "The Language of the Hebrew and Aramaic Letters of Bar-Koseva and His Contemporaries: A. The Aramaic Letters," *Leš.* XXV (1960-61) 117 ff. (Heb.).

29. For the Jewish magical texts see most recently Baruch A. Levine, "The Language of the Magical Bowls," in Jacob Neusner, *A History of the Jews in Babylonia* V (Leiden, 1970) 343 ff., as well as Neusner's chapter (pp. 217 ff.) in that volume.

In light of the substantial dialectal differences among the various Jewish Aramaic texts, whenever possible the specific text or text group to which a Jewish Aramaic reference belongs will be cited. Since the Palestinian Targums and Galilean Aramaic are definitely of Palestinian origin, however, the term Jewish Palestinian Aramaic will be used to refer to them as well as the other Palestinian Jewish texts when speaking of grammatical or lexical characteristics they share. Since the origin of Onkelos and Targum Jonathan is, for the present at least, uncertain, they will always be referred to separately. Only when an item is common to all groups of Jewish Aramaic (including both Targum groups and Babylonian Talmudic), and further subdivision seems fruitless (or impossible with the tools available), will the general term Jewish Aramaic be used.

Post-Biblical Hebrew is also an important source of Aramaic lexical items; it is necessary, however, to distinguish between two basic groups: Mishnaic Hebrew, the last colloquial Hebrew dialect, probably influenced by early Palestinian colloquial Aramaic as well as Imperial Aramaic but still a survival of older Hebrew and whatever Aramaisms and Akkadianisms might have been absorbed at an earlier time; and Rabbinic Hebrew, the Hebrew of the Amoraim, a literary language only, highly influenced by Biblical Hebrew and by the colloquial Aramaic of its users. The latter must accordingly be separated into Palestinian and Babylonian divisions.[30]

The other Palestinian Aramaic dialects, Samaritan and Chriatian Palestinian, do not present problems of the type one might hope to solve here.[31]

Mandaic is unquestionably a dialect of the Eastern Aramaic type, yet a controversy still exists over the

30. See in general E. Y. Kutscher, "Mittelhebräisch und Jüdisch-Aramäisch im neuen Köhler-Baumgartner," Suppl. *VT* XVI (1967) 158 ff. On Palestinian Rabbinic Hebrew see M. Sokoloff, "The Hebrew of *Berēšit Rabba* according to Ms. Vat. Ebr. 30," *Leš.* XXXIII (1968-69) 25-42, 135-49, 270-79 (Heb.), especially parts 2 and 3.

31. The greatest difficulty with Samaritan is the lack of critically edited texts and dictionaries. Z. Ben-Hayyim and R. Macuch have promised dictionaries, but for now one must use Ben-Hayyim's index to the Samaritan Hebrew, Arabic, and Aramaic dictionary to the Torah (*Hamēlīṣ*) in *The Literary and Oral Tradition of Hebrew and Aramaic amongst the Samaritans*, Vol. II (Jerusalem, 1957) and the index to the Aramaic prayers in Vol. III, Part 2 (Jerusalem, 1967), as well as the glossaries in A. E. Cowley, *The Samaritan Liturgy* (Oxford, 1909) and Z. Ben-Hayyim, "Samaritan," in F. Rosenthal, ed., *An Aramaic Handbook*, Vol. II, Part 2 (Wiesbaden, 1967). For Samaritan and Christian Palestinian in general see the relevant chapters in *AF*. See also J. C. Greenfield's reviews of Ben-Hayyim's work in *Biblica* XLV (1964) 261 ff., L (1969) 98 ff.

origin of the Mandeans themselves. In the past certain features of Mandaic were used to support the theory of a western origin, while today many see Babylonian origins in some of the same features.[32] We might hope to clarify some of these points.

No systematic analysis either of the Aramaic logograms in Iranian texts or of the Neo-Aramaic dialects has been attempted here. The latter, aside from a lack of adequate lexicographical tools, are too encumbered with foreign borrowings of more recent vintage to allow otherwise unknown traces of Akkadian influence to be discovered with any reasonable expense of effort at this time.[33] As for the logograms, as far as I have been able to determine, that group actually used by the scribes in literary contexts contains no Akkadianisms other than those common in Imperial Aramaic and common to the various Aramaic dialects. The Aramaic—Middle-Persian dictionary, *Frahang-i-Pahlavik,* is quite a different matter. Ebeling attempted to show that many of the Aramaic forms in this dictionary can only be explained as Akkadian or even Sumerian words and that this work is thus merely a natural extension of the cuneiform lexicographical tradition.[34] Even if one accepts some of his identifications, or even his overall analysis, such items can hardly be considered linguistic borrowings and are thus excluded from consideration here.

THE NATURE OF LANGUAGE CONTACT

The influences of one language upon another can be of many different sorts. The extent and nature of such influences naturally depend upon the nature of the relationship

32. The most recent summary is to be found in R. Macuch, "Anfänge der Mandäer," in F. Altheim and R. Stiehl, *Die Araber in der alten Welt* II (Berlin, 1965), pp. 76 f., who rejects the linguistic arguments but still argues for a western origin. Cf. also W. Baumgartner, "Zur Mandäerfrage," *HUCA* XXIII (1950-51) 41 ff., reprinted with additions in *Zum alten Testament und seiner Umwelt* (Leiden, 1959) pp. 332 ff. On the non-Western origin of the Mandaic script see J. Naveh, "The Origin of the Mandaic Script," *BASOR,* No. 198 (1970) pp. 32 ff., and P. W. Coxon, "Script Analysis and Mandaean Origins," *JSS* XV (1970) 16 ff.

33. It is to be hoped that among future studies on Eastern Neo-Aramaic will be an attempt to reconstruct its Aramaic ancestors and that the presence or absence of Assyrian traits will then be taken into account; see p. 165.

34. E. Ebeling, *Das aramäisch-mittelpersische Glossar Frahang-i-Pahlavik im Lichte der assyriologischen Forschung* (*MAOG,* Vol. XIV 1 [Leipzig, 1941]). Because of the polyvalent nature of the Pehlevi script, the actual reading of the text involves great difficulties; but lacking further studies by competent Iranologists, one can only assume that at least some of Ebeling's interpretations are correct.

between the dialects or languages involved. Not infrequently, words can be transferred from one language to another without any direct contact at all between the groups speaking those languages. In the ancient Near East such borrowings are to be expected in several spheres. Cultural objects or practices that have their ultimate or immediate origin in one or another of the language groups will often maintain their foreign name as they spread throughout an area. In the ancient Near East during the first millennium B.C. for example, one might expect to find the political terminology of the Assyrian and Babylonian empires widespread throughout the area. Yet while such terminology may give evidence for cultural and political contact which may be quite accurately datable by archeological and historical records, it does not represent evidence for the kind of direct linguistic contact we are seeking here.

It may be assumed with some certainty that during the first half of the first millennium there was large-scale contact between native speakers of various Akkadian and Aramaic dialects. In such a situation different types of linguistic influences may occur, depending on the actual nature of the contact, the degree of native or acquired bilingualism (the ultimate contact situation), and the length of the duration of that contact. Accordingly, one might hope that the material studied herein will provide some of the information needed to derive a general picture of the actual contact relationship.

One of the most perplexing aspects of the study of loanwords is the determination of the cause of the borrowing of a given word. Most commonly, perhaps, as in the cases mentioned above, the new word is borrowed in order to designate something totally new to the borrowing culture, but this is certainly not always the case. Often psycholinguistic factors beyond our powers of analysis may be at work; thus, any argument rejecting the foreign origin of a word solely because there would have been no reason to borrow it must itself be rejected.[35]

In referring to these psycho-linguistic factors, such terms as "prestige" and "higher" (or "dominant") and "lower" languages are very common in the literature on linguistic borrowing. Bloomfield uses the latter set of terms to refer to his special case of "*intimate borrowing* which occurs when

35. Reasons which I would classify in this group are the following (discussed by Uriel Weinreich, *Languages in Contact*, pp. 56 ff.): the low frequency of the word to be replaced; to resolve the clash of homonyms; the need for synonyms in certain semantic fields to increase the expressive nature of the language.

two languages are spoken in what is topographically and politically a single community."[36] Now, while it is obviously true that prestige can be a strong motive for linguistic change, one must take care not to draw any premature conclusions along that line in the case of Akkadian and Aramaic. For example, in a recent article one finds the a priori statement, "Akkadian had an enormous cultural prestige."[37] In spite of what first thoughts might indicate, why must this statement be correct? There were certainly periods when Akkadian and Aramaic fit Bloomfield's definition of "intimate borrowing"; yet if Akkadian were the more prestigious language, theory would lead us to expect to find "copious borrowings"[38] in the later Aramaic of Mesopotamia, but, as we shall see, they are not to be found. At this stage it seems best to refrain from any prejudgment of the psychology of those whose language habits, and the results of whose habits, we are trying to analyze. Our lexical analysis will allow us to reach some conclusions about the nature of the relationship between the two languages, however, since it can be shown that in different types of relationships, different classes of words are more likely to be borrowed than others.[39]

There are many different kinds of lexical interference that may occur between languages. Perhaps the most common but certainly the easiest to recognize is the outright transfer of a word from one language to another--the loanword. Most of the other varieties come under the general rubric of "loan-translation" or "calque."[40] In the lexical portion of this study I shall limit myself almost exclusively to loans of the first type, not because they are more important—they are not—but because in the great majority of cases of suspected calques it is impossible to be at all certain that Akkadian is the origin of a particular usage.[41] Accordingly, I shall omit entirely Aramaic linguistic usages which result

36. Leonard Bloomfield, *Language* (London, 1935) p. 461.

37. E. E. Knudsen, "Spirantization of Velars in Akkadian," *Lišān mitḫurti* (*AOAT*, Vol. I [Neukirchen-Vluyn, 1969]) p. 155.

38. Bloomfield, *Language*, p. 464.

39. See p. 168.

40. A good analysis of the various types of loanwords and loan-translations is to be found in Weinreich, *Languages in Contact*, p. 47 ff. For a summary of the various theoretical discussions of types of lexical interference see E. Oksaar, "Bilingualism," *Current Trends in Linguistics* IX 494.

41. Probable calques and partial calques which I have included are discussed s.v. *ina libbi, ina ṣilli, bāb ekalli, abbūtu, bēl dīni, libbatu, ṣītu, ša ekalli, tajjāru*. A particularly difficult type of loan-translation to isolate, found in pairs of closely related languages such as Akkadian and Aramaic, is the use of a term in one language according to the semantics of its cognate in the other; cf. e.g. *paqādu, pašāru*.

from the borrowing of Akkadian formulae and procedures, such as those of the legal papyri from Elephantine, which are already the subject of an excellent study by Y. Muffs.[42] As Muffs points out so well, in the great majority of cases the lines of transmission are complicated, involving prolonged and various periods of cultural and political contact and domination. This is something quite different from contact between two language populations. Actual interlinguistic contact is even less likely in the case of similar phraseology in similar genres, such as royal inscriptions or treaties.[43] Loanwords that occur in such formulae, for example *dabābu*, will be treated, however.

Even under the general term "loanword" one must distinguish among several kinds of phenomena. When a speaker of one language first uses a word of another language he usually uses it as a foreign word. As that word spreads throughout the language community and in the course of time, it soon loses its foreign connotations and often becomes totally integrated into the borrwoing language. One might expect to find words of the first type in Aramaic texts contemporaneous with Akkadian, that is Old Aramaic, Mesopotamian Aramaic, and early Imperial Aramaic. If a word is found in later dialects, however, it means that it has been absorbed completely into the fabric of Aramaic. One might also expect to find different kinds of loanwords in general Aramaic and in those Aramaic-speaking areas that had previously been Akkadian-speaking. For the Aramaic speakers of Mesopotamia were heirs to its material culture along with the terminology associated with that culture.[44]

A special problem is faced by the etymologist when confronted by the names of natural objects of wide distribution and mobility, such as flora, fauna, and minerals. Frequently these names are not susceptible of etymological analysis. In such cases, not only is the ultimate origin of the name in doubt, but even the direction and process of its spread from one language to another is less than certain. Indeed, the name of an object can be imported together with that object without any significant interlingual contact between the languages involved. Such names are conveniently

42. Yochanan Muffs, *Studies in the Aramaic Legal Papyri from Elephantine* (Leiden, 1969).

43. See Chap. IV, n. 73.

44. See Stephen A. Kaufman, "Akkadian and Babylonian Aramaic—New Examples of Mutual Elucidation," *Leš.* XXXVI (1972) 28 (Heb.). For the problem of substratum vs. loan in the later contact between Aramaic and Arabic, cf. M. T. Féghali, "La question du substrat," *RES*, 1938, No. 3, pp. 133-39.

termed "culture words" (German "kulturwörter"). In this work this term is also used to designate the names of man-made culture objects of similar distribution and unknown etymology. Except for those few names whose Aramaic forms are explicable only on the basis of Akkadian, our study must thus exclude such names of animals, plants, and minerals, even though their earliest occurrence may be in an Akkadian text.

THE EVIDENCE FOR BORROWINGS

Etymological studies in the Semitic languages are often fraught with uncertainties; the greater the scope of the work, the greater the chance for error. Recognizing this in advance, one must be extremely careful in choosing the kind of evidence upon which judgments will be based in attempting to determine whether or not a given word or feature is borrowed from Akkadian.

The strongest proof obtainable for the Akkadian origin of an Aramaic word is in the case of a Semitic word with at least one phoneme that was subject to a different development in Akkadian from that in Aramaic. If the word occurs both in Akkadian and in Aramaic, but the Aramaic has the Akkadian form, then one may be quite certain it is a loan. A difficulty with this approach is that the characteristic Aramaic sound changes were not complete until the Imperial Aramaic period, and some not even then. The following are the relevant consonantal phonemes:

Proto-Semitic	Akkadian	Old Aramaic (spelling)	Later Aramaic
ṯ	š	š	t
ḏ	z	z	d
ṯ̣ (ẓ)	ṣ	ṣ	ṭ
ḏ̣	ṣ	q	ʿ
ś	š	š	s
ḥ	ʾ/0	ḥ	ḥ*
ġ	ʾ/0	ʿ	ʿ
ʿ	ʾ/0	ʿ	ʿ
h	ʾ/0	h	h
ʾ	ʾ/0	ʾ	ʾ/0
initial w	ʾ+	y	y
initial y	ʾ	y	y

*Although the maintenance of /ḫ/ in Akkadian as opposed to its merger with /ḥ/ in Aramaic is important, when only Akkadian and Aramaic evidence is available the treatment of /ḫ/ is not significant for our inquiry.
+See p. 138.

Akkadian also reduces the diphthongs *aw* and *ay* to *ū* and *ī/ē*, while they remain unreduced in some positions in Aramaic.

Several problems complicate this analysis, however. On the one hand, in Old Aramaic the spelling may mask actual loans.[45] On the other hand, in a word known only from late Aramaic, subsequent loss of the laryngeals might have occurred, giving the impression that the form comes from Akkadian. In the case of the first four phonemes listed, the Akkadian change was the same as that in Canaanite, and, thus, other considerations are necessary to determine whether a given term is a loan from Canaanite or Akkadian.

Frequently overlooked in etymological discussions are the phonemic changes that may occur in the various Semitic languages because of the incompatibility of certain root consonants in certain positions. Analysis of this phenomenon in the Semitic languages is still in its early stages,[46] but some use can be made of it here.[47]

Other Akkadian sound changes different from those of Aramaic, such as the change of the nominal prefix *m-* to *n-* before roots with a labial radical, can also be expected to provide evidence for loanwords. (More of these will be discussed in the analysis of the phonology of loanwords, Chapter IV.)

Words that can be shown to be Sumerian loanwords in Akkadian may generally be assumed to have been borrowed by Aramaic from Akkadian.[48] One must also be on the lookout

45. So, too, in most cases of Mesopotamian Aramaic and in later historical spellings. See Spirantization of Postvocalic Stops in Chap. III.

46. The ground-breaking study is J. Greenberg, "The Patterning of Root Morphemes in Semitic," *Word* VI (1950) 162-81. For Biblical Hebrew cf. K. Koskinen, "Kompatibilität in den dreikonsonantigen hebräischen Wurzeln," *ZDMG* CXIV (1964) 16-58. In Akkadian, "Geer's Law" is an example of this, and a greater awareness is beginning to be shown of the importance of this phenomenon; cf. *GAG* § 51 (and *Ergänz.* § 51). An interesting consideration which has not yet been adequately determined is the extent to which each language alters Proto-Semitic words to fit its own sound patterns, as Akkadian appears to do most of the time, as opposed to the cases where words of the offending type are merely discarded entirely from the lexicon.

47. Cf. *sunqu, suqāqu,* and *batāqu.*

48. This includes those items with a good Sumerian etymology as well as words assigned by some to the Mesopotamian predecessors of Sumerian and Semitic, for which see most recently A. Salonen, "Zum Aufbau der Substrate im Sumerischen," *St.Or.* XXXVII 3 (1968) 1 ff., and *Die Fussbekleidung der alten Mesopotamier* (Helsinki, 1969) pp. 97-117. For the Sumerian loanwords in Akkadian there is only the long-outdated study of P. Leander, *Ueber die sumerischen Lehnwörter im Assyrischen* (Uppsala, 1903). With the increasing realization of the antiquity of Semitic settlement in Mesopotamia (see Robert D. Biggs, "Semitic Names in the Fara Period," *Or.* n.s. XXXVI [1967] 55-66) not all words common to Sumerian and Akkadian can be assumed to be of Sumerian origin.

for Semitic words that may have undergone expansions or changes of meaning under the influence of Sumerian which one might also be able to trace in Aramaic. When grammatical peculiarities of Akkadian that are attributable to Sumerian influence appear in Aramaic, they may also be assigned an Akkadian origin.

In early studies of loanwords, there was a tendency to presuppose the semantic areas where one would be likely to find loanwords. For example it was assumed that any Arabic word having to do with sedentary or urban life must necessarily be a loan.[49] The potential pitfalls of such assumptions are clear; thus, while it will prove helpful to analyze the loanwords, once determined, on the basis of semantic groups, the occurrence of an uncertain word in a specific group cannot be considered conclusive evidence for its origin. A similar argument, which must also be rejected, is that of antiquity. In the case of nouns without apparent Semitic verbal etymology, it was often assumed in the past that since the earliest occurrence of the word is in Akkadian, its origin is Akkadian, even with widespread Semitic words.[50] But this is no criterion at all, and in such a case only other evidence will allow us to suggest an Akkadian origin.

Another important consideration, but one that can be very misleading, is distribution. If, for example, a word appears in Akkadian and Aramaic but not in Canaanite, then either this word had been known in the immediate ancestor of Canaanite and Aramaic but was lost in the former, or else it was added to Aramaic after the split of the two main North West Semitic language groups, in which case it may be a loan from Akkadian. Unfortunately for our purposes, the probability of the former occurring is by no means small,[51] and there are ways to account for the latter other than as a direct loan in the period with which we are concerned (see below).

If a word occurs only in Eastern Aramaic but not in the other dialects, there is a good chance that it was borrowed by Eastern Aramaic from Akkadian. Yet here, too, aside from possible loss in the western dialects, there are other

49. Fraenkel's *Die Aramäischen Fremdwörter im Arabischen* (Leiden,1886; reprint, Hildesheim, 1962) is an excellent philological work but is not free of this flaw.

50. Notable examples are *kaspu*, "silver," *immeru*, "sheep," and *qanû*, "reed." In such cases the borrowing was assumed to have occurred at an early date.

51. Even in the most frequent vocabulary items, Imperial Aramaic and Biblical Hebrew show a lexical difference of more than 20 per cent, and the difference is correspondingly greater with more infrequent words. Another problem is the limited Canaanite vocabulary at our disposal outside Hebrew, and even in Hebrew our knowledge is far from complete. Generally we may suppose that approximately the same percentage of common Akkadian

explanations which must be considered. In the case of grammatical borrowings, distribution is often the only clue.

A final guide in the discovery of loanwords is the study of changes in the native vocabulary, for, except in the case of loanwords with entirely new content, the addition of a foreign word to a vocabulary must somehow affect that vocabulary. It may result in confusion between the semantic content of the new word and its older synonym; the old word could disappear, or both could survive but with specialization in their content.[52] Naturally such changes are often very difficult to detect.

Some of the difficulties encountered in the application of these observations have been discussed above, but there are many more. Perhaps the most important is our limited knowledge of Akkadian. While the corpus of Akkadian provides a wide-ranging scope of lexical material and a broader lexicon than is available from the other early written Semitic languages, one may be certain that there are many Aramaic terms borrowed from Akkadian words that have not yet appeared in the cuneiform texts, or perhaps have not yet been properly recognized.[53]

The problem of culture words has been mentioned above. No doubt some of them do indeed derive from Akkadian, yet provide no proof that such is the case. There are many words of a clearly Semitic nature which give every appearance of being cognate in the two languages and grant us no grounds, phonological or otherwise, for establishing their Akkadian origin.

Thus, given the uncertain nature of most of the evidence at our disposal, except when phonological considerations dictate an Akkadian origin, one can be relatively sure of attribution to Akkadian only when several other signs of a loan occur together.

THE PROBLEMS OF AKKADIAN—WEST SEMITIC CONTACTS

The determination of whether or not a given Aramaic lexical or grammatical feature has its ultimate origin in

and North West Semitic vocabulary was lost in Hebrew as in Aramaic and that we might expect to find as many cognate items common to Hebrew and Akkadian but not Aramaic as occur in Akkadian and Aramaic but not in Hebrew. Nevertheless, the reader will find that the number of exclusively Akkadian-Aramaic words whose status as loans is listed as uncertain in Chap. II is far less than the number of exclusively Akkadian-Hebrew cognates which are to be found in the Biblical Hebrew lexicon, a fact which indicates that at least in this regard I have not been overcautious.

52. Cf. Weinreich, *Languages in Contact*, p. 54.

53. See, e.g., *šē bābi*.

Akkadian is hampered by yet another group of problems that also complicate any attempt to confine research to the period of greatest Akkadian-Aramaic contact. These problems may be said to group themselves into the two interrelated subjects of "the Amorite problem" and "the Aramean problem."

It is by now well known that in early Mesopotamia the speakers of Sumerian and Akkadian were in close contact with peoples bearing mostly West Semitic personal names characterized, at least in the Ur III period, by the expression MAR.TU, Akkadian *amurru*.[54] It is also quite clear that throughout the second millennium semi-nomadic and in some cases sedentary tribes speaking West Semitic dialects or languages were spread from Babylonia to the Levant.[55] It is common practice today to use the term "Amcrite" to refer to these people and to their languages. While there is general agreement that Amorite is to be considered North West Semitic, there is little agreement over the proper divisions of that language sub-family during the second millennium. Some claim that there are three divisions: Canaanite, Aramaic, and Amorite;[56] others that Amorite and Canaanite go together as opposed to Aramaic.[57] Some suggest that Aramaic developed from Amorite, which is to be separated from Canaanite.[58] The fourth view is that during the greater part of the second millennium North West Semitic was as yet undifferentiated and thus should be referred to under the term Amorite.[59]

The view that Aramaic developed from Amorite, which is to be separated from Canaanite, is most important for our purposes, for if Aramaic is nothing more than a late Amorite dialect, then it may be said that Aramaic was in contact with

54. Cf. Giorgio Buccellati, *The Amorites of the Ur III Period* (Naples, 1966); A. Haldar, *Who Were the Amorites?* (Leiden, 1971).

55. There were certainly sedentary Amorites along the Upper Euphrates and its tributaries alongside the semi-nomadic peoples of the desert areas, as typified by the situation at Mari during the OB period (cf. M. B. Rowton, "Urban Autonomy in a Nomadic Environment," *JNES* XXXII [1973] 201-15). Though that city itself may not always have been in Amorite control, the same cannot be posited a priori for the other urban settlements of the river valleys (contra Buccellati, *Amorites*, pp. 246 f.) Even in areas of Hurrian overlordship, such as Alalakh, the basic Semitic population almost certainly preserved its language.

56. This is probably the most common view. Cf. W. F. Albright, *CAH*, fasc. 51, p. 47.

57. J. C. Greenfield, "Amurrite, Ugaritic and Canaanite," *Proceedings*, pp. 92-101.

58. Cf. M. Noth, "Mari und Israel," in Festschrift A. Alt, *Geschichte und Altes Testament* (Tübingen, 1953) pp. 127-52, and *Die Ursprung des alten Israel im Lichte neuer Quellen* (Cologne, 1961), and the response by D. O. Edzard, "Mari und Aramäer?" *ZA* n.f. XXII (1964) 142 ff.

59. M. Liverani, "Elementi innovativi nell 'Ugaritico non-letterario," *AANL, Rendiconti*, Classe . . . Morali, Series VIII, Vol. XIX (1964) p. 190.

Akkadian for a much longer period of time than we have supposed.

As a significant historical group, Arameans first appear in Near Eastern texts in 1112 B.C., and it is usually assumed that they were late invaders from the desert,[60] although recently efforts have been made to find traces of the Arameans as far back as the Ur III period.[61] But, whether or not the name "Aram" occurs prior to 1112 B.C. is really of little consequence for us. Here we must be concerned only with whether or not there can be found among the North West Semitic languages of the second millennium B.C. immediately adjacent to the Akkadian-speaking area a direct lineal linguistic antecedent of the language we call Aramaic.

Unfortunately, our knowledge of Amorite is extremely limited, based almost exclusively on personal names.[62] While it should be clear to most scholars that several different, albeit closely related languages are subsumed under the term Amorite, further analysis and separation of these dialects is extremely difficult.[63] On the evidence available, scholars have been led to different classifications of Amorite exemplified by the names East Canaanites, Canaanites, and Proto-Arameans. It is to be hoped that I. J. Gelb's soon to appear computer-aided analysis of all of the Amorite names, when studied in conjunction with the names from Ugarit and the early Aramaic names attested in both alphabetic and cuneiform texts, will lead to a better understanding of this problem.[64]

60. Cf. W. von Soden, "Zur Einteilung der semitischen Sprachen," *WZKM* LVI (1960) 177-91.

61. Most important is A. Dupont-Sommer, "Sur les débuts de l'histoire araméenne," Suppl. *VT* (1953) 40-49. A recent bibliography of works on Aramean history can be found in F. Vattioni, "Preliminari alle iscrizioni aramaiche," *Augustinianum* IX (1969) 310 ff., which ought to be supplemented by M. Liverani, "Antecedenti dell'onomastica Aramaica antica," *RSO* XXXVII (1962) 65-76 and the bibliography cited p. 65, n. 1.

62. The recent grammatical studies are I. J. Gelb, "La lingua degli Amoriti," *AANL, Rendiconti,* Classe . . . Morali, Series VIII, Vol. XIII (1958) 143-64, and H. Huffmon, *Amorite Personal Names in the Mari Texts: A Structural and Lexical Study* (Baltimore, 1965).

63. Some argument continues over whether or not the West Semitic MAR.TU names of Ur III differ from the names of the OB period (cf. Buccellati, *Amorites,* pp. 10 f.), but other divisions, especially on a synchronic level, are undetermined.

64. The Ugaritic names are collected in Fauke Grondahl, *Die Personennamen der Texte aus Ugarit* (Rome, 1967). First steps toward a comparison with Aramaic were taken by Liverani, in *RSO* XXXVII 65-76.

Clearly more work needs to be done, but based on those studies already available, I see no objection to a position which views Aramaic as the descendant of an Amorite dialect. The non-onomastic lexical material discussed by Noth and Edzard (see n. 59) is inconclusive, and there are

In the final analysis, however, even the genetic relationship between Amorite and Aramaic is not crucial, for, in any case, during the first millennium the Aramaic-speaking peoples from Babylonia[65] to northern Syria occupied the very same areas inhabited by the earlier North West Semitic peoples of the second millennium, and there can be litte doubt that, even lacking lineal descent, the Aramaic language was strongly influenced by the language of its predecessors. Thus, I shall henceforth use the term "Amorite" or "pre-Aramaic" to refer to the North West Semitic languages which preceded Aramaic and the term "Eastern Amorite" to refer to the Amorite of and immediately adjacent to Mesopotamia.

It should now be clear that some Aramaic words that appear to have been borrowed from Akkadian or words of Sumerian or pre-Sumerian origin that appear to have entered Aramaic through Akkadian may in fact have entered Aramaic through Amorite, which in turn borrowed them from Akkadian, Sumerian, or perhaps even pre-Sumerian.[66] This is especially true of words confined to Eastern Aramaic, which may have had a long history among the Eastern Amorites as well. One must also take into account the special situation of the Amarna period, when Akkadian was in widespread use in the west as well as the east.

Akkadian, too, was greatly affected by Amorite, just as it was later affected by Aramaic during the first millennium. At least from Ur III on, there was a constant movement and assimilation of West Semitic peoples into Mesopotamia.[67] The Amorites were of great importance during the Old Babylonian period, and both the Old Babylonian dynasty of Hammurapi and that of his Assyrian contemporary Šamši-Adad were of self-admitted Amorite origin. The Akkadian of Mari has many Amorite lexical items, and some have been recognized in Old Babylonian.[68] Old Assyrian connections with Amorite have been explored by J. Lewy.[69] In spite of the fact that Akkadian dialectology

no objections on grammatical grounds. Albright, for example (*CAH*, fasc. 51, p. 47) finds Amorite much closer to Aramaic than to Canaanite but apparently wants to keep it separate from Aramaic on the grounds that the sibilant shifts are different. But this is merely a problem of definition, for at least in some of the Amorite dialects the sibilants had not yet shifted at all.

65. Cf. Brinkman, *Political History*, p. 283.

66. By pre-Sumerian I mean the as yet unknown languages which preceded Sumerian and Akkadian in Mesopotamia whose traces can be found both in the lexicon and in geographical names; see above, n. 48.

67. Cf. Buccellati, *Amorites*, pp. 355 ff.

68. Most recently Johannes Renger, "Überlegungen zum akkadischen Syllabar," *ZA* LXI (1971) 26.

69. Julius Lewy, "Zur Amoriterfrage," *ZA* n.f. IV (1928-29) 243-72; "Amurritica," *HUCA* XXXII (1961) 31-74 and, in passing, in numerous other studies.

is still in its early stages, it is generally assumed that Amorite left no significant lasting imprint on the standard dialects of Akkadian. Different dialects can be detected even in Old Babylonian, however, and some of these, their descendants, and even certain genres of texts probably owe more to Amorite than do others.[70] Certain distributional clues often prompt the suspicion that a given Akkadian word is Amorite in origin, but even lacking such evidence there is always the possibility that an Aramaic term occurring commonly in Akkadian may have been an Amorite loan in Akkadian.

Another source of West Semitic influence on Babylonian was the Chaldeans, who appeared on the Babylonian scene early in the ninth century and obtained control of Babylonia under Merodach-Baladan in 722.[71] With the Aramaization of Babylonia, their name became equated with Aramaic, but there is far too little evidence to determine the proper classification of their own language.[72]

Such significant Aramaic influence on Late Akkadian requires that any word or feature common to Aramaic and Akkadian that is not found in the early stages of Akkadian must be treated with caution. The Akkadian lexical lists

70. I have in mind some of the dialects represented in poetic texts and in divination. The latter as we know it is almost certainly of Semitic origin; no Sumerian omen literature is known. The Old Babylonian prayer of the divination priest published by A. Goetze (in *JCS* XXII [1968] 25-29) is strikingly West Semitic in its word order, and there are quite a few Akkadian words apparently cognate to North West Semitic terms which are found only in omen material in Akkadian. The latter, however, might be explained as the result of chance, for a very large proportion of all the extant texts deal with omens. This is not to say that divination was not known to the Sumerians or Akkadians, only that Amorite tradition may have added a strong impetus. (For possible West Semitic mythological motifs in Old Babylonian literature see T. Jacobsen, "The Battle between Marduk and Tiamat," *JAOS* LXXXVIII [1968] 108.) Might there also be morphological clues to foreign words in Akkadian, whether Sumerian or Amorite or other, in the not infrequent noun forms with a final double consonant (*GAG* § 55 *p, q*)? These are much more frequent in Akkadian than in the other Semitic languages and are easily explained as compensatory lengthening resulting from the attempt to preserve the shape of a word which otherwise would have three short syllables and be subject to loss of the middle vowel. Note that several of the words of uncertain origin considered below (e.g. *abullu, itannu, pilakku,* etc.) fall in this category.

71. In general see Brinkman, *Political History,* pp. 260 ff.

72. According to Dr. Israel Ephʾal, who has made extensive study of the Arabs and Arabic names in cuneiform texts, previous hypotheses connecting the Chaldeans with South Arabian tribes (cf., e.g., T. C. Mitchell, "A South Arabian Tripod Offering Saucer Said to Be from Ur," *Iraq* XXXI [1969] 113 f.) can no longer be maintained. Nevertheless, cultural contact with the South Arabians certainly existed and is an important consideration in dealing with a word such as *apkallu* (see Chap. II s.v.).

warrant equal caution, for in their zeal for completeness the compilers of these materials ranged far and wide for their synonyms and, especially in particular types of lists, made extensive use of Aramaic or other West Semitic words, in most cases without any indication of the foreign origin of Aramaic words.[73]

In light of the not insubstantial hazards and handicaps discussed in this and the preceeding section, one might suppose that an accurate list of all the Akkadianisms in Aramaic can never be produced. True, our results will necessarily be far short of perfect, but careful application of the principles set forth above should result in an accurate and fairly complete sample, and the conclusions drawn from that sample should have a high degree of reliability.

EARLY AKKADIAN LOANS IN WEST SEMITIC

Since the intent of this study is to concentrate on the period of contact between Akkadian and Aramaic, words borrowed by North West Semitic at an earlier period will not be discussed in the main section of this work. As Akkadian loanwords or suggested loanwords in Aramaic, however, they are relevant to the general theme of this study and are therefore listed here.

To my knowledge there is only one Aramaic word[74] unquestionably in this category: *h(y)kl* < *ekallu*, "palace." The occurrence of *hkl* in Ugaritic shows that the word was borrowed very early, and the preservation of the *h* in all West Semitic forms shows that the borrowed word endured and was not reborrowed. There is no other example of an Akkadian initial vowel occurring as *h* in its borrowed form in West Semitic (see Phonology, in Chapter III).[75] There are Aramaic loans from both the Neo-Assyrian and Neo-Babylonian forms of the very similar word *ekurru* (see below), and neither has the initial *h*. It is not clear whether the *h* is due to an early Akkadian dialectal pronunciation of all initial vowels with heavy aspiration rather than a glottal, or, if the loan is very old and *h* derives from a Sumerian pronunciation of *é-gal*, whether the North West Semitic borrowing was directly from Sumerian or, as seems more probable, from an Akkadian which still preserved this possible phonetic trait of Sumerian.[76]

73. Cf. Anne D. Kilmer, "The First Tablet of *malku* = *šarru* together with Its Explicit Version," *JAOS* LXXXIII (1963) 423, n. 17.

74. Except for Hama *skn*; see Chap. II, s.v. *šaknu*.

75. Except for the possible occurrence of *abarakku*, "steward," as *hbrk* in the Azitawadda inscription; see Franz Rosenthal, *ANET* (2d ed.) p. 499, n. 1.

76. A. Falkenstein, *Das Sumerische*, in *Handbuch der Orientalistik*,

There are other words whose Akkadian origin is subject to doubt but whose appearance in North West Semitic in any case goes well back into the second millennium.

kitû, "flax," "linen," *ktn*—Neither the West Semitic word for linen, flax, *ki/attân*, nor the words for tunic, *kittûn*, *kuttîn*, etc., are unquestionably derived from Akkadian.[77] The old Akkadian word for linen is *kitû*, certainly related to but not necessarily a loan from Sumerian *gada*. The difference in the first vowel perhaps points most likely to separate developments of inherited culture words, or the final *-a* of the Sumerian could indicate an early loan from Akkadian.[78] While the form *ktn* occurs in Ugaritic (for both linen and garment?), a form with final *-n* does not occur in Akkadian until the Neo-Babylonian period (*kitinnu*, "linen," "linen cloth"), perhaps as an Aramaic loan.[79] The relationship with the Old Assyrian woolen garment *kutānu* (*AHw*.: *qutānu*) is uncertain.[80]

kussû, "throne," "chair," *ksʾ*, *krsʾ/kwrsy*—The Ugaritic, Hebrew, and Old Aramaic forms of this word all preserve the final *aleph*. Since the Akkadian word has final *aleph* only in Old Akkadian and Old Assyrian, if the North West Semitic form was indeed borrowed from Akkadian, the borrowing must have occurred very early. The only reason to consider the Akkadian form primary here is that it appears to be a loan from Sumerian ^{giš}GU.ZA. But the Sumerian has no satisfactory etymology, and both the long *ss* and the final *aleph* of the Akkadian are inexplicable on the basis of the Sumerian form. Yet the Sumerian can be interpreted as a loan from Akkadian,[81] and a Semitic etymology is not impossible.[82]

Vol. II: *Keilschriftforschung und alte Geschichte Vorderasiens* (Leiden, 1959) p. 24, § 7 *c*, *e*, believes the borrowing was directly from Sumerian. Cf. also I. J. Gelb, *MAD*, No. 2 (2d ed.) p. 25; E. Sollberger, "Sur chronologie des rois d'Ur et quelques problemes connexes," *AfO* XVII (1954-56) 11, n. 4.

77. Cf. Z, p. 37; *Wb.KAS*, p. 54*b*.

78. See. D. O. Edzard, "Sumerische Komposita mit dem nominal Präfix *nu*-," *ZA* n.f. XXI (1963) 94, n. 115.

79. Cf. A. L. Oppenheim, "Essay on Overland Trade in the First Millennium B.C.," *JCS* XXI (1967) 251. Von Soden (*AHw*.) and Landsberger ("Über Farben im Sumerisch-Akkadischen," *JCS* XXI [1967] 158, n. 102) read this word *kidinnû*.

80. See Oppenheim, in *JCS* XXI 251, n. 82; Landsberger, in *JCS* XXI 158, n. 102. The rare Syr. form *qeṭṭaw*, "linen," is difficult to explain but could hardly be from Akk. *kitû*. (Is the Syriac derived from the Armenian form *ktav*?) On flax in general in the ancient Near East see Oppenheim, in *JCS* XXI 244 ff.

81. Cf. I. J. Gelb, *MAD*, No. 3, p. 152, and for final *-a* words, D. O. Edzard, in *ZA* n.f. XXI 94, n. 115.

The noun form is unusual for Semitic, however, and so perhaps **kussiʾ* is a foreign or substrate word.[83] The single suggested Akkadian parallel to the Aramaic (> Arabic) form with *rs* for *ss* has remained unique despite seventy years of scholarship, and there is little reason to regard it as the same word.[84]

šipru, "message," "work"; *spr*, "document"—It is generally agreed that this North West Semitic term derives from early Akkadian, but Y. Muffs has recently raised a dissenting voice.[85] His argument, while quite correct, does not prove that *spr* is not a loan, but only that, if a loan, it must have been borrowed even earlier than the period of the Ras Shamra texts. It is quite possible that at the time that cuneiform writing first became known in the Levant the Akkadian word *šipru* (in Assyrian pronunciation) was associated with that writing. But in light of the Canaanite verb *spr*, "to count," and the lack of clear etymological connections among the various Semitic roots of the shape *spr*, *śpr* and *špr*, uncertainty still must prevail.[86]

šiqlu, "shekel," *ṯ/š/tql*—The root *ṯql*, "to weigh," is certainly Proto-Semitic, as the noun **ṯiql*, "weight," must be as well. As a specific unit of weight, however, Akkadian may have had some influence at an early date, though, as the preservation of *ṯ* in Ugaritic and Aramaic shows, it was not a complete borrowing. The frequent Egyptian Aramaic spelling *šql* (instead of *tql*), abbreviated *š* (also in late Mesopotamian Aramaic) probably represents an historical spelling rather than a borrowing of the Akkadian (or Hebrew) form.

82. Cf. A. Salonen, *Die Möbel des alten Mesopotamien* (Helsinki, 1963) p. 58.

83. Further support for the foreign origin of *kussû* can be found in the unusual Ugaritic spelling *kśu* (cf. *UT*, p. 421*b*) with the sibilant *ś* reserved usually for foreign words.

84. Cf. B. Meissner, review of Zimmern, *Beiträge zur Kenntis*, *ZA* XV (1900) 418 f. In *AHw*. the form is cited s.v. *kurṣû*. Cf. also *KBL* Supplement, p. 202.

85. Z, p. 19; *LS*, p. 493; E. A. Speiser, *Oriental and Biblical Studies: Collected Writings of E. A. Speiser*, ed. by J. J. Finkelstein and M. Greenberg (Philadelphia, 1967) p. 439, n. 16; E. Y. Kutscher, *Words and Their History* (Jerusalem, 1961) p. 67; *KBL*, p. 1104; Muffs, *Studies*, p. 207.

86. On *spr*, "scribe," see Muffs, *Studies*, p. 207.

II

THE LEXICAL INFLUENCES

In an attempt to produce an accurate list of the Akkadian loanwords in Aramaic, all those Akkadian and Aramaic lexical comparisons whose status as loanwords is relatively certain as well as other suggested comparisons deemed to merit discussion will be studied in this chapter. Only those entries which can with some degree of certainty be shown to be loanwords will be used as the basis for the conclusions in Chapter IV. *Such loanwords are marked with an asterisk in the margin next to the entry.*

I have not felt it necessary to include for purposes of refutation every comparison that has ever been suggested in print. Many, if not most, of these suggestions were adequate for their day but have been proven false by the evidence accumulated since, and therefore simple reference to the *CAD* or *AHw*. should settle the matter. In other cases common sense should serve as the final judge, though one notes with some remorse that even long-outdated suggestions are not infrequently resurrected today.[1] Words previously considered loanwords but now thought to be Aramaisms in Akkadian, for example, *qarābu*, "battle," have not been included if they are treated in W. von Soden's study of Aramaisms.[2]

For obvious reasons it was impossible to read through all of Aramaic literature for the purposes of this study. Only Old Aramaic, Mesopotamian Aramaic, Imperial Aramaic, Hatran, and Qumran texts were thoroughly scrutinized. For the other dialects the standard lexical tools served as a first step, with reference to the texts involved whenever necessary.

As previously mentioned, no extensive effort has been made to include loan-translations, and only those few names of animals, plants, and minerals whose Akkadian origin is almost certain will be discussed. Divine names (and planet names, etc.), borrowed as such, whose borrowing is a result of cultural, not linguistic, influence, will not be included here either. Such names are important, however, inasmuch as they

1. I fail, for example, to understand the reasoning behind the statement that West Semitic *śʾn*, "shoe," "is manifestly borrowed from Akkadian *šênu*" (J. Blau, *On Pseudo-Corrections in Some Semitic Languages* [Jerusalem, 1970] p. 116).

2. "Aramäische Wörter in neuassyrischen und neu- und spätbabylonischen Texten. Ein Vorbericht I [and] II," *Or*. n.s. XXXV (1966) 1-20, and *Or*. n.s. XXXVII (1968) 261-71.

are part of the corpus of Akkadian appearing in transliterated form in alphabetic texts, and as such they will be of use in matters of phonology.

Because of the great variety of Aramaic forms and spellings in which a given word may appear in the various dialects, the words have been listed alphabetically in order of the Akkadian. An alphabetic listing of the Aramaic forms can be found in the index. In citing Akkadian words that occur in more than one dialect, the reference form of the *CAD* (Standard Babylonian) is used rather than that of the *AHw*. (Old Babylonian), since the Standard Babylonian form is likely to be closer to the form actually borrowed.[3] Aramaic forms are cited in consonantal spelling only, except where the vocalization is certain or crucial to the discussion. While the writer prefers the Drower-Macuch system of transliteration for Mandaic,[4] to prevent confusion the same system used for the other Aramaic dialects will be used here for Mandaic.[5] Biblical Hebrew forms are transcribed.[6] In discussing individual forms and formations, / / is used for phonemic notation, [ ] for rough phonetic approximation,[7] and " " for graphemes. In general discussion, when phonemic and phonetic considerations are not relevant, italic type is used.

Wherever possible, all supplementary material has been collected in a single note at the end of each lexical entry. In each case references to the appropriate pages of Zimmern (Z), *Lexicon Syriacum* (*LS*) and *Akkadisches Handworterbuch* (*AHw*.) are given first followed by the most recent significant etymological discussion of the word. If it is to be

3. The dialectal divisions of Akkadian and their abbreviations are those used by the *CAD*. In general see *GAG* § 2 for the divisions, but the *CAD* uses Standard Babylonian (SB) instead of von Soden's Jungbabylonische (jB). Von Soden's division between Neo-Babylonian and Late (*ca*. 625), while perhaps linguistically more accurate than any other, is historically misleading since Late Babylonian would then be the language of the Neo-Babylonian empire. In any case the dialectal development was gradual, and I prefer to use the Late Babylonian to refer only to texts of the Achaemenid and subsequent periods, as the *CAD* does. In citing Akkadian words, I used "h" for the phoneme usually transcribed "ḫ" for typographic simplicity.

4. See *MD*, p. vi; *HM*, pp. 528 ff.

5. Where necessary in reference to specific *MD* citations the Drower-Macuch system is used. The transliteration system used for the West Semitic languages is fairly standard and should be clear. In transcriptions of Aramaic and Arabic, long vowels are indicated by a circumflex.

6. For Biblical Hebrew the system used is that proposed by W. Weinberg, "Transliteration and Transcription of Hebrew," *HUCA* XL-XLI (1970) 1-32.

7. Not to be confused with the usage of square brackets in text citations to indicate broken passages.

found in the latter, previous bibliography is not otherwise indicated. If a lexical entry has no note, it indicates that to my knowledge the connection with Akkadian was not previously made. It must be stressed here that this study is not meant to be a dictionary, either of Akkadian or of Aramaic, but on the contrary is intended to be used together with the available lexicographical tools. In Akkadian, for example, not all the meanings of a word will be cited, only those of immediate relevance; nor is any effort made to indicate recent discussions of the word in purely Akkadian contexts which are irrelevant to our study when the word is already treated in the published volumes of *CAD* or *AHw*. More complete Assyriological references will be given for those lexical entries not yet the subject of dictionary articles. Accordingly, it has not always seemed necessary to make explicit the reasons why a given word is considered to be loan in the case of words whose Sumerian etymologies are easily found in the dictionaries or wherever phonetic considerations, such as Aramaic /w/ for Akkadian "m" make a loan obvious.

LEXICAL LIST

* *abbūtu*, "a father's legal status," in the expression *abbūtu ṣabatu*, "to intercede"—Syr. *ʾbwtʾ*, "patrocinium," used with the verb *ʾḥd*. The Hebrew reflex of this expression may occur in the Manual of Discipline, col. ii l. 9, at the conclusion of a curse: *wlʾ yhyh lkh šlwm bpy kwl ʾwḥzy ʾbwt*.[8]

* *abullu*, "city gate"—Palm. *ʾblʾ*; Syr. *ʾbwlʾ*; Mand. *ʾbwlʾ*; BT *ʾ(y)bwlʾ*; rare elsewhere in JAr.: Targ. Jer. 50:26, Targ. YI Dt. 28:52, and (Hebrew) Tosefta B. Mets. XI, 10. The BH hapax *ʾûḇāl* (Dan. 8:2 f.) is taken by many ancient and modern scholars to be this word (cf. Greek, Syriac, and Saadiah Gaon). The etymology of *abullu* is unknown. It was used in Sumerian alongside the more usual *ká-gal* in the spelling *a-bul*$_x$(ZUR)*-la*, but this is probably borrowed from Akkadian. That it was almost certainly not a part of the early North West Semitic vocabulary is shown by the Amarna gloss *ša-ah-ri* (*EA* 244:16).[9]

aburru, "pasture"—Mand. *ʾbwrnʾyt (?)* (*MD*, p. 3); cf. Syr. (lex.) *ʾbrtʾ*, "reed grass"; hardly YT *ʾbryytʾ*, "rural places."

8. Z, p. 25; *LS*, p. 1; *CAD*, Vol. A, Part I, p. 50, and Vol. Ṣ, p. 24; P. Wernberg-Møller, *The Manual of Discipline* (Leiden, 1957) p. 53; J. Licht, *The Rule Scroll* (Jerusalem, 1965) p. 70; E. Y. Kutscher, "Aramaic Calque in Hebrew," *Tarbiz* XXXIII (1963) 125 f.

9. Z, p. 14; *LS*, p. 2; *AHw.*, p. 8; *KBL*, p. 7. A. W. Sjöberg, "KÁ.GAL(-a) = abulla = *abullu*," *RA* LX (1966) 91, suggests that even when spelled KÁ.GAL the Sumerian is often to be read *abulla*.

abūtu, "a kind of tool" (lex.)—Syr. *ʾbwtʾ*, "ruler," "scraper."

adê, "treaty"—Sefire *ʿdn* (pl. tantum). The relationship and etymology of the Akkadian and Aramaic have often been discussed, but no conclusive results have been reached.[10] Nevertheless, the etymological and phonetic evidence, as well as the occurrence of *adê* in late Akkadian only, almost certainly precludes an Akkadian origin for this political term.[11]

agammu, "marsh"—BH *ʾăgām*, MH, BT, Targ. Prophets, Syr., Mand. *ʾgmʾ*, "(reed) pool." This word, of unknown etymology, is foreign in Akkadian as well as in the other languages.[12]

agannu, "bowl"—BH, Common Ar. *ʾaggân(â)*. The origin of this term is unknown, but the West Semitic and Akkadian distribution (peripheral and late Assyrian) indicates a foreign loan from the West.[13]

agāru, "to hire"—There is no reason to suspect that Common Ar. (and Arab.) *ʾgr* is anything but cognate with the Akkadian verb.[14]

* *agurru*, "kiln-fired brick"—Bab. docket *ʾgw(?)rn*; Syr. *ʾgwrʾ* > Arab., Persian. Though its etymology is unknown, this architectural term was almost certainly borrowed from Akkadian.[15]

akukūtu, "a red glow in the sky"—Syr. *kwkytʾ*, "storm," and BT *kwkytʾ*, "some sort of heavenly phenomenon," are similar in form. The etymology of the Akkadian is unknown, but the phonetic differences between the Akkadian and Aramaic forms point to an origin in a third language.[16]

10. Most recently J. A. Fitzmyer, *The Aramaic Inscriptions of Sefîre* (Rome, 1967) pp. 23 f.; David B. Weisberg, *Guild Structure and Political Allegiance in Early Achaemenid Mesopotamia* (New Haven, 1967) pp. 32 ff.

11. For phonetic considerations see below, p. 142. One should not rule out a Canaanite origin for the term; cf. E. Y. Kutscher, "Samaritan Aramaic," *Tarbiz* XXXVII (1968) 410. In *CAD*, *adû* A and *adû* B should be taken as one word, as in *AHw*.

12. *KBL* (3d ed.) p. 10.

13. Z, p. 33; *LS*, p. 4; *KBL* (3d ed.) p. 11.

14. Z, p. 47; *AHw.*, p. 16. Probably *ʾgr* occurs as "hire" in *agrt* in Ugaritic in I Aqht 213 ("hired woman" [see H. L. Ginsberg, "Ugaritic Myths, Epics, and Legends," *ANET* (2d ed.) p. 155] rather than "employer" [*UT*, p. 351]). This common Semitic root apparently shifted in meaning in some Hebrew dialects and was replaced by *śkr*.

15. Z, p. 31; *LS*, p. 35; *AHw.*, p. 17; S. Fraenkel, *Die aramäischen Fremdwörter im Arabischen* (Leiden, 1886; reprint, Hildesheim, 1962) p. 5. The Babylonian docket is L. Jakob-Rost, Helmut Freydank, "Spätbabylonische Rechtsurkunden aus Babylon mit aramäischen Beischriften," Staatliche Museen zu Berlin, *Forschungen und Berichte*, Vol. XIV, Archäologische Beiträge, 1972, pp. 7-35, No. 14, l. 1.

16. *LS*, p. 320; *Aruch* IV 224*b*, *Additamenta*, p. 222.

* *amāru*, "brick pile"—BT *ʾwʾrʾ*.[17]

ameluttu, "(female) household slave" (*CAD*, Vol. A, Part II, p. 61)—The reading *ʾwltʾ* in the Babylonian docket *DEA*, No. 91: 1 is doubtful in the light of collation of the tablet.

* *amurriqānu*, "jaundice"—Syr. *mryqnʾ*, "a kind of disease." Although the nature of the rare Syriac disease is uncertain, the word must be a loan from the Akkadian term which is derived from the root *wrq*, "yellow."[18]

* *amurru*, "west"—BT *ʾwryʾ*.[19]

* *amuršānu*, "a type of pigeon"—BT *ʾwwršnʾ*, Syr. *wršnʾ* > Arab. *waršān*.[20]

ana, "to"—Some scholars have suggested that the common BT preposition *ʾa*, "on," is not, as usually interpreted, derived from the preposition *ʿal* but is to be related to Akkadian *ana*. There is little to recommend this suggestion, which has been refuted at length by Epstein.[21]

apkallu, "a priest"—Palm., Nab., Hat. *ʾpkl*. The term occurs as well in ESA and appears to have been the name of a high religious functionary among various early Arab peoples. If the Sumerain etymology is correct, it might well have been an early loan into the Arabic culture sphere and may represent an Arabic rather than an Aramaic title in the monumental texts.[22]

17. Stephen A. Kaufman, "Akkadian and Babylonian Aramaic—New Examples of Mutual Elucidation," *Leš*. XXXVI (1972) 28.

18. Z, p. 49; *LS*, p. 310.

19. Z, p. 45; *AHw.*, p. 46. For a possible occurrence of *ʾwr* as "west wind" in BH (Job 38:24) see N. H. Tur-Sinai, *The Book of Job* (Jerusalem, 1967) p. 529, *KBL* (3d ed.) p. 24*b*. The BT form with final *y* is unexpected (cf. p. 149). One might suggest derivation from a nisbe form **amurrû*, "western," though the Akkadian sources give no evidence for such a form.

20. Z, p. 51; *LS*, p. 186; *AHw.*, p. 46.

21. F. Perles, "Ergänzungen zu den 'Akkadischen Fremdwörtern,'" *OLZ* XXI (1918) 65 f.; C. Gordon, "Šamši-Adad's Military Texts from Mari," *Ar.Or.* XVIII (1950) 201, n. 6; J. N. Epstein, *Grammar of Babylonian Aramaic* (Tel Aviv, 1960) pp. 132 ff. Additional evidence not mentioned by Epstein is offered by the fact that except in set phrases like *aššum* and *appitti*, *ana* does not generally assimilate in the late dialects; cf. *CAD*, Vol. A, Part II, p. 100.

22. Z, p. 29; *DISO*, p. 21; *AHw.*, p. 58; R. Borger, "Assyriologische und altarabische Miszellen," *Or.* n.s. XXVI (1957) 8 ff.; J. Teixidor, "Notes hatréenes," *Syria* XLIII (1966) 91 ff., No. 3; T. C. Mitchell, "A South Arabian Tripod Offering Saucer Said to Be from Ur," *Iraq* XXXI (1969) 111 f. The *apkallu* occurs as the name of a profession in Akkadian only in the first millennium, and thus, one might suspect that the loan could only have taken place then; but it is attested as a Sumerian profession

* *appāru*, "reed marsh"—JPA and MH *ʾpr*, "marshy meadow." MS Kaufmann, one of the most reliable of Mishnaic manuscripts, gives the vocalization *ʾappār* for the Hebrew. This term was originally a Sumerian (derived from a substrate?) loanword in Akkadian.[23]

appitti(mma), "accordingly(?)," "certainly(?)"—This modal particle occurring only in NB and LB has been compared to two problematic words in Imperial Aramaic: *ʾpyty* (*AP*, No. 26:9) and *ʾptm* (Ezra 4:13). Unfortunately, the meaning of the Akkadian is by no means certain, though the meaning "accordingly" (*CAD*, Vol. A, Part II, p. 184) seems to fit the Akkadian contexts better than "sicherlich" (*AHw.*, p. 60). Neither meaning fits nicely into the context of *AP*, No. 26, however. In any case the first *y* of the Aramaic form is difficult to explain, and the preservation of the final *i* is unusual (see Phonology in Chap. III). BA *ʾptm* has possible Persian etymologies and is probably not connected with the Akkadian word.[24]

apsu, "deep water"—see below, p. 152.

aptu, "window"—BT *ʾptʾ*, "balcony." Cf. as well *appātu* in *bīt appāti*, the Akkadian translation of "Amorite" *bīt hilāni*, "a type of building with a columned portico and a balcony above."[25]

* *arad ekalli*, "builder"—Eg., Hat., JAr. (Targ. Prophets, Targ. Hagiographa, BT [Erub. 26*a*]), Syr., Mand., *ʾrd(y)kl(ʾ)*; RH also *ʾdrykl*, "architect." Oppenheim's thorough study of this term leaves little doubt that NB *arad ekalli* was a professional involved with building and that the Aramaic is a loan from Akkadian.[26]

* *argamannu*, "red purple wool"—Common Ar. *ʾargwân* > Arab. *ʾurǧwân*, "purple." This culture word of as yet uncertain origin occurs first in the west during the Late Bronze Age and then in Mesopotamia in the first millennium. If Hebrew and

as early as Old Sumerian (see *CAD*, Vol. A, Part II, p. 173*a*). Thus, its development and cultural importance in South Arabian leads us to look for a loan significantly earlier than the NA reference to a South Arabian priestess as *apkallatu*.

23. E. Y. Kutscher, "Marginal Notes to the Mishnaic Lexicon and a Grammatical Note" (Heb.), *Leš.* XXXI (1967) 107, and "Mittelhebräisch und Jüdisch-Aramäisch im neuen Köhler-Baumgartner," Suppl. *VT* XVI (1967) 163.

24. *DISO*, p. 21; *KBL*, p. 105; F. Rosenthal, *A Grammar of Biblical Aramaic* (Wiesbaden, 1963) p. 59.

25. Z, p. 32; *Additamenta*, p. 61.

26. Z, p. 26; A. L. Oppenheim, "Akk. *arad ekalli* = 'Builder,'" *Ar.Or.* XVII (1949) 227 ff. Oppenheim himself concluded only that it was probably a loanword in Aramaic. His hesitation and that expressed in the *CAD* are unwarranted.

Ugaritic forms with *m* represent the original form, the Aramaic appears explicable only on the basis of a loan from Babylonian, with intervocalic /m/ > [w]. Though purple wool was a precious commodity and was often used for royal tribute, one cannot be certain that Mand. *ʾrgbʾ*, "money(?)," reflects this word, for it presents a phonetic as well as a semantic problem, especially inasmuch as a correct Mandaic reflex occurs as *rgwʾn*.[27]

* *arhu*, "half-brick"—Syr., JAr. *ʾrḥʾ*; MH *ʾ(w)ryḥ*.[28]

* *arittu*, "canal"—BT, Targ. Onk., and Targ. Psalms *ʾrytʾ*. Although this word occurs only in Neo-Babylonian, both its distribution in Aramaic and its presumed etymology from *warittu* (< *wrd*) indicate that it is a loanword.[29]

* *arru*, "decoy bird"—Hapax Syr. *ʾrʾ*, hapax BT *ʾrʾ*.[30]

* *arsānu*, "groats"—Syr. *ʾrsnʾ*. This is almost certainly the same word as MH *ʿrsn*, but it is not clear whether the Hebrew represents the continuation of an old form of this culture

27. Z, p. 37; *LS*, p. 46; *CAD*, Vol. A, Part II, p. 253; Wagner, p. 28; C. Rabin, "Hittite Words in Hebrew," *Or*. n.s. XXXII (1963) 116 ff.; B. Landsberger, "Über Farben im Sumerisch-akkadischen," *JCS* XXI (1967) 155 ff., and in general A. L. Oppenheim, "Essay on Overland Trade in the First Millennium B.C.," *JCS* XXI (1967) 244 ff. The form with *w* occurs in Qumran Hebrew as well.

28. *LS*, p. 48; *AHw*., p. 67. Cf. N. H. Tur-Sinai, *The Language and the Book* I (2d ed.; Jerusalem, 1954) 146 ff. The Hebrew could have been borrowed directly from the Akkadian: *arhu* [arēh] > *ʾărē/īăḥ* or from the Aramaic absolute form before the sound law final eG(uttural) > aG took effect (or where it did not operate at all). A phonetic change by analogy with *yārēăḥ* is also feasible. (Is this the correct etymology as well, < *arhu*, "moon"?) The forms with "y" in Jewish Aramaic are either incorrect textual variants (cf. the dictionaries) or Hebraisms. (Cf. *Additamenta*, p. 66.) There may be confusion between two words here, however, for a development into "carrying pole" (Targ. Onk.) is unlikely, though not impossible; half-brick > lath > pole. Cf. G. Hoffmann, "Lexikalisches," *ZAW* II (1882) 70 ff. For *ʾrḥ* in Ahiqar (Eg.) see Chap. IV, n. 83.

29. Z, p. 44; F. Perles, review of J. Levy and L. Goldschmidt, *Nachträge und Berichtigungen*, *OLZ* XXVIII (1925) 320; *CAD*, Vol. A, Part II, p. 269.

30. Z, p. 15; *LS*, p. 45*b*; *AHw*., p. 71; and most recently D. Weisberg, "Some Observations on Late Babylonian Texts and Rabbinic Literature," *HUCA* XXXIX (1968) 76 f., who however, overlooks the Syriac (Ahiqar 69,4) which gives a clear description of the *ʾarrâ* as something which "saves itself not from death, but brings its comrade to the net with its voice." Though the origin of *arru* is unknown, it is well attested in Akkadian, while its limited Aramaic distribution points strongly to a loan.

word of uncertain etymology, or is an assimilation (orthographic?) to BH *ᶜărîsāh*.[31]

* *asītu*, "tower (of a city wall)"—BH **ʾošyāh* (said of Babylon); BT, Mand. *ʾšytʾ*, "wall"; Syr. *ʾšytʾ*, "column" > Arab. *ʾâsyah*, "column." This word also occurs in Targ. Psalms, but similar-looking words elsewhere in JPA seem all to be from *ʾ(w)šʾ*, "foundation"; see *uššu*. Syr. *ʾstʾ* (pl. *ʾsʾ*), "wall," is probably cognate; otherwise the Syriac form with *s* would indicate a loan from Babylonian, while *asītu* occurs only in Assyrian.[32]

* *askuppu/atu*, "threshold," "doorsill"—Syr., JPA, CPA *ʾskwptʾ* > Arab. *ʾuskuffah*; Mand. *ʾsqwptʾ*; JPA *ʾ(y)sqwph*; Mand., Targ. Prophets *sqwptʾ* > Eastern Neo-Aramaic *squpt/ṯa*; The Heb. and JAr. forms *šqwp* and *šqpʾ* may be the result of assimilation to the form of the BH cognates *šeqep̄* and *mašqôp̄* or may be legitimate Hebrew forms.[33]

asmarû, "lance"—see below, p. 153.

* *asû*, "physician"— Common Ar. *ʾsyʾ* (> Arab., Ethiopic). Except for the uncertain Imp. Ar. occurrence in *AG*, No. 67:1, the earliest attestations are in Qumran, Palmyran, and Nabatean (hardly BH *ʾāsôn* as a euphemism). Note that the denominative verbs are later developments in Aramaic as no verb is known in Akkadian. The traditional Sumerian etymology as "one who knows the water" has recently been challenged,[34] but lacking a good Sumerian etymology, it must be considered to be of pre-Sumerian origin and thus still a Sumerian loanword in Akkadian.[35]

31. Z, p. 56 and *AHw.*, p. 71 (Heb. only); B. Landsberger and O. R. Gurney, "Practical Vocabulary of Assur," *AfO* XVIII (1957-58) 339; *Aruch* VI 271.

32. Z, p. 14; *LS*, p. 52*b*; *AHw.*, p. 74; *KBL*, p. 91; Wagner, p. 30. The meaning of the Biblical Hebrew term is uncertain. M. Ellenbogen's suggestion (*Foreign Words in the Old Testament* [London, 1962] p. 41) that it refers to a glacis is highly unlikely, for the passage refers to Iron Age Babylon, not Bronze Age Palestine. The lexical term *aṣītu*, "part of a building," is apparently to be differentiated from *asītu*. With the former compare Syr. *yᶜytʾ* (*ᶜᶜytʾ*), Targ. Proph. *npqtʾ* (and BT *npqy(?)*, cf. J. Levy, *Chaldaisches Wörterbuch über die Targumim* [Leipzig, 1881] II 122) "projection of a wall."

33. Z, p. 31; *LS*, p. 35*a*; *AHw.*, p. 74; A. Salonen, *Die Türen des alten Mesopotamien* (Helsinki, 1961) p. 57. According to I. Löw, "Lexikalische Miszellen," in *Festschrift zum siebzigsten Geburtstage David Hoffmann's* (Berlin, 1914) pp. 119 f., and A. Kohut, *Aruch*, s.v. *šqwp*, *ʾsqwph* is "sill" and *šqwp* is "lintel," suggesting that the latter is a legitimate Hebrew form. Note that a borrowing from Assyrian is precluded, for the form there is *aksuppu*.

34. Cf. *CAD*, Vol. A, Part II, p. 347*b*.

35. Z, p. 49; *LS*, p. 31; *AHw.*, p. 76; *KBL*, p. 71; Wagner, p. 27.

* *asumittu*, "stele"—Teima *swt*.[36]

* *asuppu*, "portico"—BH *ʾāsōp̄*; Qumran Ar. (5Q15 I 16-19) *ʾspʾ*; BT (and RH) *ʾsy/wpʾ*; Syr. *ʾswpʾ*. The etymology is unknown.[37]

aṣītu, hapax in a broken lexical text for "prostitute" and related connotations of the verb *aṣû*, "to go out"—Targ. Onk., Prophets, Neofiti *npqt br* (RH *ywṣʾt hḥws*); Syr. *npqt šwqʾ*, "prostitute" (see also Sam. Targum *lmtbrʾh* for BH *lznwt*, Lev. 21:9, 14). The noun form cited was certainly not one of the many common Akkadian words for women of this type and may even be a calque from Aramaic. Although the use of the verb with this connotation is very old, it is unlikely that such a connotation would have been borrowed, especially into a non-cognate verb.[38]

* *ašāšu*, "reed basket(?)," "reed shelter(?)" (lex. only)—Mand. *ʾšʾšʾ*, Syr. lex. *ʾššʾ*, "reed raft." Though the mean- of the Akkadian is uncertain, it clearly is some kind of reed construction, presumably originally made by water fowl. The similar sphere of meaning of the Aramaic term and its limited distribution leaves little doubt that it represents the developed meaning of an inherited culture word.

ašgandu—Occurring in Akkadian only in Neo-Babylonian as a non-Akkadian family name, it may or may not be connected with the Iranian loan in Syr. *ʾyzg(n)dʾ*, Mand. *ʾšgʾndʾ*, "messenger."[39]

* *āšipu*, "exorcist"—BA and BH *ʾšp* (noun); Syr. *ʾšpʾ* and *ʾšwpʾ* and verb *ʾšp* (pʿal); Mand. verb *ʾšp* only. Note that this word does not occur in JAr. As the Akkadian comes from a root with initial *waw*, there can be no question of a cognate here. It is noteworthy that none of the Aramaic forms reflect the active participle form of the Akkadian but rather other "professional" noun forms. The unusual BA vocalization *ʾāšap̄* could

36. Z, p. 8; *DISO*, p. 191; Koopmans, *Aramäische Chrestomathie* (Leiden, 1962) p. 163. For very uncertain Punic attestations see *DISO*, s.v. *sywʿt*.

37. *AHw.*, p. 77; E. Y. Kutscher, "Marginal Notes to the Biblical Lexicon" (Heb.), *Leš.* XXVIII (1963) 183 f., XXX (1965) 24; G. Sarfatti, "ʾsp = 'portico,'" *Leš.* XXXI (1966) 79; J. C. Greenfield, "The Small Caves of Qumran," *JAOS* LXXXIX (1969) 133; *KBL*, p. 72.

38. J. J. Finkelstein, "Sex Offenses in Sumerian Laws," *JAOS* LXXXVI (1966) 362 f. and n. 29. His discussion of similar uses of *yṣʾ* in old Biblical Hebrew texts supports the position that the use of the verb "to go out" in this connection is ancient. For Old Babylonian compare also *CAD*, Vol. A, Part II, p. 360*a*.

39. *CAD*, Vol. A, Part II, p. 427; H. Happ, "Zu ásgándēs, áskandēs, ástandēs = 'Bote,'" *Glotta* XL (1962) 198-200.

conceivably be a reflex of the original Akkadian form, but there are unfortunately no other loanwords of similar phonetic shape with which to compare it. Since the word does not occur in JAr., however, one might consider assigning the BA vocalization to Masoretic error.[40]

aširtu, "santuary"—see below, p. 153.

* *aškāpu*, "leatherworker"—Hat. No. 212 *[ʾ]škpʾ* (*Sumer* XX [1964] 79); Syr. *ʾškpʾ*; MH (Tosephta), JPA *(ʾ)škp*; BT *ʾwškpʾ* > Arab. *ʾsk(ʾ)f*, *sakkâf*, "shoemaker."[41]

* *ašlu*, "tow rope," "measuring rope"—Eg. *ʾšl* (see *DISO*, p. 27), "area measure"; Syr. *ʾyšlʾ*, BT, Targ. Job (canonical), Targ. YI, Mand. *ʾšlʾ* > Arab. *ʾašl*, "rope," "tow rope," "measuring rope." Though the word itself may well be cognate in Aramaic and Akkadian (cf. Arab. *ʾsl*, "rush" = Akk. *ašlu* B [in *CAD*] and the unexpected form of the Syriac), Akkadian was almost certainly of some influence in its use as a standard measure and perhaps in the meaning "tow rope."[42]

aššum, "concerning," "because of" (< *ana šum*)—Kutscher has compared the Akkadian to Eg. *bšm* (Demotic *n-rn*), "concerning (the object of a suit)"; MH *mšwm*, *ʿl šwm*; Syr. (hapax) *ʿl šmʾ*, "because." The Egyptian Aramaic form cannot legitimately be compared with the Akkadian, however, for the latter occurs in a similar context only once, in an Old Babylonian Alalakh text; thus, the Demotic should be considered primary here.[43]

40. Z, p. 67; *LS*, p. 53; *KBL*, p. 93. Sum. *išib* is also a loan from *āšipu*; cf. *CAD*, Vol. I/J, p. 243*a*. The suggestion by Ellenbogen (*Foreign Words*, p. 43) that this word can be found in II Kings 5 *ʾsp* is not without some merit. On the basis of other uses of this verb in the sense of "remove," we might expect "leprosy" to be the direct object (as it is once in v. 11) and not the man (as in vv. 3, 6, 7). Note as well that the verb is used only to describe the cure as conceived by Naaman (v. 7) and not the actual cure by immersion.

41. Z, p. 28; *LS*, p. 777; A. Salonen, *Die Fussbekleidung der alten Mesopotamier* (Helsinki, 1969) p. 92. The loss of initial *aleph* in the Palestinian forms has parallels. Cf. H. L. Ginsberg, "Zu den Dialekten des Talmudisch-Hebräischen," *MGWJ* LXXVII (1933) 427 f.

42. Z, p. 35; *LS*, p. 53; Fraenkel, *Aramäischen Fremdwörter*, p. 93; *DISO*, p. 27; *AD* (2d ed.) p. 68. The phonetic similartiy between *ašlu* and Sum. *eše*, "rope," is probably coincidental; nevertheless, that similarity may have been at least partially the cause for the development of "rush" into "rope" in Akkadian.

43. Z, p. 70; E. Y. Kutscher, "New Aramaic Texts," *JAOS* LXXIV (1954) 242; Y. Muffs, *Studies in the Aramaic Legal Papyri from Elephantine* (Leiden, 1969) p. 31, n. 2. The various Mishnaic uses of *mšwm*, *ʿl šwm*, and *lšwm* are complicated, as are the meanings of the noun *šwm* itself, hardly a back-formation from the prepositions.

Kutscher ("Two 'Passive' Constructions in Aramaic in the Light of Persian," *Proceedings*, p. 133) has also pointed out the problem of deter-

The Akkadian may either be a native construction or a loan from Sumerian *mu . . . šè*; compare Geʾez *ʾesma*, "because."[44]

* *atappu*, "small canal"—Syr. *tpʾ*, "canal."[45]

* *attalû*, "eclipse"—Syr. *ʾtlyʾ*, Mand. *tʾlyʾ*, Medieval Hebrew *tly*, "the mythical dragon or constellation which causes eclipses," "eclipse."[46]

* *bābu*, "doorway," "gate"—Eg., Ahiqar narrative, Uruk, Palm., Pehlevi logogram, Mand., BT, and Targ. Hagiographa (> Arab.) *bāḇâ*. The Neo-Babylonian usage in the sense of "account entry," "sector of a field" occurs in *AP*, No. 81, where the meaning must be "account entry" and in a developed form in BT, Mand., and the Pehlevi logogram (and late Arabic) "section of a written work," section."[47] The strictly eastern attestation of this word in the late dialects presents an extremely strong case for borrowing, and there is no reason to suggest (cf. *AHw*. p. 95*b*) that the new NB meanings should be the result of a reborrowing from Aramaic or that the borrowing from Akkadian should have taken place any earlier than the NB period. That it is still a fairly recent borrowing is shown by the confusion prevailing in Eg. and Ahiqar between *bbʾ* and *trʿ*. (Note especially the borrowed Akk. phrase *bāb ekalli*, twice rendered *bb hyklʾ* [ll.

mining the origin of the construction NN *šmh*, used in Egyptian, Biblical Aramaic, and Old Persian and in the Akkadian version of the Behistun inscription at the first appearance of proper names. In spite of the somewhat doubtful observation of H. Bauer and P. Leander (*Grammatik des Biblisch-Aramäischen* [Halle, 1927] p. 358) that this construction seems to have "eine degradierende Bedeutung," this practice can scarcely be connected with the Old Babylonian use of Sum. mu-ni-im after the name of slaves in contracts. Note that precisely this construction (NN *rn-f*) is the regular one in all stages of Egyptian.

44. See F. Rundgren, *Über Bildungen mit š- und n-t- Demonstrativen im Semitischen* (Uppsala, 1955) pp. 19 ff.

45. Z, p. 44; *LS*, p. 830; *AHw.*, p. 86.

46. Z, p. 63; *LS*, p. 55; *AHw.*, p. 54; *MD*, p. 479; T. Nöldeke, "Aus einem Briefe des Herrn Prof. Th. Nöldeke an C. Bezold," *ZA* XXV (1911) 355 ff.; C. Bezold, "Aus der Antwort auf diesen Brief," *ZA* XXV (1911) 357 f.; W. Baumgartner, "Zur Mandäerfrage," *HUCA* XXIII (1950-51) 60, n. 73; J. Buxtorf, *Lexicon Chaldaicum, Talmudicum et Rabbinicum*, ed. by B. Fischer (Leipzig, 1875) p. 1288*a*; A. Even-Shoshan, *HaMilon HeḤadash* (Jerusalem, 1970) p. 1454. The most complete study of this term and its history is that of G. Furlani, "Tre trattati astrologici siriaci sulle eclissi solare e lunare," *AANL, Rendiconti*, Series VIII, Vol. II (1947) pp. 576 ff. For a relatively early Neo-Assyrian statement on the nature of eclipses see *HABL*, No. 437 r. 11-12 (cited by K. Deller, "Zur Syntax des Infinitivs im Neuassyrischen," *Or.* n.s. XXXI [1962] 228): TA du-ri AN.KU$_{10}$ ^{d}XXX te-ḫe-e DINGIR.MEŠ, "from of old an eclipse of the moon is a conjunction of gods."

47. Cf. the use of Syr. *pṯâḥâ* in the sense of "capitulum (libri)" (*LS*, p. 616) and of *tarʿâ* as a literary division.

17, 23] and once by *trʿ hyklʾ* [l. 44].) This conflict might well account for the retention of *bâḇâ* only in the East, where the conflict was resolved by limiting the sense of the word *trʿ* (cf. *daltu*).[48]

* *balaggu*, "drum"—Syr. *plgʾ* (*plaggâ*).[49]

* *bārānû*, "rebel"—BT *brywnʾ*, "rebel." One must separate, as Jastrow does, this strictly BT word both semantically and etymologically from the identical Rabbinic Hebrew form, apparently of Latin etymology, meaning "palace guard." On the other hand, relating the talmudic word to its Neo-Assyrian semantic equivalent entails considerable phonetic difficulty. One might suggest that the attested Aramaic form is the result of confusion with and subsequent graphic assimilation to the Hebrew word. Note the unique Akkadian orthography *ba-ra-a-nu-ú*, suggesting a pronunciation with a *y* glide.[50]

bārû, "diviner"—Mand. *bʾrʾyʾ*, "exorcizer(?)." Unfortunately, the two Mandaic attestations are in unpublished texts. One would expect the Mandic form to be *bʾryʾ*, however; thus its correct interpretation may well be "foreigner."[51]

batāqu, "to cut through"—There is no reason to consider BH *bedeq*, "fissure," "breach," or JAr., Mand. *bdq*, "to burst" (let alone the more common Aramaic meaning "to search," "to repair") as "under strong Akkadian influence."[52]

48. Z, p. 30; *AHw.*, p. 95; *DISO*, p. 32; Fraenkel, *Aramäischen Fremdwörter*, p. 14; P. Jouon, "Notes grammaticales, lexicographiques et philologiques sur les papyrus araméenes d'Egypte," *Mélanges de l'Université Saint-Joseph* XVIII (1934) 17. The Arabic borrowing was probably very early, from a dialect still under the influence of Imperial Aramaic. For the limitation of the meaning of *trʿ*, cf. especially Palm. *bbʾ wtrʿwh* (*DISO*, p. 32). That *bbʾ* was considered indicative of the Babylonian dialect is demonstrated by the story related in BT Nedarim 66*b*.

49. *LS*, p. 571. The late Akk. forms often have "p." For the history and nature of the instrument see *CAD*, Vol. B, p. 39*a*.

50. This etymology has not been previously suggested. On the Jewish forms, cf. M. Jastrow, *A Dictionary of the Targumim, the Talmudic Babli and Yerushalmi, and the Midrashic Literature* (reprint; New York, 1950) p. 193; *Additamenta*, pp. 106 f. For Akkadian, *CAD*, Vol. B, p. 103. An etymology from *bryʾ*, "outside," "foreign," and mere chance similarity to the Akkadian cannot be ruled out; compare MH *bôr*.

51. *MD*, p. 50. The old emendation (cf. Z, p. 67) of BH *bdym* in Isa. 44:25, Jer. 50:36 "diviners" to **brym* is far superior to Driver's etymology adopted by *KBL* (3d ed.) p. 105 and M. Wagner, "Beiträge zur Aramaismenfrage im alttestamentlichen Hebräisch," Suppl. *VT* XVI (1967) 358 (= Mari *baddum*, a military official of some sort, attested nowhere else); but it is by no means certain in view of the uses of the verb *bd* in Ugaritic, the nouns *bd* in Phoenician, and *bd* IV in Hebrew (and Syr. *beḏyâ*).

52. J. C. Greenfield, "Lexicographical Notes I," *HUCA* XXIX (1958) 221, n. 4. Cf. *KBL* (3d ed.) p. 106. Indeed Akk. *batāqu* (and the BH hapax

* *bēl dabābi*, "adversary"—Syr., CPA, Mand., BT, Targ. Hagiographa, and RH *bᶜldbb*ʾ, "enemy," and derived forms of adjectives, abstracts, and the like in these as well as JPA, Targ. Onk., and Sam., all in the sense of "enmity." This is to be kept separate from the form *dbb* occurring in Egyptian Aramaic in the hendiadys *dyn wdbb*, a loan from the NA expression *dīnu u dābabu*, "suit and process," which is the only place in Aramaic where the juridical meaning of *dbb* is preserved. For "adversary in court" the term *bᶜl dyn*ʾ is the usual expression. This fact militates against the possibility that the highly uncertain Mandaic verb *dbb* (pael), "to accuse(?)," is correctly interpreted or that the Akkadian semantic development from "adversary" to NB "enemy" could be the result of Aramaic influence.[53] More difficult to determine is the relationship between Akk. *dibbu*, "report," "rumor," and BH *dibbāh*, Syr., JAr., Mand. (conjectured for BH? cf. *KBL* [3d ed.] p. 352) *ṭebbâ* with the same meaning.[54] If, with von Soden (*AHw.*, p. 146), one assumes that Akk. *dabābu* is cognate with Heb. *dibbēr*, then a loan relationship must be posited, since Hebrew would then not have had a verb **dbb*, "to mutter." There is no reason to accept this suggestion, however, for the Heb. verb *dibbēr* is certainly a denominative from the word *dāḇār*, as substantiated by its nonexistence in Ugaritic and Aramaic. Thus, there could have been a Hebrew/Aramaic cognate to Akk. *dabābu* which persisted in a nominal form, leaving only a trace as a verb.[55] Several facts support this position: The Hebrew has a feminine form as opposed to the Aramaic and Akkadian masculine forms. A loan correspondence Akk. *d* > Ar. *ṭ* is otherwise unknown (though such a development within Aramaic is equally difficult to explain). The meanings "report," "gossip," "matter" occur fully developed in NA and NB, but the term is extremely rare in earlier texts and only in the sense "word." One might even suggest possible Aramaic in-

btq) appears at first to be the unexpected form in the group of roots composed of a labial, dental, and velar stop meaning "to split": Arab., Ethiopic *btk*; Arab., Ar. *f/ptq*; Ar., Heb. (and Ug. *bdqt*?) *bdq*. But *batāqu* is in fact the correct Akkadian reflex of original *bdq*; cf. *GAG Ergänz.*, p. 8**, § 51*d*.

53. So E. S. Rimalt, "Wechselbeziehungen zwischen dem Aramäischen und dem Neubabylonischen," *WZKM* XXXIX (1932) 122; but cf. BH *bᶜl dbrym* in Exod. 24:14.

54. MH *ṭyb*, "nature," "character," is derived from the Aramaic form. Good manuscripts of the Mishna do indicate a doubled *b* before suffixes, e.g. *ṭibbô* (E. Y. Kutscher, orally).

55. The Rabbinic interpretation of Cant. 7:10 *dôḇēḇ* and their use of the verb *dbb* with "lips" in the clear meaning "to murmur" may well reflect more than just etymology by exegesis (cf. Jastrow, *Dictionary*, p. 276, and Targ. Canticles). Such an interpretation of the Biblical passage, to be translated "makes lips of sleepers murmur," is superior to some of the modern attempts to understand the phrase (see *KBL* [3d ed.] pp. 199 f.). Also see Arab. *ḏbḏb* and *ṭbṭb*.

fluence on the semantic development in late Akkadian![56] If it were a loan from Akkadian, the Hebrew form with *ḏ* (as against Aramaic *ṭ*) and its frequent occurrence throughout the Old Testament would point to a very early loan indeed, a situation not in agreement with the nature of the word, which was clearly not borrowed in any juridical sense (see Chap. IV, n. 77).[57]

* *bēl dīni*, "adversary in court"—Qumran, Syr., Mand., JAr. *bʿldynʾ*; possibly an early calque in Isa. 50:8 *bʿl mšpṭ*. Though presumably *bēl dīni* was the most common expression for this concept in both NB and NA, the early peripheral attestations of the Akkadian form point to a possible Assyrian origin for the loan at a relatively early date.[58]

* *bēl piqitti*, "commissioner," "overseer"—Imp. Ar.: Caquot, "Inscription" *bʿl pqt*. Although the Aramaic text itself dates from the period of Babylonian control of Syria, this Akkadian term is apparently used here in its Assyrian sense of "royal commissioner" rather than the Babylonian usage as a temple official.

bīʾu (bību), "drainage opening" MA, NA, SB—MH, JPA, Syr. *bîḇ*, Arab. *bîb*, "pipe," "gutter." The history of this term of uncertain origin is difficult to trace. The Akkadian orthographies indicate a pronunciation *[bīw(u)]*. Thus, unless spirantization of *b* was already operative at the time of borrowing, it could not be a loan into Aramaic. Syriac and BT (Sabb. 29*a*) also use the form *bwbyʾ* in a similar if not identical meaning as well as a homonym meaning "frying pan." (The Akkadian lexical list entry *bubû*, "part of an oven," is probably to be connected with the latter.) Note that *bîb* is found only in Syriac and Western Aramaic and in Assyrian, whereas *bwbyʾ* is only in Syriac and Babylonian Talmudic, suggesting that *bwbyʾ* may originally be a Babylonian form of the Assyrian and Western *bīb*. Cf. the hapax OB *bubû*, a topographical feature.[59]

56. It must be remembered that *ṭebbâ* and its several related verbal forms (but peal only three times?) are generally connected with Arab. and Ethiopic *ṭbb* (cf. *LS*, p. 265). The Ar. root *dbb* could have assimilated to the root *ṭbb* of similar meaning, thus accounting for the shift *d* > *ṭ*.

57. Z, p. 24; *LS*, p. 83; *AHw.*, p. 146; *CAD*, Vol. B, pp. 132 f.; *KBL* (3d ed.) p. 200; Muffs, *Studies*, p. 31 n. and p. 196.

58. Z, p. 24; *AHw.*, p. 119. Earlier suggestions that the word *dîn* itself and the corresponding verbal root were borrowed from Akkadian (cf. Z, p. 24, *LS*, p. 145) have been shown incorrect by its common occurrence in Ugaritic. For *bʿl dyn* in Qumran Aramaic see J. T. Milik, "Turfan et Qumran, Livre des Géants juif et manichéen," in *Tradition und Glaube, Festgabe K. G. Kuhn* (Göttingen, 1971) p. 124.

59. *AHw.*, p. 134.

* *biltu*, "tribute"—BA *blw*. The BA form is probably a corruption from **blt*. Occurring in sequence with *hlk* and *mndh*, it can scarcely be anything but a foreign word in Aramaic. It should be noted, however, that the three terms never occur together in Akkadian. Although *biltu* and *maddattu* are common together in NA, the BA group seems to be a reflex of the threefold list of Persian taxes represented in LB by the forms *ilku*, *bāru*, and *nadi/anātu*, the middle term being a loanword from Old Persian **bhara*. It is thus conceivable that *blw* is a corruption of the latter term rather than Akk. *biltu*. None of the attempts to find *biltu* in any other Aramaic texts or in Hebrew are convincing. The word *blw* does occur in Jewish Aramaic, but only in reference to the Ezra passages.[60]

* *birītu*, "alley"—Syr. *brytʾ*, Mand. *byryʾ*, Qumran 5Q15 I *bryt* (const.), BT, and Targ. Proverbs 1:21 *brytʾ*. Jewish lexicographers have confused this word with others, but its use in Baba Bathra 40b together with *šwqʾ* to describe the types of streets in a city perfectly parallels Mandaic and Akkadian occurrences.[61]

* *birtu*, "citadel," "fort"—Eg., Persepolis, Behistun, BA, BH, Syr., JAr. *byrtʾ*, "palace," "fortress," Nab. *byrtʾ*, "temple." Albright's suggested etymology from a root *wbr* may be correct, but that does not rule out the possibility that we are dealing here with an Old Amorite word.[62] Note the NB plural *biranātu*, corresponding to BH *bîrāniyyôṯ* (and JAr. *byrnytʾ*), both best explained as borrowed from Aramaic.[63]

bītu, "an area of land (requiring a given amount of seed)"—There are similar usages in Aramaic and Hebrew, but since the Akkadian is limited to Neo-Assyrian, one cannot determine in which language this method of area measurement originated.[64]

60. Z, p. 10; W. Henning, "Arabisch ḫarāǧ," *Or.* n.s. IV (1935) 291 ff.; *AF*, p. 51, n. 3; G. R. Driver, "Problems in Aramaic and Hebrew Texts," *An.Or.* XII (1935) 54 f., and *AD* (abridged) p. 97; *KBL* (3d ed.) p. 127.

61. Z, p. 43; *LS*, p. 88; *MD*, p. 62; Jastrow, *Dictionary*, p. 167; M. Baillet, J. T. Milik, and R. de Vaux, *Discoveries in the Judaean Desert III* (Oxford, 1962) 187.

62. W. F. Albright, "The Nebuchadnezzar and Neriglissar Chronicles," *BASOR*, No. 143 (1956) p. 33.

63. Z, p. 14; *LS*, p. 69; *AHw.*, p. 129; Wagner, pp. 34 f.; *KBL* (3d ed.) p. 119. The possibility that *bîrâ* is an old word in Aramaic is not ruled out by the form *byrt* in *AP*, No. 13:4, as would be the case if the scribe confused the form *byrh* and *byrt* in the absolute state (cf. *egirtu*), for the obvious meaning requires the determined state. Thus, as usually interpreted, the form must be in error. See *Persepolis*, p. 20 for the same phenomenon in the Persepolis texts.

64. Cf. H. L. Ginsberg, "Aramaic Letters," *ANET* (3d ed.) p. 633, n. 3, and *CAD*, Vol. B, p. 292.

bubû, see *bīʾu*.

* *bukānu*, "pestle"—Syr., BT (JPA rare) *bwknʾ*, RH *bwknh*. The etymology is uncertain, but the long *û* in the Aramaic forms points to a loan (see Phonology, in Chap. IV).[65]

* *bulṭītu*, "termite"—Syr. *blṭytʾ*, Targ. Proverbs and Job *b(w)lṭytʾ*. The earlier Akkadian form is *bušṭītu*.[66]

* *burû*, "reed mat"—Syr. *bwryʾ*, pl. *bwrwtʾ*, Mand. *(ʾ)bwryʾ*, BT *bwryʾ*, > Persian *būryā*. Note (*CAD*, Vol. B, p. 340*b*) that the Akkadian reading with *b* rather than *p* is based on the Aramaic form, but this evidence is inconclusive, for BT and Mandaic also have the form *pwryʾ*.[67]

buṣinnu, "lamp wick" SB, NA—Syr., JPA, Sam., CPA *bwṣynʾ*. In light of the western distribution of the Aramaic and the *-innu* ending, indicative of a foreign word in Akkadian, this may well be a foreign word in both languages in spite of the Semitic-looking *ṣ*.[68]

* *dabābu*, see *bēl dabābi*.

dajjālu, "scout," "inspector," (attendant?)—BT *dyʾlʾ*, "constable"; hardly > Ar. *ṭayyel*, "to walk about." The *CAD* and von Soden differ as to the meaning and origin of the Akkadian, found only in the later dialects.[69]

daltu, "door"—Eg. *dš*, pl. *dššyn*; BT, Targ. Onk., and Targ. Hagiographa *dšʾ*; Sam. *dršh*; Mand. *dyštʾ*, *dʾštʾ*. The excellent suggestion of Zimmern's relating the Aramaic form *dš* to the necessary Assyrian reflex of *daltu : dassu*, has been less widely accepted than some of his more unlikely associations.[70] The phonetic correspondence is perfect, and this etymology is far superior to a derivation from the root *dwš*, "to thresh," "to tread." Interestingly the old Semitic word *dalt* occurs in Aramaic only in the Sam. and Y. Targums, as a translation of BH *delet̠*.[71]

65. Z, p. 36; *LS*, p. 73; *AHw.*, p. 136.

66. Z, p. 52; *LS*, p. 75; *AHw.*, p. 143.

67. Z, p. 35; *LS*, p. 95; *AHw.*, p. 141.

68. Z, p. 35; *LS*, p. 63; *AHw.*, p. 143; *CAD*, Vol. B, p. 348. The story related in BT Nedarim 66*b* indicates that the Rabbis knew that in the West *bwṣyn* meant "lamp," whereas it was a pumpkin-like vegetable in the East (cf. Mandaic). The latter may be related to the Akk. *buṣinnu* plant.

69. Z, p. 7; *LS*, p. 271; *AHw.*, p. 150; von Soden, in *Or.* n.s. XXXVII (1968) 270 (where "nicht echt akkad." must be an error for "echt akkad.").

70. Not cited in *DISO* or *AHw*.

71. Z, p. 30; *Additamenta*, p. 153; E. Y. Kutscher, *Words and Their History* (Jerusalem, 1961) p. 25. The Mandaic forms could represent new formations after assimilation of the word *daššša* to the root *dwš*. Note the

* *dannatu,* "valid tablet"—*dnt,* passim in Assyrian endorsements. It has been suggested that Nabatean *tqp,* "valid document," is a calque of the Assyrian form.[72]

dannu (*AHw. tannu,* always spelled DAN-nu), "vat"—Syr., BT *dnʾ,* Mand. *dʾnʾ,* Arab. *dann,* "jar" (cf. also RH *dwn* and JAr. *dny*). According to *CAD,* Vol. D, p. 99*a,* the word derives from the Akk. adjective *dannu,* "strong," but this etymology is by no means certain. The term is restricted to NA and NB but may occur in Ugaritic as a container for bread. For the reading *tannu* compare Mand. *tʾnʾ,* "primeval matrix."[73]

dappu, "(wooden) board"—Syr., JAr., and MH *dp(ʾ)* > Arab. *daff(ah),* "board," "tablet," "column," "page." The relationship here is difficult to analyze. The Akkadian, attested only for late NA, NB, and LB, looks very much like a loan from Aramaic. In addition there is the unusual NA by-form *adappu.* This word is generally treated together with *ṭuppu,* "tablet" < Sum. DUB (which appears to have been borrowed into ESA *ṭp*). In OB one finds the form *dibbu/dippu* for "plank" from Sum. DIB. Thus, it is assumed that *dappu,* too, is a Sumerian loanword from a form DAB, but all this is extremely uncertain. The form *ṭp* occurs in Aramaic, in *AP,* No. 26, but there the context involves wood. Why doesn't Sum. *DAB or Akk. *dappu* occur earlier if there really is such a Sumerian form? Taken as a whole, the evidence suggests that in the case of *dappu* we are dealing with a very old loanword (or an old culture word) which, after independent development in Aramaic, was re-borrowed into Akkadian.[74]

dibbu, see above, s.v. *bēl dababi.*

* *diqāru,* "bowl"—BT *dqwrʾ,* "jug." As long recognized, the phonetic similarity between the names of the common household

modern Mandaic use of the verb meaning "to enter" (*MD,* p. 109). For Sam. *šš* > *rš* note *uššu* > Sam. *ʾrš.*

72. Z, p. 19; *AP,* p. 32; Muffs, *Studies,* pp. 187 ff., 208. *AP,* No. 10:23 *dnh,* which Muffs (p. 184) terms "the most conclusive proof of the historic link between the docket tradition and the Elephantine papyri," is not unquestionably a form of this word. It may just mean "this"; cf. Palm. *ṣlmʾ dnh dy ʿgylw* (*CIS* II, No. 3922:1). For *tqp* compare as well BH *tqp* in Esther 9:29.

73. Z, p. 33; *LS,* p. 159; *CAD,* Vol. D, p. 99*a*; D. Weisberg, in *HUCA* XXXIX 77; *KBL* (3d ed.) p. 218. For the western Jewish Aramaic forms see *Aruch* III 94. Note that in Akkadian it is a large vat, while in Aramaic and Arabic it is a much smaller vessel.

74. Z, p. 19; *LS,* p. 102; *CAD,* Vol. D, p. 106*b*; C. Conti-Rossini, *Chrestomathia arabica meridionalis* (Rome, 1931) p. 159. The Mand. hapax *dwpʾ* (var. *dpʾ*?) may be correct (with *a* > *u* before a labial) or corrupt. That Mand. hapax *dʾpʾ* means "parchment" (*MD,* p. 100) is very uncertain. On the variability of vowels in CVC signs in Sumerian, see W. W. Hallo, review, *Bi.Or.* XVIII (1961) 60.

vessels Akk. *diqāru* and Ar. (and Arab.) *qidr*, "pot," is almost certainly not coincidental. There is, however (contra Z, p. 33, *LS*, p. 649), no reason to regard the Aramaic as anything but cognate with Akkadian. The Akkadian word has no other etymology, whereas the metathesis and difference in form indicate a long history of separation. A descendant of the Akkadian form is apparently found in BT *dqwrʾ*, however, a term of uncertain meaning but clearly a vessel of some sort. Is *dqwrʾ* also the same word as BT *d(y)qwlʾ*, "basket," "vessel"?[75]

ebbūbu, "flute"—Syr., JAr. *ʾbwbʾ*, MH *ʾ(y)bwb*, Mand. *ʾm/nbwbʾ*, all "flute," "tube"; Arab. *ʾunbûb*, "reed." Possibly cognate; cf. BH *nbb*, "to be hollow."[76]

ebūru, "harvest," "crop"—This is clearly cognate with and not a loan into Heb., Ar. *ʿbwr*, etc.[77]

* *ēdiltu*, "door" (hapax lex.)—Syr. *ʾdltʾ* and *ʾydltʾ*, "door leaves."[78]

* *edû*, "high water"—BT *ʾ(y)dw(w)tʾ*, "foam of the sea."[79] BH *ʾēḏ* (Gen. 2:6) has frequently been connected with this Akkadian term, itself a loanword from Sumerian. If this identification is correct, it is unusual to find no final vowel preserved in the loan (see Phonology in Chap. IV). One might suggest emendation, perhaps to *ʾdw*, as in Job 36:27, possibly to be interpreted as an absolute form.[80]

75. Y. Brand, *Klei HaḤeres BeSifrut HaTalmud* (Jerusalem, 1953) p. 109. For the Akkadian and the literature see A. Salonen, *Die Hausgeräte der alten Mesopotamier* II (Helsinki, 1966) 71.

76. Z, p. 29; *LS*, p. 1; *AHw.*, p. 180. A. Ungnad, "Lexikalisches," *ZA* XXXI (1918) 248 argues on the basis of the OB (hapax) spelling e-bu-bi-im that the doubling and "m" are secondary, but in Old Babylonian we would expect assimilation, and single spellings of doubled consonants are common (cf. *GAG*, p. 9).

77. Z, p. 41. Still so cited without any foundation by A. Salonen, *Agricultura Mesopotamica* (Helsinki, 1968) p. 258, and Ellenbogen, *Foreign Words*, p. 128. The Ugaritic form cited in *AHw.* is highly suspect and very probably does not mean "harvest." In its original meaning *ʿbwr* occurs in a seventh century B.C. Arad ostracon; see Y. Aharoni, "Three Hebrew Ostraca from Arad" (Heb.), *Eretz Israel* IX (1969) 18.

78. Z, p. 30; *LS*, p. 5.

79. Perles, in *OLZ* XXI 67. J. N. Epstein, *Prolegomena ad litteras amoraiticas* (Jerusalem, 1962) p. 199, suggests that Mand. *ʿdyʾ* is the same word as the BT. Though the translation in *MD* differs, corresponding to other attestations of the word, Epstein's interpretation cannot be ruled out. I am unable to find a meaning "flood" for Syr. *ʿdyʾ*, as given by Epstein.

80. *KBL* (3d ed.) p. 11; Ellenbogen, *Foreign Words*, p. 13. Note (Chap. IV, p. 149) that no final vowel is preserved in two loans from Assyrian. Perhaps the Hebrew word is to be considered a loan from Assyrian as well.

* *egirtu*, "letter" NA—Aššur Ostracon, *DEA*, No. 19 (Ass.), Eg., *AD*, BA, BH, Palm., Syr., CPA, JAr. *ʾ(y)grh/t(ʾ)*; Mand. *ʿngyrtʾ*. The origin and direction of borrowing of this word have been widely debated. A convenient summary of the history of scholarship can be found in Wagner, p. 19.[81] I find it difficult to interpret the evidence as pointing to anything but an Akkadian etymology here. A Persian etymology is ruled out by the relatively early Akkadian and Aramaic occurrences. Von Soden considers *egirtu* Aramaic in origin, saying that it "zu den nicht deverbalen Substantiven zu gehoren scheint."[82] This is highly improbable. Not only is the noun form *qittal* unusual in Aramaic,[83] but the word itself was still foreign to the scribes of Elephantine, who were uncertain of the absolute form of the word, while in the Driver texts only the absolute form with *t*, *ʾgrt*, is found, the same error which occurs in the certain loanword *lbt* < *libbatu*. Nevertheless, a convincing Akkadian etymology has yet to be proposed.

* *ekurru*, "temple"—Eg. *ʾgwrʾ*, "temple"; Targ. Proph. *ʾgwrʾ*, "pagan altar"; Mand. *ʿkwrʾ*, "pagan temple." The two forms with *k* and *g* are loans from Babylonian and Assyrian, respectively (cf. Phonology in Chap. IV). The JAr. word must be separated from the similar BA, Targ., and Syr. word *ygr*, "heap," which has a good Semitic etymology, Ethiopic *wgr*, "mound."[84]

**eliltu*—This supposed model for Mand. *hʾlʾltʾ*, "purification," "rinsing," does not exist. The correct Akkadian form is *tēliltu*. The roots are clearly cognate.[85]

elippu, "ship"—Common Ar. *ʾ(y)lpʾ*. Since this word lacks an obvious Semitic etymology, perhaps it is an old culture word for "boat" along the upper Euphrates and thus cognate in the two languages.[86]

81. Subsequent bibliography: von Soden, in *Or.* n.s. XXXV 8; *KBL* (3d ed.) p. 11; Muffs, *Studies*, p. 187, n. 4. As pointed out by E. Y. Kutscher (orally), one must also take into account the similar Greek words *ággaros*, *àggérios*, *ággelos*.

82. Von Soden, in *Or.* n.s. XXXV 8.

83. R. Köbert, "Gedanken zum semitischen Wort- und Satzbau, 1-7," *Or.* n.s. XIV (1945) 278 ff.

84. Z, p. 68; *AHw.*, p. 196; B. Porten, *Archives from Elephantine* (Berkeley and Los Angeles) pp. 109, 155. Note that in Egyptian Aramaic *ʾgwrʾ* serves as the term for the Jewish temple.

85. Cited by Baumgartner, in *HUCA* XXIII (1950-51) 58. Ar. *ḫll* cannot possibly be a denominative from *ʾ(w)ḫlʾ*, *uhulu*, "alkali" (as in *MD*, p. 148).

86. Z, p. 45; *LS*, p. 22; *AHw.*, p. 198; A. Salonen, *Die Wasserfahrzeuge in Babylonien* (*St.Or.*, Vol. VIII:4 [Helsinki, 1939]) p. 12. Both *spynh* and *ʾlp* are general terms for "boat" but presumably had varying com-

* *emēdu*—In NB *imittu emēdu* means to estimate and impose a tax on a garden or field (cf. *CAD*, Vol. I/J, p. 123*b*), deriving from the old Akkadian usage of *emēdu* in the sense of "to impose (taxes)." As Kutscher has shown, MH *ʾmd*, "to estimate," "to evaluate," and its derivatives must be borrowed from this Neo-Babylonian technical term. The BT forms *ʾmd* and *ʾwmdnʾ* most probably derive from the Hebrew usages, though a separate development from Akkadian cannot be excluded.[87]

In Syriac *ʾmd* means "to flee," which is clearly derived from the well known idiomatic usages of Akk. *emēdu* in the sense "to take refuge," "to flee to."

ērib bīti, see below, p. 153.

* *errēšu*, "tenant farmer"—JAr. and RH (Western), Sam. *ʾrys(ʾ)* (rarely *ʿrys*) > Arab. *ʾirris*; Sam. *ʾrs*, *ʿrs*, "to work." According to the *CAD*, Vol. I/J, p. 54*a* the interpretation "tenant farmer" can no longer be upheld after the Old Babylonian period on the basis of the Akkadian texts, but this loan suggests that this meaning was indeed maintained, at least in Assyrian, for the change *š* > *s* shows that this word was borrowed from Assyrian.[88] The spellings with *ʿayin* are either merely late orthographic confusions or false etymologies from the root *ʿrs*. The connection between this Akkadian word and the proposed reading *[ʿ]rsth* in Caquot, "Inscription," l. 3 remains uncertain.

erṣetu, "earth," used in the sense "underworld"—This has been suggested as the etymology for Nerab *ʾrṣtʾ*, "sarcophagus," and, although problematic, is far superior to the usual interpretation of the latter as a development from *ʿrś*, "couch."

plementary meanings in relation to each other at different periods. For Eg. see J. T. Milik, "Les papyrus araméens d'Hermoupolis et les cultes syro-phéniciens en Égypte perse," *Biblica* XLVIII (1967) 555.

87. E. Y. Kutscher, "ʾmd, ʿmd, ʿmdh," *Leš*. X (1939-40) 295-99. J. C. Greenfield, "The Lexical Status of Mishnaic Hebrew" (Ph.D. diss., Yale University, 1956) p. 275, suggests that *ʿmdh* in Mic. 1:11 is to be understood as "tax," from *imittu*, and compares Arab. *ʾmt*, "to conjecture," "to determine," as well. Cf. also Soqotri *ʾímdehin*, "estimation," "approximation" in W. Leslau, *Lexique Soqotri* (Paris, 1938) p. 63.

88. Z, p. 40; Fraenkel, *Aramäischen Fremdwörter*, p. 128; *Additamenta*, p. 68, Jastrow's BT form *ʾryšʾ* is incorrect (*Dictionary*, p. 120); see E. S. Rosenthal, "A Contribution to the Talmudic Lexicon," *Tarbiz* XL (1970-71) 187 ff. Except for the hapax *ārišūtu*, the dictionaries do not list *errēšu* in NA. Since the Aramaic and Arabic forms preserve the long vowel in the second syllable, the borrowed form must have been *errēšu* and not **ārišu* as the abstract NA form might suggest. Apparently, in spite of *CAD*, Vol. I/J, p. 54*b*, *errēšu*, as a borrowed Babylonian term, is to be found in NA in the spelling LÚ.ENGAR.

It seems, however, that the correct interpretation of the Aramaic is yet to be found.[89]

* *esittu*, "mortar"—BT *ʾsytʾ*, *ʾsyntʾ*, Syr. (lex.) *ʾstʾ*, Eastern Neo-Aramaic *sitta*.[90]

Another word for mortar, the hapax Targ. Y II *mzwktʾ* (not in Neofiti!), should be viewed either as a mere orthographic error or as a pseudo-correction of the standard form *mdwktʾ*. A derivation from the rare Akk. form *mazuktu* is almost impossible in light of the common cognate form.

eṭemmu, "ghost"—A reflex of the Akkadian is perhaps to be found in BH *ʾṭym* but certainly not in MH *ṭymyn*, JPA *ṭmyʾ*, "bones" < *ʿṭm*; nor is the Akkadian to be connected with Mand. *ʿwdʾmyʾ*.[91]

eṭēru, "to remove"; in NB "to pay"—BT *ʿ/ʾyṭd/rʾ*, a document indicating complete payment and transfer of property.

89. Proposed by G. R. Driver, in *An.Or.* XII 49 and "Brief Notes," *PEQ*, 1945, p. 11; E. Y. Kutscher concurred in "Contemporary Studies in North-Western Semitic," *JSS* X (1965) 42. Driver's proof in *PEQ*, 1945, that *erṣetu* means "grave" is incorrect, however. The lexical passage cited (incorrectly given as *CIWA* V 30, which is a broken parallel to the correct *CT* XVIII, No. 30 rev. 28-30; cf. *CAD*, Vol. E, pp. 308*d*, 309*a*) only shows that Sum. arali (É.KUR.BAD) can mean *erṣetu*, "underworld," as well as *bīt mūti* and *naqbaru*, "grave," and not that those items on the Akkadian side of the list are equivalent.

A cuneiform parallel to Nerab *ʾrṣtʾ*, whatever its etymology, may actually occur. In a contemporary funerary inscription of an Aramean tribal chief, we find the word *e-ṣi-it-ti* in a precisely identical context (*YOS* I, No. 43:5, 13). This has been treated by the modern dictionaries as a form of *eṣemtu*, "bone," "body frame" (cf. *CAD*, Vol. E, p. 342*b*), but the occurrence would be only the second time that that word is spelled with "tt" for /mt/ or /nt/ (cf. *BWL*, p. 44, l. 93), though one might expect the Assyrians always to have pronounced it with [tt]. Albright treated the cuneiform word ("Notes on Assyrian Lexicography and Etymology," *RA* XVI [1919] 177) but translated "burial cairn," relating it to the Arab. *waṣîdah*, "stone enclosure." This is unlikely, however, for, just as in Nerab, the *eṣittu* is something moveable. The dictionaries may be correct, and in fact for Nerab *ʾrṣtʾ* a meaning "skeleton," or "corpse" is not excluded by the context. This could be the NA equivalent of Bab. *šalamtu*, "corpse," borrowed into Aramaic (and when used in *YOS* I, No. 43, used as an Aramaic word). The "r" of the Aramaic form is disturbing but not impossible to account for. For a possible parallel see the usage of *ṭmy*, "bones," in the Uzziah inscription (see n. 91).

90. S. A. Kaufman, in *Leš*. XXXVI 30 f.

91. For the BH, see *KBL* (3d ed.) p. 36. The meaning of the Mandaic is uncertain. The famous Uzziah plaque (E. L. Sukenik, "An Epitaph of Uzziahu, King of Judah," *Tarbiz* II [1930-31] 288 ff.) has proven that *ṭmy* is "bones," but for earlier comparisons see J. N. Epstein, "Gloses babylo-araméenes," *REJ* LXXIII (1921) 58.

But the verb *ʿṭr*, "to remove," does occur elsewhere in JAr., whereas such a noun form is unknown in Akkadian.[92]

gabbu, "all"—See below, p. 152.

* *gagû*, "a building or section of the temple district reserved for the women of the *nadītu*-class"—Syr. *ggwyʾ* (lex.), "harlot." Note that this word is attested only in OB texts primarily from Sippar and in SB omen texts, which certainly preserve an old tradition; so although this etymology seems certain, the history of the borrowing remains obscure.[93]

gallābu, "barber"—BH, Phoen., and Ar. *glb*, "barber"; JPA and Syr., "razor." Evidence to determine whether these terms are borrowed or merely cognate is lacking.[94]

* *gāmiru*, "(door) bolt"—Mand. *gʾwrʾ*.[95]

gammidatu, NA, LB "a kind of garment"—Imp. Ar. (Kraeling, *Brooklyn Museum*, No. 7:7) *gmydh*; MH *gwmdyt*. Probably an old Aramaic loanword in Akkadian, but certainly not an Akkadian word.[96]

* *ganūnu*, "living quarters," "bedroom"—Genesis Apocryphon, JAr. and RH, Syr., CPA *gnwn(ʾ)*; Syr. and CPA *byt gnwnʾ*; Mand. *gnʾnʾ*, BT *gnnʾ*, "bridal chamber." It remains to be seen whether the Aramaic meaning is the result of independent semantic development of this loanword or represents a borrowing of a specific meaning of the Akkadian term not actually attested yet in our texts. If the latter, it could have been taken from a popular term or one used specifically in the cult (see *CAD*, *ganunu* A, mng. 2*b*).[97]

gašīšu, "stake"—There is no reason to connect this with BT, RH *gšwš(ʾ)*, "sounding pole," "sounder" < *gšš*, "to feel."[98]

* *gâšu*, NA "to come near"—BT, Mand. *gw/ys*. The NA form seems to be a development of *nagāšu*.[99]

92. D. Weisberg, in *HUCA* XXXIX 74 f.; cf. Muffs, *Studies*, p. 126, n. 2, and p. 201.

93. Z, p. 68; *LS*, p. 103.

94. Z, p. 28; *LS*, p. 117; *AHw.*, p. 274.

95. *MD*, p. 75.

96. *CAD*, Vol. G, p. 36. For the Eg. reading, see E. Y. Kutscher, in *JAOS* LXXIV 236, and B. Porten, *Archives*, p. 88, n. 132. For the Mishnaic Hebrew cf. *Additamenta*, p. 125.

97. Z, p. 32; *LS*, p. 122. In Aramaic the word was probably frequently confused with the root *gnʾ*, "to lie down," "to sleep."

98. Z, p. 31; Salonen, *Wasserfahrzeuge*, p. 110. The meaning "sounding pole" for the Hebrew is uncertain. The BT references seem to refer to those who make the soundings.

99. The relation between *gw/ys* and Syr. *gawsâ*, "refuge," is uncertain.

* *gerû*, see below, s.v. *rāšû*.

* *ginû*, "regular offering"—Mand. *gynyʾ* (pl.), "pagan sacrifices." The form was probably borrowed as a collective.[100]

* *gišru*, "bridge"—Syr., JAr. *g(y)šrʾ*, MH *gšr*, > Arab. *ǧisr*. The term occurs only in Neo-Assyrian and Neo-Babylonian but has a feasible etymology only in Akkadian. It is to be considered the same word as the one found earlier in the meanings "log" and "barricade" (with *AHw*. contra *CAD*) and cannot possibly be separated from the word *gušūru* (q.v.).[101]

* *giššu* (*gilšu*), "hip," "flank"—Syr. *gsʾ*, BT *gysʾ*, Targ. Onk. and Targ. Isaiah pl. *gyssyn*, "hip," "flank," "side"; Mand. *gysʾnʾ*, "cheeks." Note especially its use for translating BH terms for "loins" in Peshitta Jer. 30:6 and Targ. Onk. Lev. 3:4, 15. Except for the Targums, the word is restricted to Eastern Aramaic, developing into one of the common words for "side."[102]

* *giṭṭu* (KUŠ.GÍD.DA), "parchment document" LB—JAr. and MH *geṭ*, *giṭṭâ*, "document," "bill of divorce"; Mand. *gyṭʾ*, "document," and in magic bowls, "document of expulsion"; Syr. *gṭʾ*, "will." The term was borrowed only in its general meaning of a parchment document, so-called because it had only one column, like a cuneiform *giṭṭu*. It use as the term for "bill of divorce" was a Jewish development, no doubt deriving from its frequent usage in transactions involving women, perhaps as a euphemism. The earliest attestation is Murabbaʿat (*DJD* II) 19 I:9, II:21, *gṭ šbqyn*, already in the context of divorce, but it is still used in contexts other than divorce in BT. Note the independent development in Syriac to another specific type of document. The Mandaic magic bowl usage is definitely a

100. *MD*, p. 91; if this translation of the form *gynʿyʾ* is correct, it represents an assimilation to the verb *gnʾ* II; cf. *gynyʾnyʾ*.

101. Z, p. 44; *LS*, p. 137; *AHw*., p. 293; Fraenkel, *Aramäischen Fremdwörter*, p. 285.

102. This comparison was first suggested by W. F. Albright (*RA* XVI 180), who correctly termed it a loan from Assyrian. Not yet aware of the construct form *giliš*, he was led into a false etymology. R. Campbell-Thompson ("Assyrian Prescriptions for Stone in the Kidneys," *AfO* XI [1937] 339, n. 13) also compared the Aramaic with the Akkadian but gave no other etymology and did not specifically mention borrowing. When the forms with *l* turned up, F. R. Kraus (*Texte zur babylonischen Physiognomatik* [*AfO* Beiheft III (Graz, 1939)] p. 27, n. 28) showed that the likelihood of a cognate relationship was slim, though he was not aware of Albright's proposal of a loan relationship. To my knowledge this suggestion has never been reconsidered, yet the relationship is obvious, especially since the Aramaic form is characteristic of Eastern Aramaic. Etymologically, *giššu* is probably to be connected with Arab. *ǧls*, "to sit."

borrowing from Jewish Aramaic and not an independent word from the root *gṭʾ* (< *qṭʿ*).[103]

* *gušūru*, "log," "beam"—Eg. *gšr*, *gšwr*, Syr. *gšwrʾ* (lex.), *kšwrʾ*, JAr. *kšwrʾ*, Mand. (modern form?) *kyšrʾ*. Probably of Sumerian etymology (see *gišru*). The change of *g* to *k* before the unvoiced sibilant is an Aramaic development which occurred after the reduction of the vowel in the initial syllable.[104]

habû, "earthenware jug"—MH, BT, Syr. *ḥbyt(ʾ)*; Arab. *ḫâbiyah*; Ethiopic *ḫabay*. The relationship is unclear, but the view that the western forms derive from an as yet unattested Akkadian feminine form **habītu* is unfounded. The attested Akkadian form is rare and limited to Standard and Neo-Babylonian. The Arabic form with "ḫ" also makes a loan through Aramaic unlikely though not impossible (see below, p. 142). No satisfactory etymology has been proposed for any of the forms, and the origin of *habû* remains obscure.[105]

halīṣu, "some leather object" rare SB lex. and NB—Syr. *ḥlyṣʾ*, "skin bottle." Cf. also RH *ḥlyṣ*, "loop" or "knot(?)."[106]

* *hāmū*, "straw"—*AP*, No. 15, Kraeling, *Brooklyn Museum*, No. 2 *ḥm*. The etymology of the Akkadian word is unknown, but as it occurs nowhere else in Aramaic, one may safely assume that *hāmū* was borrowed in the process of an Aramaic remodeling of the NA phrase *lū hāmū lu huṣābu*, "be it straw of splinter," into *mn ḥm ʿd ḥwṭ*, "from straw to string."[107]

harîṣu, "moat"—Old Aramaic (*KAI*, No. 202 A 10) *ḥrṣ*, BH *ḥrwṣ*, "moat"; MH *ḥryṣ*, "trench"; Targ. *ḥryṣʾ*, channel." All

103. Z, p. 19; *LS*, p. 113; *AHw.*, p. 294; *HM*, p. 534. The various Aramaic meanings are hardly derived from another LB usage of *giṭṭu*, "quitclaim" (cf. *AHw.*, p. 294).

104. Z, p. 31; *LS*, p. 137; *AHw.*, p. 300. For the sound change cf. J. N. Epstein, *Grammar of Babylonian Aramaic* (Tel Aviv, 1960) p. 18; T. Nöldeke, *Compendious Syriac Grammar*, J. A. Chrichton, trans. (London, 1904) § 22. The form *gšr* in Targ. Ezek. 27:5 may actually be meant for "bridge," not out of place in the context of Tyre (see as well Kimchi's commentary on the verse), but if "ship beam" is meant, it may be a development from "bridge" (note the English nautical term) rather than a survival of the old form. For the uncertain Mand. *kšwrʾ* see *MD*, p. 224.

105. Z, p. 33; *LS*, p. 209; *CAD*, Vol. H, p. 20; Fraenkel, *Aramäischen Fremdwörter*, p. 168. D. Weisberg, in *HUCA* XXXIX 77 f., proposes that the hapax variant *ḥbyh* cited in the *Aruch* represents the missing link in the Akkadian "parental development" **habiatu* > **habītu*. This is incorrect. The Hebrew variant, at best, is only a back-formation from the plural form *ḥbywt*. In addition, a form **habiatu* is impossible in late Akkadian.

106. *AHw.*, p. 312.

107. Muffs, *Studies*, p. 59, n. 1, p. 182.

the evidence points toward a native North West Semitic formation for this word.[108]

harurtu, hapax NA "throat"—Syr. *ḥrwštʾ*. The relationship is very uncertain. The Syriac word would have to have been borrowed from an unattested Babylonian form, while an etymology from *ḥrš* is not ruled out.[109]

* *haṣbu*, "clay," sherd," "pot"—BA, JAr., CPA *ḥsp*, Mand. *hʾspʾ*, "sherd," "clay"; MH, BT, Syr. *ḥṣb*, Mand. *hʾṣbyʾ*, *hʾṣwbyʾ*, "pot"; Syr. *ḥṣp*, "pot," *ḥzb*, "tub"; Arab. *ḫzf*, "pottery." It is difficult to determine the relationships among these many forms. The earliest attested meaning of the Akkadian appears to be "sherd." The best explanation of the various forms appears to be to consider *haṣbu* and *ḥsp* as parallel developments of an old culture word and take *ḥṣb* and *ḥṣp* as loans from Akkadian perhaps from different periods or dialects.[110]

haṣṣinnu, "axe"—There is no reason to suppose that this old culture word, Ar. *ḥaṣṣīn* (Arab., Ethiopic *ḫaṣîn*) necessarily entered Aramaic through Akkadian.[111]

hašāhu, "to need," "to desire"—BA, Syr. *ḥšḥ*, CPA *šḥšwḥ*, *ʾštḥšḥ*, "to be required, needed, useful." The limited distribution of the Aramaic is the only reason to suspect a loan here. The shape of the root *ḫšḫ*, with *ḫ* in first and third positions, is as unusual in Akkadian as it is in Aramaic.[112]

**hašālu*, "to pay the *ilku*"—*AD*, No. 8:6 *ḥšl*. Driver's attempt to relate the Aramaic to Akkadian makes faulty use of the Akkadian lexical material. It is true that the logograms used for the verb *hašālu*, "to crush," are also used for verbs

108. Cf. *KBL* (3d ed.) p. 338. The corresponding sense of the verb *ḫrṣ* is at home in North West Semitic, not in Akkadian, where *herû* and *herītu* are the native forms. Note as well the limited distribution of the Akkadian.

109. W. F. Albright, "Notes on Egypto-Semitic Etymology II," *AJSL* XXXIV (1917-18) 240; H. Holma, *Die Namen der Körperteile im Assyrisch-Babylonischen, eine lexikalisch-etymologische Studie* (Helsinki, 1911) p. 42; *LS*, p. 259; *AHw.*, p. 329; *CAD*, Vol. H, p. 121a. Von Soden, in *Or.* n.s. XXXV 10, considers the Akkadian to be a loan from Aramaic and is thus forced to accept a Babylonian origin for the change to *št* in Syriac.

110. Z, p. 33; *LS*, p. 251; Fraenkel, *Aramäischen Fremdwörter*, p. 169; Salonen, *Hausgeräte* II 99; E. Y. Kutscher, "*kwk (uvne mišpaḥta)*," *Eretz Israel* VIII (1967) 276. The Old Babylonian occurrence in *MSL* VII 207, l. 32 is uncertain, but the word does occur in an Old Babylonian mathematical text from Susa, *MDP* XXXIV 27, l. 65, where it probably means sherd, since its coefficient is different from that for clay as given in the similar text *MCT* Ud.

111. Z, p. 12; *LS*, p. 251; Salonen, *Agricultura*, p. 150.

112. Z, p. 70; Rosenthal, *Grammar*, p. 58; *KBL* (2d ed.) p. 1077.

meaning "to give," but whatever other values its logograms may have, when equated with *hašālu* they only mean "to crush." There is, however, one Neo-Babylonian text in which the verb *hašālu* might occur in a precisely identical context. In *VAS* VI, No. 188:13 we read *i-ha-pa-la-ʾ* (*CAD* and *AHw.*, s.v. *hapālu*, a hapax), but in Neo-Babylonian script PA and ŠÁ are rather similar signs, so we may have a modern copyist's error here. In any case the origin and etymology remain obscure.

Some Eastern Aramaic noun forms from the root *ḥšl* may in fact be continuations of similar Akkadian forms. Compare BT *ḥšyltʾ* and Akk. *hašlatu*, kinds of beer.[113]

haštu, *haltu*, "pit," "grave"—Compare the Mandaic hapax *hʾltʾ*, the location of the throne of the lord of the underworld.

hašû, "lungs," "entrails"—Mand. *hʾšʾ*, *ḥʾšʾšʾ*, Arab. *ḥašâ*, "bowels." These can hardly be cognate since the Akkadian is almost certainly cognate with the word for "chest," Heb. *ḥāze*, Ar. *ḥădē*, Arab. *ḥidaʾ*. Thus a loan is possible.

hâṭu, "to search carefully," "to pay out"—Possibly in the meaning "to examine" in Ezra 4:12 *yḥyṭw*; compare the use of the Akkadian with *temennu*, "foundation" (*CAD*, Vol. H, pp. 160*b*, 161*a*). In the meaning "to pay" this verb has been suggested for Sabbath Ostracon, l. 6, but the reading and the meaning are uncertain.[114]

* *hazannu*, "mayor," "chief magistrate"—Aššur tablet, No. 4:2; Caquot, "Inscription," "mayor"; JAr., MH *ḥzn(ʾ)*, "overseer."[115]

hibištu, "cuttings"—Syr. *hbšʾ*, "wood shavings."[116]

* *himētu*, "butter," "ghee"—Syr. *ḥʾwtʾ*, Targ. Proverbs 30:

113. *AD* (abridged) pp. 70 f. Cf. also S. Funk, "Beiträge zur Kulturgeschichte Babyloniens," *Jahrbuch der Jüdisch-Literarischen Gesellschaft* VII (1909) 220, n. 1.

114. *KBL* (2d ed.) p. 1074; B. Levine, "Notes on an Aramaic Dream Text from Egypt," *JAOS* LXXXIV (1964) 20; F. Rosenthal reads *hāṭu*, "cash" ("Aramaic Texts from Achaemenid Times," *An Aramaic Handbook* [Wiesbaden, 1967] Vol. I, Part 2, p. 10).

115. Z, p. 6; *AHw.*, p. 338; *CAD*, Vol. H, p. 165; Kutscher, *Words*, pp. 47 f. The reading *ḥzn ʾglh* < *hazan ekalli* in Aššur Tablet 4:2 was pointed out to me by Prof. E. Lipiński; see below, n. 364. Although the origin of *hazannu* remains obscure (not from *ḥzy*, cf. *CAD*, Vol. H, p. 165*b*; Gelb, *MAD*, No. 3, p. 136), its limitation outside of Akkadian to the Aššur Tablet, to the Babylonianizing Syrian inscription, and to late Jewish sources makes a loan quite certain.

116. *LS*, p. 213. The Syriac term is not used at all as the Akkadian is. Cf. Arab. *ḫašab*, "wood."

33 ḥʾytʾ (read ḥʾwtʾ, var.: ḥmʾtʾ [Hebraism]). The loan from Babylonian is shown by the *w* for the original *m*. It is noteworthy that the expected cognate form with *m* occurs nowhere in Aramaic.[117]

* *himṣu*, "fatty tissue"—Mand., BT (Hull. 49*b*) *hymṣʾ*.[118]

hinnu, "ship's cabin" (lex.)—*AP*, No. 26:11 *ḥn*, Arab. *ḫinn*(?) < Persian? This is a culture word of uncertain origin.[119]

* *hirītu*, "ditch," "canal"—Syr. *ḥʾrytʾ* (*ḥêrîṯâ*).[120]

* *hittu*, "architrave"—Syr. *ḥtʾ* (*ḥeṭṭâ*), "plank" (supported by columns, cf. I Kings 7:3).[121]

* *hubullu*, NB "interest"—Syr. *ḥwblʾ*; Mand. *hbwl*, *hbwlyʾ*; Targ. Onk. and Targ. Hagiog., BT *ḥ(y)bwlyʾ*. This noun is to be separated from the BH verb *ḥbl*, "to seize a pledge," which is not a loan.[122]

hultuppû, "whipping rod"—J. N. Epstein, whose reading *hulduppû* is not inconsistent with the known Akkadian spellings, connected this word to the rare BT *hrdwph*, traditionally interpreted as a kind of reed cage. The only thing certain about the *hrdwph*, however, is that it is an instrument or mode of punishment. Since no other satisfactory etymology is known, Epstein's identification may be correct in spite of the inexact phonetic correspondence.[123]

117. Z, p. 38; *LS*, p. 208.

118. *AHw.*, p. 346. The BT form with *h* is the form cited in the *Aruch*; variants have *ḥ* (see Jastrow, *Dictionary*, p. 347).

119. Z, p. 45; *AHw.*, p. 347; Salonen, *Wasserfahrzeuge*, p. 82.

120. Z, p. 44; *LS*, p. 208. See n. 108.

121. Z, p. 31; *LS*, p. 263; *AHw.*, p. 349. The meaning of *hittu* as accepted in the *CAD*, *AHw.*, and Salonen, *Türen* was challenged by Röllig, in *WZKM* LXII (1969) 299 f.

122. Z, p. 18; *AHw.*, p. 351; *KBL* (3d ed.) pp. 274 f. All consider the BH to be a borrowing from Akkadian as well, but this is clearly not the case. Akk. *hubullu* has two meanings, the older "debt" (maintained in NA *habullu*) and the MB and NB "interest"; and the related verb *habālu* B means "to borrow." There is clearly no connection here with the meaning of BH *ḥbl*, "to seize a pledge," though granted both are aspects of the loan transaction. The fundamental element of *ḥbl*, as opposed to *ʿrb* and *ʿbṭ*, is the seizure, not a voluntary pledge, and it should be considered a cognate of Akk. *habālu* A, "to ravage (a person)," Ar. (and LB) *ḥbl*, "to despoil," "to damage." The similarity of the BH nouns (only in Ezekiel) *ḥăḇōl* and *ḥăḇōlāh* to NA *habullu* may be coincidental or a Masoretic assimilation to the Aramaic word "interest." Note that they are always spelled defectively.

123. J. N. Epstein, "Babylonisch-aramäische Studien," in *Festskrift i anledning af professor David Simonsens 70-aarige fødselsdag* (Copenhagen, 1923) pp. 305 f.

hūqu, "rung of a ladder" (SB, NB, NA)—Syr., BT *ḥawqâ* (JPA also *ᶜwwq*). The origin of the term is uncertain, but in light of the apparent borrowing of the word for ladder, *simmiltu*, a loan here is not unlikely.[124]

* *hurdu*, "reed mat"—Mand. *hwrdʾ*; BT *hwrdʾ*, *hwdrʾ*, "reed mat"; Arab. *ḫ/hurdiyy*, "reed roof."[125]

huṭṭimmu, *hulṭimmu*, "snout," "muzzle"—Syr. *ḥrṭwmʾ*; MH *ḥrṭwm*, *ḥwṭm*, *ḥṭm*; Targ. Y *ḥwṭmʾ*; Arab. *ḫaṭam*, *ḫurṭûm*, The Akkadian occurs only in Neo- and Late Babylonian; its etymology is unknown.[126]

* *igāru*, "wall"—Eg. *ʾgr*, "wall"; Uruk *ig-ga-ri*, "wall" or "roof"; Syr. *ʾeggârâ*, JAr. *ʾîgâr* and *ʾiggâr*, Sam., CPA *ʾgr*, Mand. *ʾ/ᶜngʾrʾ* > Arab. *ʾiǧǧâr*, *ʾinǧâr*, all in the meaning "roof." That the Egyptian Aramaic word means "wall" is shown by the phrase *ʾgr bʾgr*, "wall to wall," in describing property lines and even more conclusively in *AP*, No. 5:5, where an *ʾgr* is described as joining another house "from the ground upwards." Thus, it would seem at first glance that this is a late loanword occurring first in its original sense and then developing a different meaning. The circumstances are not so clear, however. Although the Akkadian is attested only in the meaning "wall," the Sumerian word from which the Akkadian was presumably borrowed is translated in an Old Babylonian lexical text by the word "roof." It is possible, therefore, that we are dealing with a very old culture word taken into Aramaic meaning the entire superstructure of a building, occurring in Egyptian Aramaic with exactly this meaning or more specifically "wall" under the influence of Akkadian. Its use as the only common Aramaic word for "roof" is also suggestive of an ancient borrowing.[127]

124. Cf. B. Landsberger, "Lexikalisches Archiv 3. Nachträge," *ZA* XLII (1934) 166, n. 4. The correspondence of Akkadian *ū* to Aramaic *aw* would seem to speak against a loanword relationship here. To be sure, Syriac has *mawtânâ* and *šawtâpâ* corresponding to Akk. *mūtānu* and *šutappu*, but the first is not unquestionably a loan and the diphthong of the second can be explained (see p. 150). In any case Jewish Aramaic has *u* in these cases, while it, too, clearly has a diphthong in *ḥwwq*, as indicated by the spelling with double *waw*.

125. S. A. Kaufman, "Akkadian and Babylonian Aramaic—New Examples of Mutual Elucidation," *Leš*. XXXVII (1973) 102 f.

126. *LS*, p. 256.

127. Z, p. 31; *LS*, p. 5; *AHw*., p. 366; *CAD*, Vol. I/J, p. 39; *DISO*, p. 4. The word is possibly pre-Sumerian. The Old Babylonian text (in two copies), as shown now by *MSL* XII 201, is to be read: lú E.SIG_4-da-šub-ba : *maḫṣam bēl ūrim*, "one felled by a roof." (For the construction see von Soden, *GAG Ergänz.*, p. 12**, citing the old incorrect reading *maḫṣam igārim*.) G. R. Driver, "The Aramaic Papyri from Egypt: Notes on

* *ikkaru*, "farmer"—BH *ʾikkār*, MH, JAr. *ʾ(y)kr*, Syr. *ʾkrʾ* (and denom. verb), CPA *ʾkr* (translates BH), Mand. *ʿ/ʾkʾrʾ*, > Arab. *ʾa/ikkâr*.[128]

* *īku*, "ditch"—Syr. *ʾygʾ*, "stream."[129]

* *ilku*, "duty (on land or produce)"—Bab. dockets, *AD*, No. 8, BA *hlk* . Note that in *DEA*, Nos. 73 and 79 the cuneiform text actually has *ilku* and the Ar., *hlkʾ*.[130]

* *immati* (mostly Assyrian and peripheral), "when"—Common Ar., MH *ʾ(y)mt(y)*. (Perhaps in *UT* 67 I: 18 *imt*.) This rather unexpected borrowing may result from the common occurrence of *immati* in Neo-Assyrian legal terminology.[131]

ina libbi, "within," "there"—In Egyptian Aramaic *bgw* is used without a suffix in a very similar fashion.[132]

* *ina ṣilli*, "under the protection of"—In the Behistun inscription *bṭllh zy* is a direct loan-translation from the Akkadian text. Note, however, that *zy* rather than the construct state is used.

* *inbu*, "fruit"—BA *ʾnbʾ*, "fruit"; Targ. *ʾnbʾ*, *ʾybʾ*, Syr. *ʾb(b)ʾ*, "fruit," "produce." In spite of Heb. *ʾēḇ*, "blossom," *ʾāḇîḇ*, "fresh grain," Arab. *ʾabb*, "meadow," and Amharic *ʾbb*, "blossom," there is good reason to assume that the cited forms have been influenced by Akkadian: The dissimilation *bb* > *nb* is otherwise unknown in Imperial Aramaic, the meaning is al-

Obscure Passages," *JRAS*, 1932, p. 77, suggested that the feminine gender of the word in Egyptian Aramaic was the result of Akkadian influence.

128. Z, p. 40; *LS*, p. 20; *AHw.*, p. 368; *CAD*, Vol. I/J, p. 54. Salonen, *Agricultura*, p. 343, suggests reading the Akk. form *ikkāru* on the basis of the Aramaic and Biblical Hebrew forms with long *ā*, but the length could be secondary in Aramaic. The word is almost certainly one of the pre-Sumerian group (cf. Salonen, *Fussbekleidung*, pp. 109, 115) > Sum. engar > Akk. *ikkaru*, but could there be any relationship between *ikkaru* and MH *ḥwkr*, *ḥkyr* etc., "tenant farmer" (cf. Arab. *ḥkr*, Fraenkel *Aramäischen Fremdwörter*, p. 189)?

129. Z, p. 44; *LS*, p. 14; *AHw.*, p. 370. This comparison is probably correct. Highly doubtful, however, are the possible connections with MH *ʿwgyh*, BT *ʾ(w)gyʾ*, and Mand. *ʾ(w)gʾ* because of the clear MH "ʿ". Perhaps the BT and Mand. forms are to be separated from the Mishnaic word, in which case they might be from an LB form *īgu*.

130. Z, p. 10; *AHw.*, p. 371; *KBL*, p. 1069. The model is clearly the common term which occurs in LB; cf. *CAD*, Vol. I/J, p. 78.

131. Z, p. 70; *LS*, p. 27. E. Y. Kutscher's study of the Aramaic forms of this word ("Leshon Ḥazal," in *Sefer Henoch Yalon*, ed. S. Lieberman [Jerusalem, 1963] pp. 267 f.) is authoritative and fairly convincing, but many uncertainties still remain. Note, for example, the clear long vowel in the Neo-Syriac form *ʾīman*. There seems to be no reasonable alternative to an Akkadian origin, however.

132. Z, p. 70; *AP*, p. 6; *DISO*, p. 48.

ways "fruit" and not "blossom" or "freshness," and Syriac has the cognate to *ʾbb* in the form *hbbʾ, hbb,* "blossom," alongside of the word *ʾebbâ,* "fruit." In Mandaic we have the opposition *ʿby/ʾbyʾ,* "fruits," and *ʿnybtʾ,* "grape," but the former might possibly belong with Syr. *hbb.* The Mand. form *ʿm/nbʾ* could mean either "grape" or "fruit," but the context favors the latter.[133]

isinnu, "festival"—BH?, Targ. Y and CPA *ʾšwn,* "season," "time." This etymology is hardly convincing, but neither are the other proposed etymologies for *ʾšwn.*[134]

* *iškaru,* "assigned quota, tax, field (on which *iškaru* work is to be performed)"—BH *ʾeškār,* "tribute"; Persepolis *ʾškr,* meaning uncertain; Targ. Isaiah 5:10, Syr. *ʾškrʾ,* Iraqi and Lebanese Arab. *škar, škareh,* "field." Because of the sibilant (see Phonology, in Chap. IV) both the Hebrew and Persepolis forms must derive from Babylonian, that is from the meaning "quota" and not the specific Neo-Assyrian tax. For the Persepolis formula I would suggest a meaning like "as part of the (ritual offering) quota of year X." Since the meaning "field" for the Akkadian is restricted in the texts we know now to OAkk., OB, and Nuzi, it is not unlikely that the borrowing in this meaning took place at that early time in the vernacular of northern Mesopotamia, especially as this meaning is restricted almost entirely to Syriac.[135]

* *išparu,* "weaver"—BT (Ab.Zar. 20b) *ʾšpry,* Syr. (lex.) *ʾšprʾ, šprʾ.*[136]

133. Z, p. 55; *LS,* p. 1; *KBL,* p. 1017; *KBL* (3d ed.) p. 2. The view expressed here follows B. Landsberger, *The Date Palm and Its By-products according to Cuneiform Sources* (*AfO* Beiheft XVII [Graz, 1967]) p. 18, n. 52*b.* The Akkadian is usually considered cognate with Sem. *ʿinab,* "grape" (cf. *AHw.,* p. 381), which is reasonable, but there are even difficulties with this: cf. Ug. *ǵnb* and the unique to Akkadian *hanābu,* "to sprout luxuriously." The nasalization "np" is found in Hat. *šnpyr* < *šappîr.*

134. Z, p. 63; B. Landsberger, *Der kultische-Kalendar der Babylonier und Assyrer* ("Leipziger semitistische Studien," Vol. VI:1-2 [Leipzig, 1915]) pp. 6 ff.; *KBL* (3d ed.) p. 91. For other etymologies see the older dictionaries. F. Schulthess' comparison with *simānu* ("Aramäisches IV," *ZA* XXVII [1912] 230 ff.), based on a unique spelling *ʾšwwn* in Targ. YI Gen. 35:16, is phonetically impossible. Neofiti *ʾšwn* shows the correct spelling.

135. Z, p. 38; *LS,* p. 52; *AHw.,* p. 395; *KBL* (3d ed.) p. 92; A. Frayha, *A Dictionary of the Non-Classical Vocables in the Spoken Arabic of Lebanon Collected and Annotated* (Beirut, 1947) p. 97; *Persepolis,* p. 54. For *ʾškr* in Targ. II Esther 1:3, see *Additamenta,* p. 70. Persepolis *ʾškr* is hardly to be related to *škr,* "intoxicating drink"; nor is there any reason to consider Akk. *šikāru,* "beer," to be anything but cognate to Ar. *sḵar,* Heb. *šēḵār,* etc. (apparently contra Bowman, in *Persepolis*).

136. Z, p. 27; *AHw.,* p. 397; R. Payne Smith, *Thesaurus Syriacus* (2 vols.; Oxford, 1879, 1901) p. 410; F. Perles, "Babylonisch-talmudische

* *ištānu*, "north"—Syr. *ʾstnʾ*, Mand. *(ʿ)stʾnʾ*, BT and Targ. Job 37:22 *ʾstnʾ*, "north wind."[137]

* *ištaru, ištartu*, "goddess"—Magic bowls *ʾ(y)strtʾ* Mand. *ʿst(y)rʾ*; Syr. *ʾstrʾ*.[138]

ištēn, "one"—Though this suggestion was long ago shown to be incorrect, the Akkadian form is still often cited as the origin of BH *ʿšty* in the word for "eleven." The Ugaritic and South Arabian evidence leaves absolutely no doubt that all these terms are merely cognate. The Eg. form *ʿštʾ* used in measuring terminology, whether or not it indeed has something to do with the meaning "one," has no other connections with Akkadian.[139]

* *itannu*, "interstice (of a net)"—Mand. *ʾ/ʿtʾnʾ*, "mesh," "network."[140]

ittimāli, "yesterday"—BH *ʾeṯmôl* (I Sam. 10:11 *ʾitteᵉmol*); Common Ar. *ʾtml(y)*. The initial *aleph* of the Hebrew-Aramaic forms can hardly be anything but prothetic, for all of the West Semitic forms except for the Hebrew hapax have a single, not a double *t*. The Akkadian form, traditionally explained as coming from *ina timāli*, occurs only in Neo-Assyrian.[141]

iz/šqāti, "fetters"—The relationships here are difficult, and several separate words have been confused in the literature. The *CAD* and *AHw*. differ on whether the Akkadian is native or a late borrowing folk-etymologized as *iṣ qāti*. In any case there is absolutely no evidence to support the theory

Glossen," *OLZ* VIII (1905) 385. This word was also previously read in the Babylonian docket *DEA*, No. 96: *zy ʾyšpr*. Collation of the tablet reveals that the correct reading is *zy tʾšṭr*, corresponding to the cuneiform *sa* ¹*Tēšî-eṭir*.

137. Z, p. 45; *LS*, p. 38; *AHw*., p. 399; *CAD*, Vol. I/J, p. 270*a*. Except for peripheral OB, the Akkadian form is always spelled *iltānu*. This does not rule out a loan, however; see Phonology, Sibilants in Chap. IV.

138. Z, p. 61; J. A. Montgomery, *Aramaic Incantation Texts from Nippur* (*PBS* III [Philadelphia, 1913]) p. 71. For the Syriac see A. Caquot, "La déesse Šegal," *Semitica* IV (1951-52) 56.

139. The refutation of the loanword theory was stated most clearly by J. Lewy, "Apropos of the Akkadian Numerals *iš-ti-a-na* and *iš-tí-na*," *Ar.Or.* XVII (1949) 111, n. 8. Nevertheless, in *KBL* (2d ed.) and Ellenbogen, *Foreign Words*, p. 129, there is still agreement voiced with Z, p. 65. For Eg. see *DISO*, p. 224.

140. Z, p. 15; *AHw*., p. 403; *MD*, p. 42; M. Lidzbarski, *Das Johannesbuch der Mandäer* (Giessen, 1915) p. 155, n. 2.

141. Z, p. 70; *LS*, p. 827; *KBL* (3d ed.) p. 99. For the Akkadian see *GAG* § 72*b*. The Aramaic form with final *y* is limited to Syriac and Targums Onkelos and Jonathan. Thus, one may assume that the form with -*y* was the Imperial Aramaic form, showing a remnant of a final long vowel or diphthong (cf. Geʾez *timalem*).

that the Akkadian word is the source of the hapax Targum Jeremiah *ᶜzqyʾ*, "fetters," let alone the Common Ar. *ᶜzqh/tʾ*, "signet ring." The BH hapax *ʾzqym* (for which *ᶜzqyʾ* is the targumic translation) is more difficult to explain, but its Qrê reading, the common Hebrew and Aramaic *zi/eqqîm/n* (Syr. also *zanqâ*), is hardly a loan from a nonexistent Akk. **sinqu*. Similarly, there is no reason to regard the Aramaic and Arabic root *znq*, "to make tight," as a denominative verb or as anything but cognate to Akk. *sanāqu*.[142]

kakku, "club," "weapon"—Syr., Targ. YI and BT, Mand., Pehlevi logograms *kkʾ*, "molar," "tooth." Since the only possible semantic development would seem to be "molar (tusk?)" > "club," the Aramaic term would appear to be cognate with Akkadian, not a loan from it.[143]

kalapp/bbu, "pick," "axe"—BH *kēlappôṯ*; JPA, Targ. Proph., Hagiog., Syr. *kwlbʾ*, "axe." This is an old culture word of indeterminate origin; note that in Akkadian it is limited to Assyrian and that it occurs in Hittite. The differences in the vowels preclude a loan.[144]

* *kalakku*, "raft" NA—Syr. *klkʾ*, Iraqi Arabic *kalak*.[145]

142. For the Akkadian controversy: *CAD*, Vol. I/J, p. 205; W. von Soden, "Izqātu, išqātu 'Kettenringe,' ein aramäisches Lehnwort," *AfO* XX (1963) 155; von Soden, in *Or*. n.s. XXXV 12. For the loan theories: Z, p. 35; *LS*, pp. 201, 203; *KBL* (3d ed.) p. 266. Von Soden's interpretation is highly preferable. As he suggests, the Akkadian and the late Targumic words for "fetter" could be derived from Ar. *ḥizqâ*, but there is no way that the "ᶜ" of *ᶜzqth*, "signet ring," already attested in Imperial Aramaic, could be derived from /ḥ/ at such an early period. Further, one can understand semantic developments from "ring" into "fetter" and "signet ring," but a development from "fetter" into "signet ring" is very difficult; *ᶜzqh*, "signet ring," could be a completely separate word. Compare Arab. *ᶜḏq*, "to mark," "to stigmatize," Ar. *ᶜdqʾ*, "curl" (and BT *ᶜdq*, "press together"?).

143. Z, p. 12; *LS*, p. 326; *AHw*., p. 422. See especially *Additamenta*, p. 221. While not indicated in *AHw*., there is some agreement among Sumerologists that *kakku* is a loan from Sum. GAG, the famous Mesopotamian cone-shaped nail or peg. On the one hand there is no textual or lexical support for this theory, though GAG does mean "arrowhead" (see E. Salonen, *Die Waffen der alten Mesopotamier* [*St.Or*., Vol. XXXIII (Helsinki, 1965)] p. 123), nor do I know of any significant archeological evidence that any standard macehead was of this shape. On the other hand, the canine teeth and pre-molars are rather similar in shape to a GAG, and some relationship here cannot be ruled out; nevertheless, there remains little likelihood that the Aramaic word was a late borrowing from Akkadian.

144. Z, p. 12; *LS*, p. 328; *AHw*., p. 424; *KBL* (2d ed.) p. 433; C. Rabin, in *Or*. n.s. XXXII 124.

145. Z, p. 45; *LS*, p. 329; *AHw*., p. 423; A. Salonen, *Hausgeräte* I (Helsinki, 1965) 200.

* *kalakku*, "storehouse," "grain silo"—BT *ʾklkʾ* (correct variant of *ʾklbʾ*).[146]

kalūbu, "hook(?)"—Mand. *kwlʾbʾ*, "hook." The Akkadian occurs only in one broken context.[147]

* *kamāru*, "a fish"—BT, Targ. YI, Targ. Hagiog., YT, *kwwrʾ*, Mand. *kʾwʾrʾ*, *Phrah.* iii 2 *kwr*, "(salt-water?) fish." This is certainly from Akkadian (< Sumerian), but except for rare lexical attestations the Akkadian is known only from Old Babylonian texts.[148]

kamāṣu, "to bow down"—Greenfield derives BT *kwṣ*, "to contract," "to shrink," from this. His suggestion must be considered rather unlikely, for *kwṣ* is clearly just another by-form of the more normal BT form *qwṣ*, Mand. *kbṣ*.[149]

* *kannu*, "a large vessel"—Mand. *kʾnʾ*, "vessel." This meaning of the word is found only in Akkadian and Mandaic and is thus apparently an inherited word in the latter. In its primary meaning "base," it is to be considered cognate with and not a loan into Heb. *kēn*, Syr. *kannâ*, etc.[150]

* *kanūnu*, "brazier"—Palm. *knwn*, Syr. *knwnʾ*, BT *knwnʾ*, Mand. *kʾnwnʾ* > Arab. *kânûn*.[151]

146. J. N. Epstein, in *Festskrift*, pp. 297 ff. There would not appear to be any connection between this eastern term and MH *klyk/bh*, "box," "bier."

147. Z, p. 42; A. Salonen, *Hippologica Accadica* (Helsinki, 1955) p. 158.

148. Cf. A. Goetze, "The Vocabulary of the Princeton Theological Seminary," *JAOS* LXV (1945) 227; B. Landsberger, *The Fauna of Ancient Mesopotamia* (*MSL*, Vol. VIII, Part 2 [Rome, 1962])p. 113, n. to l. 95. For the Akkadian see *AHw.*, p. 430, where the Aramaic is not cited. For the JAr. see *Additamenta*, p. 219. Targ. Neofiti has *nwn* wherever Pseudo-Jonathan has *kwwr* (Gen. 1:26, 28; 48:16).

149. J. C. Greenfield, "Studies in Aramaic Lexicography I," *JAOS* LXXXII (1962) 296. The original form of the root is *qpṣ* (Akk. *kap/bāṣu*). We must posit the development *qpṣ* > Proto-Babylonian Aramaic *qbṣ* > *kbṣ*, *kwṣ*, and *qwṣ* as dialectal variants. BT *k(w)bsʾ*, "cluster of dates," probably represents a form derived from a related root (compare Syr. *qps*), and hardly derives from hapax Akk. *kibsu*, "pressed," said of dates (for which see Landsberger, *Date Palm*, p. 54, n. 188).

150. Z, p. 33. The relationship between what appears to be a reduplicated form of this word, *kankannu*, and MH *qnqn* is uncertain. The Akkadian seems originally to mean "stand" but is also used as a "storehouse for beer." The Hebrew word means a large vessel in the cellar for liquids. Complicating the situation is Ug. *kknt*, also a vessel for liquids.

151. Z, p. 32; *LS*, p. 333; *AHw.*, p. 481; A. Salonen, "Die Öfen der alten Mesopotamier," *Baghdader Mitteilungen* III (1964) 108. The Akkadian, whose older (or Babylonian?) form is *kinūnu*, may be a loanword from Sumerian KI.NE, but its use almost exclusively in the North suggests that it is a northern culture word. Even so, the Aramaic form with a long initial vowel indicates a loan (see p. 146). See s.v. *kanūnu*, p. 115.

kanzuzu, "chin(?)"—Mand. *kᵓnzwzᵓ*, *kᵓnkwzᵓ*; Syr. *klzwzᵓ*, "chin." Origin unknown.[152]

karballatu, "cap"—Eg., BA, JAr., Syr. *krblh/tᵓ*. In Akkadian it is a late word of foreign origin.[153]

karpatu, "vessel"—This is an old culture word (cf. Ug. *krpn*), but Syr. *krptᵓ*, "vessels," might be a loan. Cf. also MH *q(w)rpy/ᵓwt*, "cups" or "bowls," and BT *krwpyytᵓ*.[154]

karṣillu, "scalpel(?)"—BT *kwsyltᵓ*, Syr. *kwsltᵓ*, "a sharp instrument for blood-letting or operating." The phonetic difficulties almost certainly preclude a loan, but the similarity can hardly be coincidental. Perhaps the Akkadian is to be read *karsillu*, for the few times that it is spelled syllabically the NUN sign, which has the reading *síl*, is used. The word is obviously foreign (compare *parzillu*); thus the Aramaic form probably derives from an intermediary other than Akkadian.[155]

karṣu, "slander"; especially in the idiom *karṣī akālu*, "to slander"—Imp. Ar. (*KAI*, No. 269) *krṣy* (pl. const. with *ᵓmr*), BA *ᵓkl qrṣyn*, JAr. (mostly Targ.) *ᵓkl q(w)rṣ(yn)*, Mand. *ᵓkyl kyrṣᵓ* (participle), Syr. *ᵓkl qrṣyn*. Note that the Carpentras and Mandaic forms have *k*, as does the Akkadian, whereas the others have assimilated the expression to the correct Ar. cognate *qrṣ*. Although the earliest attestation of this loan occurs with *ᵓmr* and not *ᵓkl*, one may safely assume that the entire idiom was the element borrowed here. Note that Aramaic follows Akkadian using the plural of the noun (except rarely in JAr.).[156]

* *kāru*, "quay"—Syr. *kr d*, "(place) where." The Syriac usage may have developed from the numerous Assyrian geographical names beginning with the element *kār*.[157]

karû, "grain heap," "storehouse"—MH, Common Ar. *kry(ᵓ)*, "heap." This is probably a common Semitic word rather than a loan from Sum. GUR(U)$_7$.[158]

kilīlu, "wreath," "crown"—Common Ar. *klylᵓ* > Arab.

152. *MD*, p. 199; *HM*, p. 536.

153. Z, p. 36; *LS*, p. 343; *KBL* (2d ed.) p. 1087.

154. Z, p. 33; *LS*, p. 348; *Additamenta*, p. 236; F. Perles, in *OLZ* VIII 384.

155. Not previously compared. Syr. *krzylᵓ*, "shepherd's crook," and BT (hapax) *krzylᵓ*, "shepherd(?)," are strikingly similar to the Akkadian in form, but the required semantic development is difficult to imagine.

156. Z, p. 25; *LS*, p. 17; *AHw.*, p. 450.

157. *LS*, p. 342. This is probably not related to the predominantly late Mand. *qᵓrᵓ*, "chez." (Cf. *MD*, p. 402, where Nöldeke's interpretation is preferable to that of Drower-Macuch.)

158. Z, p. 41; *LS*, p. 345; *AHw.*, p. 452; Salonen, *Agricultura*, p. 280.

ʾiklîl. Since the form with *ī* is found only in Old Akkadian and Old Babylonian (cf. *kulīlum*) and the later common form is *kulūlu*, the terms would appear to be only cognate.[159]

* *kimahhu*, "grave"—Palm. *gwmḥ*, *gmḥ*, Nab. *gwḥ*, Syr. *byt gmḥʾ*, BT *gwhʾ*, MH, JPA, Targ. Judges, Hagiog. *kwk*, "grave niche." This has been thoroughly treated by E. Y. Kutscher.[160]

kimtu, "family"—Mand. hapax *kymtʾ*(?). Since *kimtu* does not occur in Akkadian in an astronomical use, it appears to be only cognate with Heb., Ar. *kîmâ*, Ethiopic *kêma*, "Pleiades."[161]

* *kinattu*, "colleague"—Eg., *AD*, Ahiqar, BA, BH, CPA, Syr. *kntʾ*, pl. *knwtʾ*.[162]

kippatu, "circle," "circumference"—There is little reason to suspect that any of the Hebrew or Aramaic nouns from the root *kpp* in the meaning "arch," "dome," "vault (of the heavens)," "cap" were influenced by Akkadian.[163]

* *kišādu*, "neck," "necklace" (see *AHw*., p. 490*a*, mngs. 5 ff.)—Mand. *kšʾdʾ*, "a neck ornament." The Mandaic word hardly means "throat," as given in *MD*.[164]

159. Z, p. 36; *LS*, p. 327; *AHw*., p. 476; *Wb.KAS*, p. 299*b*. Cf. R. Borger, "Gott Marduk und Gott-König Šulgi als Propheten," *Bi.Or*. XXVIII (1971) 19.

160. Z, p. 68; *LS*, p. 120; F. Rosenthal, *Die Sprache der palmyrenischen Inschriften und ihre Stellung innerhalb der Aramäischen* (*MVAG*, Vol. XLI [Leipzig, 1963]) p. 14; E. Y. Kutscher, in *Eretz Israel* VIII (1967) 273 ff. The rare Syriac form may actually derive from the attested *bīt kimahhi*. Kutscher's treatment still leaves several points unclear. What is the origin of the initial *k* in the Jewish form? He seems to attempt to overcome this difficulty merely by citing the Akkadian as *k/gimahhu*, yet the other Aramaic forms all have *g*. I would return to a solution similar to Nöldeke's ("Palmyrenische Inschrift," *ZA* IX [1894] 266): Ass. [gimaḫ] > Palm. *gumaḥ*. Bab. *kimah* [kiwaḫ] > *kuwaḫ* > *kûḫâ* (emphatic) > *kûḵ/ḫ* (absolute). This derivation considers the BT form found by Kutscher uncertain and regards Nab. *gwḥ* either as a mixed form or, in view of the frequent historical spellings of Nabatean, as an historical spelling for *kûḫ/ḵ* and the immediate model of Heb. *kwk*.

161. *MD*, p. 213; cf. *AHw*., p. 479, *KBL* (2d ed.) p. 434, and W. Leslau, *Ethiopic and South Arabic Contributions to the Hebrew Lexicon* ("Publications in Semitic Philology," Vol. XX [Berkeley and Los Angeles, 1958]) p. 26.

162. Z, p. 46; *LS*, p. 334; *Ahw*., p. 479; *KBL*, p. 1086. Is this the origin of MH, JAr. *kt(ʾ)*, *kytʾ*, "group"?

163. Cf. *LS*, p. 339. The etymology for *kippatu* proposed by M. Bravmann, "Akk. *kipru(m)* pl. *kipratu(m)* and Ethiopic *kanfar*," *JCS* XXII (1968-69) 85 ff., is unconvincing.

164. *MD*, p. 224; cf. M. Lidzbarski, *Ginzā, der Schatz oder das grosse Buch der Mandäer* ("Quellen der Religionsgeschichte," Vol. XIII [Göttingen, 1925]) p. 347, n. 1. A translation "Saturn unbinds his loins and frees the *k*. from his neck" is certainly preferable to ". . . and cuts his (own!) neck in two." The Akkadian is used for a neck ornament as early as OB.

* *kiššu*, "bundle of reeds"—BT *kyšʾ*, "bunch."[165]

* *kukku*, "cake"—Syr., Mand., BT *kwkʾ*.[166]

* *kurru*, "a dry measure"—Bab. dockets, BH, BA *kr*, MH, JAr., Syr., Mand. *kwr* > Arab. *kurr*.[167]

kūru, "furnace"—This word, which occurs in Hebrew, Aramaic, Arabic (all *kûr*) and Ethiopic (*kawr*), is almost certainly of Common Semitic origin, yet it is often assumed to be the same word as *kīru* (Heb. and Arab. *kîr*), which has a corresponding Sum. form GIR_4. The latter may be an old culture word and cannot conlusively be proven to be a Sumerian loanword.[168]

kusiʾu (*AHw.*, *kusīu*) lex. only, "turban" or "crown"—This occurs on the left side of the synonym list and represents the foreign (probably Aramaic) word for "full moon," Ug. *ksa*, BH *kese*, Syr. *k(ʾ)sʾʾ*.[169]

kusītu, "garment"—Syr. *kwsytʾ*, "hood." The root is common, but the unusual form of the Syriac suggests a loan.[170]

* *kuspu*, "residue of ground dates"—BT *kwspʾ*.[171]

* *kutallu*, "back of the neck," "backside"—Syr., Mand. *kwtlʾ*, "ship's stern" > Arab. *kwṯl*; BT *kwtly* (*dḥzyry*), "bacon." This is to be separated from the word "wall," occurring rarely in Akkadian (*kutlu*), common in western Aramaic (*koṯlâ*), late Biblical and Mishnaic Hebrew (*kōṯel*), to be considered a native Aramaic word, lost in eastern Aramaic, where it was replaced by Akkadian words such as *asītu* and *igāru*.[172]

165. *AHw.*, p. 492.
166. *LS*, p. 326; *Additamenta*, p. 221.
167. Z, p. 21; *AHw.*, p. 511; *KBL*, p. 453. The distribution pattern favors the accepted view that *kurru* is a loanword from Sum. gur, which became an official Imperial Aramaic measure.
168. Z, p. 32; *LS*, p. 323; *AHw.*, pp. 484, 512; Salonen, in *Baghdader Mitteilungen* III 118 ff.; *Wb.KAS*, pp. 487*b*, 431*a*.
169. Z, p. 63; *KBL*, (2d ed.) p. 446. For Ugaritic cf. *Ugaritica* V 584 and M. C. Astour, "Some New Divine Names from Ugarit," *JAOS* LXXXVI (1966) 282.
170. Z, p. 36; *LS*, p. 337.
171. Z, p. 39; *Additamenta*, p. 229; *AHw.*, p. 509. The earlier publications preceded recognition of the proper Akkadian form.
172. Z, pp. 32, 45; *LS*, p. 352; *AHw.*, p. 518*b*; W. von Soden, "Der hymnisch-epische Dialekt des Akkadischen," *ZA* n.f. VII (1933) 171, n. 4; Salonen, *Wasserfahrzeuge*, p. 76, n. 2, and *Hippologica Accadica*, p. 118; *Wb.KAS*, p. 70. The opinion expressed here follows von Soden and Salonen. With Salonen I also reject a Sumerian etymology for *kutallu* but for the additional reason that it is probably cognate with the common Aramaic word for "back of the neck," *qḏâl* > Arab. *qaḏâl* (but previously unrecognized as such). (For Arab. *ḏ* for Ar. *ḏ* cf. Fraenkel, *Aramäischen Fremdwörter*, p. xix and *tilmīḏ* < *talmîḏ*.) It is difficult to account for changes in

* *kutimmu*, "gold- and silversmith"—Bab. docket *kdm*.[173]

labāru, "to be old"—Cf. *AP*, No. 26:13, 17 *lwbr*.[174]

lahannu, "drinking dish"—This may be a Sumerian loanword in Akkadian but could hardly be a loan into Syr. *laqnâ*, which must be from Greek *lekánē*.[175]

* *lahhinu*, fem. *lahhinatu*, "a temple or court official," "steward(?)"—Eg. *lḥn*, *lḥnh*, "x of the temple"; BA *lḥnh*, "x of the court"; Targ. *lḥ(y)ntʾ*, "concubine."[176]

* *libbatu*, "wrath"; in the idiom *libbati malû*, "to be angry with"—Aššur Ostracon, Eg. *lbt* (absolute) *mlʾ*. This idiom is frequently proposed for BH in Ezek. 16:30 but definitely occurs as a loan-translation in Dan. 3:19, Esther 3:5, 5:9 in the form *mlʾ ḥmh*.[177]

libittu, "brick"—There is no compelling reason to assume that Akkadian is the origin of the Common Semitic term and its related forms.[178]

* *lilītu*, "female demon"—BH, JAr., Syr., Mand. *lîlîṯ*, "Lilith."[179]

both of the stops, but perhaps there was some assimilation to Sumerian. Note that the BT *kwtly*, "back parts (of pigs)," has the variant *qdly*. The resulting mixed form *qōtel* (based on the form found in the *Aruch*) is used in Modern Hebrew for "bacon."

173. G. R. Driver, "A Babylonian Tablet with an Aramaic Endorsement," *Iraq* IV (1937) 18. The reading is not certain.

174. F. Perles, in *OLZ* XXI 69; *AP*, p. 95; *DISO*, p. 136.

175. *AHw.*, p. 527; Salonen, *Hausgeräte* II 225.

176. *DISO*, p. 137; *KBL*, p. 1090; B. Landsberger, "Akkadisch-hebräische Wortgleichungen," Suppl. *VT* XVI (1967) 204; Porten, *Archives*, pp. 200 f. Attempts to find other than Akkadian etymologies, especially for the Eg., have not been fruitless, but are much less convincing. Note that the NA *lahhinu* (*alahhinu* in *CAD*) is something like a temple steward (cf. J. V. Kinnier Wilson, *The Nimrud Wine Lists* [London, 1972] pp. 80 f.), certainly identical in function with the Elephantine *lḥn* and his female counterpart (wife?) the *lḥnh*, while the *lahhinatu* is a woman of the queen's court, just like the *lḥnh* of BA. The targumic usage of *lḥyntʾ* is merely the result of a misinterpretation of the BA term.

177. *AHw.*, p. 548; *DISO*, p. 134; *KBL*, p. 471. To the Eg. examples in *DISO* add Hermopolis 1:6; cf. B. Porten and J. C. Greenfield, "The Aramaic Papyri from Hermopolis," *ZAW* LXXX (1968) 228. Might there be any relation here to MH *libbāh*, "to set ablaze"? Cf. N. M. Waldman, "A Note on Canticles 4:9," *JBL* LXXXIX (1970) 215 ff.

178. Z, p. 31; *LS*, p. 357. It is, in fact, difficult to account for the derivation of the Heb. form *lᵉḇēnāh* from any of the Akkadian forms.

179. Z, p. 69; *LS*, p. 366; *AHw.*, p. 553; *KBL*, pp. 480 f. Lilith probably occurs in Arslan Tash (*KAI*, No. 27:20) *lly*, now read *llyn* by F. M. Cross and J. Saley, "Phoenician Incantations on a Plaque of the Seventh Century B.C. from Arslan Tash in Upper Syria," *BASOR*, No. 197 (1970) p. 46.

* *limmu/līmu*, "eponym official"—Assyrian dockets *lʾm, lm.*[180]

litiktu, "a measuring vessel"—This probably belongs together with Ug. *lṯḥ*, BH and Syr. *ltk*, "a measure," but as such is probably of foreign origin, to be separated from the root *latāku*, "to test," cognate with Syr. *lâṯeḵ*, "suitable."[181]

* *lumāšu*, "constellation," "zodiacal position"—Syr. *mlwšʾ*, Mand. *mʾlwʾšʾ*, "sign of the zodiac." The Aramaic derives from this word, apparently preceded by the pronounced determinative MUL, "star," though in the Akkadian texts *lumāšu* usually occurs without the determinative, and I know of no spellings *mu-* or *ma-lumāšu* that would indicate that it was actually pronounced. The development *mu(l)wâš* > *malwâš* is probably due to the absence of a noun preformative *mu-* in Aramaic.[182]

* *maddattu*, "tribute"—Eg., *AD*, BA *mndh*; BA, BH, Genesis Apocryphon *mdh*; Syr. *mdʾtʾ* (pl. *maddatê* and *mdʾtwtʾ*). The only JAr. reference I know of is the *Aruch* citation of Targum Proverbs 12:24 *mdʾtʾ* (< Syriac), while the Rabbinic Hebrew use of *mndh* is based directly on the Biblical passages.[183]

magannu, "gift," "gratis"—Ug., Phoen., BH *mgn*, "to offer," "to present"; Common Ar. (and Arab.) *maggân*, "gratis." This foreign word has been studied by von Soden. It occurs in early Akkadian in the sense of "gift," but only as a Hurrianism, and in late Akkadian in the meaning "gratis" as an Aramaism. The western forms were probably also borrowed directly from Hurrian.[184]

mahāru, in *mithuru*, "to be equal," "to be square"—The connecting link between the many Akkadian uses and Syr.

180. Cf. *DISO*, p. 134. The *aleph* of the Aramaic is difficult, but for another possible example of *aleph* to indicate internal ê/î, see n. 136. Since no other etymology is known for the Akkadian, perhaps this is an old North Semitic word for "ruler" (which possibly exists in BH as well; cf. James Barr, *Comparative Philology and the Text of the Old Testament* [Oxford, 1968] p. 329, s.v. *lʾm*).

181. W. von Soden, "Zum akkadischen Wörterbuch," *Or.* n.s. XX (1951) 162 ff.

182. To my knowledge this is the first time that the correct model for Ar. *malwâšâ* has been found, for the word *lumāšu* itself is a fairly recent addition to the Akkadian lexicon. Formerly (cf. Z, p. 62; *LS*, p. 390) Sum. mul-maš was cited, which is only the name of one particular constellation.

183. Z, p. 9; *LS*, pp. 374-75; *AHw.*, p. 572; *DISO*, p. 158; *KBL*, p. 1091; Wagner, p. 71. For discussion see above s.v. *ilku* and *biltu*.

184. W. von Soden, "Vedisch *Magham*, 'Geschenk'—neuarabisch *maǧǧānīja*, 'Gebührenfreiheit,'" *JEOL* XVIII (1964) 339 ff.; C. Rabin, "Milim BeIvrit HaMiqrait MiLašon HaIndo-Aryim ŠeBeMizraḥ HaQarov," in *Sefer Shmuel Yeivin* (Jerusalem, 1970) pp. 484-86.

maḥḥârâ, "architect," has not yet been discovered, so one must reserve judgment on the nature of the relationship. The general semantic similarity between Akk. *mahāru* and Ar. *qbl*, both originally meaning "to stand over against," requires further study. Both occur in their original sense in similar juristic usage, and both become the common word for "to receive."[185]

* *māhāzu*, "major town," "city"—Palm., Syr., BT (and possibly Targ. Onk. Num. 22:39) *mḥwzʾ*, Mand. *mʾhwzʾ*, "walled city." In spite of the many articles and notes devoted to this word, the relationship and development of the various forms and meanings remain obscure. It is clear, however, that in the West Semitic languages there are two separate words. In BA, Targ. Onk., JPA, and Nab. *mâḥôz* means "harbor" and is an ancient word in the West as now attested by a Sumerian, Akkadian, Hurrian, and Ugaritic vocabulary text from Ugarit: KAR : *kāru* : *ma-ḫa-[z]i* : *ma-aḫ-ḫa-[ ]*. Although the evidence of this vocabulary text would suggest that this word is either Hurrian or North West Semitic in origin, it may in fact be an early loan from the Akkadian term in its original meaning (see R. Kutscher; note, however, that the Ugaritic harbor-town name *Maʾḫadu* shows the reflex of the etymologically correct *ḏ*). The later Ar. *mâḥôz*, "city," must be a development of the late and common Akkadian usage. Nevertheless, the *o* vowel of the second syllable is inexplicable unless one allows for Canaanite influence, perhaps by formal assimilation to *mâḥôz*, "harbor."[186]

* *mahrat elippi*, "ship's bow"—Mand. *mhʾrʾ*.[187]

* *makkī/ūtu*, "a tow barge or cargo ship"—Mand. *mʾkwtʾ*, BT, Syr. (lex) *mkwtʾ*, "a kind of boat."[188]

185. On the Syriac, cf. *LS*, p. 381.

186. Z, p. 9; *LS*, p. 219; *AHw.*, p. 582; Rosenthal, *Die Sprache*, p. 90; E. Y. Kutscher, "LeSheelot Milloniyot Maḥoz = Namal," *Leš.* VIII (1937) 136 ff., *Words*, pp. 41 ff., and "The Language of the Hebrew and Aramaic Letters of Bar-Koseva and His contemporaries: B. The Hebrew Letters," *Leš.* XXVI (1962) 9 f.; J. Starcky, "Un Contrat nabatéen sur papyrus," *RB* LXI (1954) 163, l. 2; W. L. Moran, "A New Fragment of DIN.TIR.KI = *Bābilu* and *Enūma Eliš*," *Analecta Biblica* XII (1959) 258, n. 2. New studies taking into account the evidence of the new vocabulary, *Ugaritica* V, No. 137 ii 21, are E. Y. Kutscher, "Ugaritica Marginalia," *Leš.* XXXIV (1969-70) 5 ff.; R. Kutscher, "The Sumerian Equivalents of Akkadian *māḫāzu*," *Leš.* XXXIV 267 ff.; R. Borger, "Weitere ugaritologische Kleinigkeiten III. Hebräisch MḤWZ (Psalm 107, 30)," *UF* I (1969) 1 ff.; and M. C. Astour, "Maʾḫadu, the Harbor of Ugarit," *JESHO* XIII (1970) 113 ff.

187. Z, p. 45; Salonen, *Wasserfahrzeuge*, p. 76.

188. J. N. Epstein, "Sride Sheʾeltot," *Tarbiz* VI (1935) 487, n. 36. Some early scholars incorrectly compared the Aramaic with Sum. ^{giš}ma-ku-

* *makkasu*, "a kind of date"—*Mks* appears in an unpublished Babylonian docket in the British Museum.[189]

mala, "as much as"—Porten and Greenfield and Kutscher interpret Hermopolis 1:7 *mlw* in this fashion, retaining the reading of the editors but interpreting it differently. Milik's reading, *hlw*, seems preferable, however, on both syntactic and paleographic grounds. The phrase *kᶜn(t) hlw* is previously known from Imperial Aramaic.[190]

* *malāhu*, "sailor"—Common Ar., BH, Arab. *mallâḥ*.[191]

* *manû*, "mina (weight)"—Assyrian weights (*CIS* II, Nos. 1-15) *mnh*; *AP*, No. 26:17 (pl.) *mnn*; BA *mnᵓ*; BH *māne* > MH; JAr., Syr. *mnyᵓ*; Mand. *mnyᵓ* > perhaps Arab., Greek, etc. Most scholars now consider Sum. MA.NA to be an old loan from Akk. *manû*,[192] but is the West Semitic word a cognate or a loan? The lack (or at most questionable occurrence) of the term in both alphabetic and syllabic texts at Ugarit is significant evidence that it is a loan, as is the rare and obviously late usage in the Bible (though large numbers of shekels are often listed, as at Ugarit). The irregularities in the plural formations in the various dialects also point toward a loan here.[193]

manzaltu, "(star) position"—BH *mazzalot* (pl.), RH. JAr. *mazzāl*, "planet," "constellation," "luck"; CPA *mzlyᵓ* (pl.), "*stoixeîa*"; Syr. *mwzlᵓ*, *mwzltᵓ*, "sphere," "heavenly zone";

a (see Jastrow, *Dictionary*, p. 782, and now Salonen, *Wasserfahrzeuge*, p. 61). For *makkī/ūtu* see *Wasserfahrzeuge*, p. 21. Although the Mandaic term unquestionably means "boat," some of the commentators took the talmudic word to mean "mast," which Salonen (*Wasserfahrzeuge*, p. 8; *Die Landfahrzeuge des alten Mesopotamien* [Helsinki, 1951] p. 134; cf. Z, p. 32) thinks is from *makūtu*, "pole." Zimmern (Z, p. 32) and von Soden (*AHw.*, p. 591) compare this latter word with the rare Syr. *mk/ḥwtᵓ*, "parapet," a connection which is uncertain at best.

189. British Museum No. 82-9-18 403, dated to Darius 19.

190. Porten and Greenfield, in *ZAW* LXXX 228, and Porten, *Archives*, p. 270; E. Y. Kutscher, "The Hermopolis Papyri," *IOS* I (1971) 113; J. T. Milik, in *Biblica* XLVIII 549. Cf. *DISO*, p. 65. The letter in question is neither a good "m" nor an "h." Milik suggests that an original "m" was corrected to "h." Considering the varied forms of "h" in this text when compared with the rather uniform shape of "m," the reading *hlw*, in my opinion, is much to be preferred. Whatever the correct reading, however, there is probably no connection with Akk. *mala*, especially in light of CPA *l-mlw d-*.

191. Z, p. 45; *LS*, p. 391; *AHw.*, p. 592; Wagner, p. 76.

192. Gelb, *MAD*, No. 2 (2d ed.) p. 141; *AHw.*, p. 604; *KBL*, p. 1095; contra E. A. Speiser, *Oriental and Biblical Studies: Collected Writings of E. A. Speiser*, ed. by J. J. Finkelstein and M. Greenberg (Philadelphia, 1967) p. 157.

193. Z, pp. 20 f.; *LS*, p. 394; *AHw.*, p. 604.

Mand. *mʾnzʾlʾ*, "constellation," "star of destiny" (perhaps the origin of Arab. *manzil*, "lunar phase").[194]

* *maqlūtu*, OB (omens), SB, NA, "burnt offering"—*AP*, No. 33:10 *mqlw*. Although the root is common in Aramaic (see, too, MH *mqlh*), this isolated and unusual Aramaic form would appear to be a borrowing from Akkadian.[195]

mār bīti, LB "administrator," "steward"—Eg., *AD*, JAr. *br bytʾ*; BH and MH *bn byt*. Both the Akkadian and Aramaic are calques from Iranian.[196]

* *marru*, "spade"—Syr., BT *mr* > Arab. *marr*, Egyptian *mr*, late Greek *márra*, Latin *marra*, French *marre*.[197]

* *maruštu*, *marultu*, "sickness," "trouble" (root *mrṣ*)—Mand. *mʾrwlʾ*, "trouble."[198]

mašāhu, "to measure"; *mišihtu*, "measurement"—A careful analysis yields the conclusion that the root *mšḥ*, "to measure" (Arab. *msh*) is the native Aramaic word for this activity.[199]

* *maškanu*, "pledge"—Nab. *mškwn*, vb. *mškn*; JAr. and MH *mškwn(ʾ)*, vb. *mškn*; Syr. *mšknʾ*, vb. *mškn*.[200]

194. Z, p. 62; *LS*, p. 10; *KBL*, p. 509; omitted in *AHw.*, p. 638. *Manzaltu* is the MB/LB form of original *manzaztu*, *mazzaztu*.

195. *AP*, p. 126; *DISO*, p. 165.

196. *AD* (abridged) pp. 40 f.; W. Eilers, "Neue aramäische Urkunden aus Ägypten," *AfO* XVII (1954-56) 335; *idem*, "Die altiranische Vorform des Vāspuhr," in *A Locust's Leg: Studies in Honor of S. H. Taqizadeh* (London, 1962) pp. 55-63. As shown by Eilers in the latter article, the occurrence of the Iranian loanword *ú-ma-as/su-pi-it-ru-ú* in Achaemenid LB texts proves the Persian origin of the expression. At Elephantine a term of completely different origin may be involved; cf. Porten, *Archives*, p. 230, n. 89, and J. B. Segal, review of Porten, *Archives*, *BSOAS* XXXIV (1971) 142.

197. Z, p. 41; *LS*, p. 400; *AHw.*, p. 612; *Additamenta*, p. 266; Salonen, *Agricultura*, p. 118.

198. Previously unrecognized. The Mandaic has no other convincing etymology, and the development *-uštu* > *-ultu* > *-wlʾ* is identical to that shown in *manzaz/štu* > *manzaltu* > *mʾnzʾlʾ*.

199. Z, p. 22; E. G. Kraeling, *The Brooklyn Museum Aramaic Papyri* (New Haven, 1953) p. 163. In *LS*, p. 406, we find the suggestion that *mšḥ* might derive from the Akkadian form of an original **mṯḫ*, Ar. *mtḥ*, "to stretch," but there is absolutely no evidence for a root other than *mtḥ* (as in Arabic and Hebrew, for which see J. C. Greenfield, "The Etymology of *ʾmtḥt*," *ZAW* LXXVII [1965] 90 ff.) The common Akkadian and Hebrew root for "measure" is *mdd*, which does not occur in Aramaic, so *mšḥ* must be the correct original verb for this activity in Aramaic. Further, the Akkadian is attested only from Middle Babylonian on and could be an Aramaic loanword. Whatever the construction of *mšḥt* in Kraeling, *Brooklyn Museum*, No. 4:12 and No. 12:28, it definitely is not a singular absolute and hence cannot be used to show treatment as a foreign word here.

200. Z, p. 18; *LS*, p. 776; H. Petschow, *Neubabylonisches Pfandrecht* (Berlin, 1956) pp. 52 ff. Although in this meaning the Akkadian term is

* *mātu*, "country," "land"—Adon, l. 9 (*KAI*, No. 266), Ahiqar, l. 36 *mtʾ*, "country," "land"; Syr., BT *mtʾ*, "region," "native land" or "town," pl. "small towns"; Mand. *mʾtʾ*, "home," "town," pl. "towns"; Neo-Syriac *mâtâ*, "village," "countryside." The etymology of the Akkadian is still uncertain, but we can be quite sure of a loan here on the basis of distribution and meaning. In the Imperial Aramaic texts the correct meaning "country," "land" is still preserved, indicating familiarity with the normal Akkadian use of the term. Later this word is limited to Eastern Aramaic, where it is found in a limited meaning derived perhaps from the rarer Akkadian usage in the sense of "countryside" or "region" (see *AHw.*, p. 634, *mātu(m)* I A2) or perhaps even from the use of the Akkadian word in the actual name of regions such as *Māt-Akkadi*, which occurs in Assur Ostracon, l. 2 as *mtkdy* and probably as *mt ʾkdh* in Caquot, "Inscription," l. 2. (Cf. *mtbbšqn* in *DEA*, No. 30:2)[201]

mazūru, "fuller's mallet"—Syr. *mzwrʾ*. The root is common. Any relationships with the Hebrew and JAr. forms listed by Epstein are extremely doubtful.[202]

mēdelu, "bolt"—Syr. (lex.) *mdlʾ* may be from Greek

limited to Neo-Babylonian and Late Babylonian, it is very unlikely that this word could be anything but an Akkadian development, given the nature of the difference in meaning of the root *škn* between Akkadian and North West Semitic (cf. *AHw.*, p. 627, "auch Aram."). The western forms with an "o" vowel in the second syllable presumably derive from the common western pronunciation of /ā/ as a middle back, but the /ā/ itself is difficult to explain (see Vowels, in Chap. IV).

201. Z, p. 9; *LS*, p. 408; *AHw.*, p. 633; H. L. Ginsberg, "An Aramaic Contemporary of the Lachish Letters," *BASOR*, No. 111 (1948) p. 26, n. 10; Kutscher, *Words*, p. 20. The precise meaning in the broken context of Adon is uncertain, but there can be no doubt about the Ahiqar passage. For Sum. ma-da as a loan from Akkadian, cf. *AHw.*, p. 633, and Gelb, *MAD*, No. 3, p. 168. Kutscher has another suggestion to explain the semantic developments (or rather limitations) in the Aramaic forms, but I do not agree that BT *mtʾ* means "city" or is used any differently from the Syriac. In fact the example he gives, Mata Meḥasiah, was certainly not a city. Cf. Ketubot 4*a*, where it is specifically said to be neither a city nor a village. While it might have been a vague suburban area around Sura, more likely it was a small town; see the Syriac source cited in J. Neusner, *A History of the Jews in Babylonia* V (Leiden, 1970) 21. J. A. Fitzmyer finds *mt* in the difficult Gen. Apoc. 2:23, which he reads *lʾrk mt lprwyn* (see *The Genesis Apocryphon of Qumran Cave I* [2d ed., rev.; Rome, 1971] pp. 94 f.). Aside from being a unique occurrence in Western Aramaic this reading is difficult to support both orthographically and syntactically. One would expect *lʾwrk mtʾ lprwyn*. Though not without difficulties, the reading *lh qdmt* (read *lh lqdmt*?) is preferable.

202. *LS*, p. 379; J. N. Epstein, "Biblisch-Talmudisches," *OLZ* XX (1917) 274 ff.; *AHw.*, p. 637. The meaning "crush," "pound" is more common to North West Semitic, while in Akkadian it is basically "to twist."

mandalos. The Greek word could hardly be derived from Akkadian.[203]

* *mesû*, "to wash"—Eastern Aramaic *mšʾ*, "wash," "rub clean."[204]

* *midru*, "watercourse"—BT *mdrʾ*.[205]

* *miksu*, "tax"—BH *meḵes*, *miḵsāh*; *AP*, No. 81; Palm. (also as "tax collector"), RH, JPA, BT, CPA, Syr. all *mks(ʾ)*, "tax," "toll"; Mand. *mʾksʾ*, "tax," "tax collector" > Arab. *maks*. The form *mâḵsâ* for "tax collector" in Palmyran and Mandaic may possibly be a loan from Akk. *mākisu* and not a secondary development. The Arabic verb and noun forms appear to be secondary, but is the Akkadian verb *makāsu* without cognates?[206]

mīlu, "flood"—The Akkadian is cognate with, but possibly had some influence on Syr. *mlyʾ* (same meaning). On the other hand, the Akkadian word, normally *mīlu*, occurs as *milʾu* in Neo-Assyrian, perhaps under Aramaic influence.[207]

mindēma, "perhaps"—Imp. Ar. *mndᶜm* > *mdᶜm*, *m(y)dm*, *mydy*, "something." In light of the semantic difference, a relationship between the Akkadian and Aramaic forms is highly unlikely.[208]

* *miṣru*, "boundary"—Old Ar. *mṣr*, MH *myṣr*, JAr., Mand. *miṣrâ* (note the JAr. plural in *-ân*), with verbal meanings of *mṣr* "to make a boundary" in JAr. and Mand. and "to stretch" in

203. Z, p. 30; *LS*, p. 375.

204. The form *mšʾ*, in Targ. II Sam. 12:20, is probably a corruption; cf. A. Tal, "The Language of the Targum of the Former Prophets and Its Position within the Aramaic Dialects" (Diss.; Hebrew University, 1971) p. 237.

205. Previously unrecognized, and for good reason. The Akkadian has not yet been properly isolated in the dictionaries. The *AHw*. references are cited s.v. *miṭirtu* and (incorrectly) *bertu* (MID = BE). For the present see *CAD*, Vol. B, pp. 206-7, and R. Borger, *Die Inschriften Assarhadons Königs von Assyrien* (*AfO* Beiheft IX [Graz, 1956]) p. 91, n. 11.

206. Z, p. 10; *LS*, p. 385; *AHw*., p. 652; Fraenkel, *Aramäischen Fremdwörter*, p. 283; *KBL*, p. 522; Wagner, p. 76; A. Malamat, "The Ban in Mari and the Bible," *Biblical Essays* (Stellenbosch, 1966) p. 48, n. 23. Malamat points out that in the Bible the *meḵes* is exclusively devoted to the religious authorities, whereas the Akkadian is purely secular in nature. I fail to see why this reasoning supports his contention that the terms are cognate. In any case the Aramaic and Arabic forms are used in secular contexts.

207. *LS*, p. 389.

208. Cf. R. Macuch, "Anfänge der Mandäer," in F. Altheim and R. Stiehl, *Die Araber in der alten Welt* II (Berlin, 1965) 85; *LS*, p. 375. The early scholars were apparently unaware of the correct meaning of the Akkadian.

Syr., Mand. and JAr.[209] The verbal uses seem more at home in Aramaic than in Akkadian, but, as demonstrated by Tadmor, the use of *mṣr* in the Sefire inscriptions alongside the usual North West Semitic term *gbl* suggests that it is indeed a loan from the common Akkadian term.[210] Syr. *mzrʾ*, "stocks," appears to be a development from the root *mṣr* and should not be connected with Akk. *maṣṣaru*, "guard."[211]

mizru, "matted wool(?)" (lex.)—MH *myzrn*, "bedding material." Except for the rare SB lexical forms *mazru* and *mizru*, the root *mzr*, "to twist wool," is known only in Mishnaic Hebrew.[212]

mukku, "low quality wool"—The meaning of the Akkadian was established on the basis of MH *mwk*. Is the Sumerian form original here? Compare as well Mand. *m(ʾ)wkʾ*, "bedding."[213]

mulūgu, "dowry"—The form *mlwg* occurs in Mishnaic and Rabbinic Hebrew although never in Aramaic itself. The aim of Levine's study of this word is to prove contemporary Mesopotamian influence on late first millennium B.C. Palestine, but the history of this word proves no such thing. Its earliest occurrences are at Nuzi, Ugarit, and Amarna, and only later is it found in Mesopotamian Akkadian, indicating that it was of foreign origin, borrowed into Palestinian and Babylonian culture through separate channels. Most significantly, it cannot be shown that the Hebrew use of the word or of the cultural institution which it signifies presupposes the development of the term which took place in the Babylonian area.[214]

muqaru (not *muqāru*), "a soft mass"—Syr., Mand., JAr. *mwqrʾ*, "egg yolk," "brain matter." The ultimate origin of this word is unknown. In Akkadian it occurs only in divinatory texts and might therefore derive from Amorite.[215]

* *mušannītu*, "irrigation dam or dike"—BT *mšwnytʾ*, "a pile or bank of earth or stones" > Arab. *musannâh*, "irrigation

209. Z, p. 9; *AHw.*, 659. Any relationship with the Semitic name for Egypt remains uncertain. For the Aramaic meaning "rope" compare LB *māṣīru*, *AHw.*, p. 620, and von Soden, in *Or.* n.s. XXXV 19, and see J. N. Epstein, "Stricke und Leinen," *MGWJ* LXV (1921) 357 ff.

210. H. Tadmor, "Notes to the Opening Lines of the Aramaic Treaty from Sefire," *Sefer Shmuel Yeivin*, pp. 397 ff. (Heb.)

211. *LS*, p. 379.

212. *LS*, p. 379. D. Weisberg, in *HUCA* XXXIX 73.

213. *AHw.*, p. 670; Benno Landsberger and T. Jacobsen, "An Old Babylonian Charm against *Merḫu*," *JNES* XIV (1955) 19.

214. Baruch A. Levine, "*Mulūgu/Melûg*: The Origins of a Talmudic Legal Institution," *JAOS* LXXXVIII (1968) 271-85.

215. See the dictionaries: none suggest a loan.

dam." The spelling of the talmudic form as well as the single western occurrence in Midrash Genesis Rabbah 10:10 are to be considered contaminations from JPA *šwnyt*, etc., "cliff," "crag."[216]

* *mušarû*, "garden bed"—Syr. *mšrtʾ*, pl. *mšrytʾ*; BT *mšʾrʾ*, "garden bed"; Mand. *mšʾrʾ*, "garden bed," "habitation," "zone," > Arab. *mašârah*. The Babylonian Talmudic form is confused in the dictionaries and the editions with *myšrʾ*, "plain." The common Mandaic meaning, "habitation," probably reflects assimilation to the root *šry*, which appears correctly in the hapax *mʾšrytʾ*, "habitation"; cf. Syr. *mašryâ*, *mašrīṯâ*.[217]

* *muškēnu*, "a dependent class," NA and SB "destitute"—BH, Common Ar. *miskēn*, "destitute" > Arab., Ethiopic, Italian, French, Portugese.[218]

mūtānu, "plague"—Common Ar. *mwtnʾ*; Arab. *mûtân*. The evidence suggests that this is not a loanword: The form seems to occur in ESA;[219] the Syriac vocalization *mawtâna* is difficult to account for if it is a loanword (see n. 124); and the Akkadian distribution points to a possible Amorite origin.[220]

* *muterru*, "oven poker"—BT *mtʾrʾ* (var. *mtwʾrʾ*, *mtwrʾ*), Syr. *mtrʾ*, *mtwrʾ*, *mtyrʾ*.[221]

216. A. Salonen, in his excellent study of this word ("Akkad. *mušannītu* = Arab. *musannāh*," *Or.* n.s. XXXII [1963] 449 ff., and cf. *Agricultura*, p. 222), was led astray by his acceptance of the western dictionaries' interpretation of *mšwnyt* as identical to *šwnyt* (based on Rashi); hence, he thought the BT word at best was a related word influenced by Ar. *šnn*, "rock." Omitting the Akkadian material, a complete study of the JAr. references and their meanings can be found in *Aruch* V 279 f., where the relationship to the Arabic was already noted. The BT form is to be corrected to *mšnyt*.

217. Z, p. 40; *LS*, p. 408; *Additamenta*, p. 273; Fraenkel, *Aramäischen Fremdwörter*, p. 129. Note (*AHw.*, p. 681) that the Akkadian occurs with or without final long vowel. The etymology suggested by J. Lewy, "The Old Assyrian Surface Measure *šubtum*," *Analecta Biblica* XII (1959) 220 ff. (ESA *mauṯâr*, "foundation") is not convincing.

218. Z, p. 47; *LS*, p. 474; *AHw.*, p. 684; Wagner, pp. 79 f. Discussion over the etymology and meaning of the OB *muškēnum* (see the recent bibliography in R. Yaron, *The Laws of Eshnunna* [Jerusalem, 1969] p. 83, n. 1) continues, but there can be little doubt that the Aramaic was borrowed from NA, where it already meant "poor man," "destitute" (for which see *AHw.* and G. R. Driver and J. C. Miles, *The Babylonian Laws* I [Oxford, 1952] 90-95). I am unable to isolate or comprehend the linguistic forces which caused this specific value term to become the most widespread and long-lived of the Akkadian loanwords.

219. Cf. A. Salonen, review of *AHw.*, fasc. 8, *AfO* XXIII (1970) 96.

220. Z, p. 49; Fraenkel, *Aramäischen Fremdwörter*, p. 265.

221. To my knowledge the connection between the Akkadian and Ara-

* *nabārtu*, "cage," "trap"—Syr. *nmrt*ʾ > Arab. *namirah*, *nâmûrah*.[222]

* *naggāru*, "carpenter"—Bab. docket, Eg., Common Ar. *naggâr* > MH *naggār*; Punic; Arab. *naǧǧâr*. Note Mand. *n*ʾ*g*ʾ*r*ʾ and *n*ʾ*ng*ʾ*r*ʾ.[223]

nagû, "region"—Targ. Onk. and Proph. *ngwwt*ʾ; Mand. ʾ/ʿ*ng*ʾ*wy*ʾ, "islands," "coastlands"; possibly also in *KAI*, No. 266:8 *ngw*ʾ, but the exact meaning is uncertain there; Arab. *naǧwah*, "rising ground." This could be a loanword, but there are indications that it is cognate: the preservation of the "w" in all the western forms (cf. Phonology, in Chap. IV), and the distribution of the Akkadian, especially in Middle and Neo-assyrian, where it is always used of foreign areas, especially those in the West. On the other hand, the Aramaic distribution points to a loanword.[224]

* *naktāmu*, "cover," "lid"—BT *nktm*ʾ.[225]

nâlu, *niālu*, "to lie down"—Possibly related to Syr., BT, and Mand. *nâlâ*, "incubus"; compare the Akkadian causative stem. See as well Mand. *nywl*ʾ, "torment," and Syr. *nawwel*, " to afflict."[226]

* *nāmaru*, "mirror"—Syr. (lex.) *nwr*ʾ (*nawrâ*), Mand. *n*ʾ*wr*ʾ.[227]

namṣaru, "angular stick(?)"—Compare Targ. Isaiah *nṣwr*ʾ, "joiner's frame."

maic terms was recognized only by R. Campbell-Thompson, *A Dictionary of Assyrian Chemistry and Geology* (Oxford, 1936) p. xxvii. The only possible etymology is Akkadian, a participle of *turru*, "to turn" (transitive).

222. Z, p. 15; *LS*, p. 431. The shift *b* > *m* is difficult. See Labials in Chap. IV.

223. Z, p. 25; *LS*, p. 415; *AHw.*, p. 710; *DISO*, p. 174; A. Salonen, *Die Möbel des alten Mesopotamier* (Helsinki, 1963) p. 273. The word *ngr* is found in Ugaritic as the title of the god *ilš* and his wives in the KRT epic and is generally translated "carpenter" (cf. *UT*, p. 441; H. L. Ginsberg, in *ANET* [2d ed.] p. 148), but the context is broken, and the word could as well be *nāgiru*, "herald," or even an as yet unknown epithet. If it is "carpenter," there is no way to determine whether the word persisted in North West Semitic from that time on or was later reborrowed.

224. Z, p. 43; *AHw.*, p. 712; on Adon: *DISO*, p. 174. The reading *ngd*ʾ should be granted equal probability.

225. Z, p. 34; *Additamenta*, p. 280. In addition to the fact that the root *ktm* has quite a different meaning in Aramaic, the preformative *n*- proves certain Akkadian influence.

226. T. Nöldeke, *Neue Beiträge zur semitischen Sprachwissenschaft* (Strasbourg, 1910) p. 216, recognized that this type of word should have an Akkadian etymology, though he separated the Syriac verb, comparing it with Arab. *nw/yl*, "to grasp," "to obtain."

227. Z, p. 36; *LS*, p. 421.

* *nam/zzītu*, "mash tub"—BT *nzyytʾ*, Syr. (lex.) *nzytʾ* Arab. *nazîyah*.[228]

* *napharu*, "total"—Behistun 47 *npḥr*. Although this is the only attested occurrence in Aramaic, its use in this important document of wide circulation suggests that at least for a short time this word was a functioning lexical item in Imp. Ar.[229]

* *nappāhu*, "smith"—MH, Targ. Prophets, BT, Syr. (only in Assyria and Beth Garmai, see *LS*, p. 436) *npḥʾ*. Note Mand. *nph/nhp*, "to fan a flame," as against *npʾ*, "to blow." Though the root is common Semitic, the distribution, especially the Syriac, indicates a loan for this derived form.[230]

nappāṣu, "beating stick(?)"—BT *npṣʾ*, "carder," is a *qattāl* professional formation, while the Akkadian certainly is **manpaṣ* > *nappas*.[231]

nāqidu, "shepherd"—Rare Syr. *nqdʾ* but well known from Ug. *nqd* and Heb. *nôqēḏ*. The origin of this word is still uncertain, but Sumerian *nagada* is certainly a loan from Akkadian.[232]

* *natbāku*, *nadabāku*, "a course of bricks"—BA *ndbk*; Targ. Prophets *ndbk*; MH *ndbk* (rarely *mdbk*, cf. Jastrow, *Dictionary*, s.v. *mrbk*, Dalman *mdbk*), "brick course," "frame" > Arab. *midmak*.[233]

* *nērebu*, Ass. *nērabu*, "defile"—Syr. *nʾrbʾ*, "peak," "deep valley"; Mand. *nyrbʾ*, "crag." The Akkadian, literally "entrance," refers to a "pass" between high mountains and is commonly used to describe treacherous mountain terrain. In Aramaic, accordingly, it can mean, depending on one's perspective, either a high mountain or a deep valley.[234]

228. *LS*, p. 422; *Additamenta*, p. 277; *AHw.*, p. 730; Salonen, *Hausgeräte* II 189 f.

229. *AP*, p. 264; this is restored correctly in the main text from a fragment. The word is used to translate *napharu* in the Akkadian text.

230. Z, p. 27; *LS*, p. 436; *AHw.*, p. 739. The Syriac word is not listed in Payne Smith, *Thesaurus Syriacus*, and the *LS* references are faulty, so I have been unable to trace the Syriac attestations. Note Ug. *mpḫm*, "bellows."

231. *AHw.*, p. 739.

232. Z, p. 41; *LS*, p. 445; *AHw.*, p. 744; *KBL* (2d ed.) p. 632; S. Segert, "Zur Bedeutung des Wortes nōqēd," Suppl. *VT* XVI (1967) 279-83. A. Salonen, in *AfO* XXIII 96, thinks that *nāqidu* is the original Semitic word for "Schafhirt" as opposed to *rēʾu*, "Rinderhirt."

233. Z, p. 31; *AHw.*, p. 766 (incorrect Arab. form); *KBL*, p. 1098.

234. Z, p. 43; *LS*, p. 449; *AHw.*, p. 780. This word is found as the name of a town near Mosul as well as one near Aleppo (see *MG*, p. 135, n. 2) and two others in Syria (see C. Clermont-Ganneau, *Études d'archéologie*

nibzu, "document," "receipt" NA, NB—*AP,* No. 11:6 *nbz,* "receipt"; Sam., YT, CPA *nbz,* "lot"; Mand. *nybzʾ,* "portion." No etymology is known, but it certainly is a loanword in Akkadian. Perhaps this is related in origin to BA *nbzbh,* gift."[235]

* *nikassu,* "account" > NB/LB "property"—BA *nksyn,* BH *n^e^ḵāsîm;* Eg., *AD,* Genesis Apocryphon, Bar Kochba Heb., MA, JAr., CPA, Syr. all pl. *nksyn,* "property."[236]

* *nindabû,* "offering"—Mand. *nʾndbyʾ,* "offerings."[237]

niqû, "libation," "sacrifice" (used commonly of sheep, cf. *AHw.,* p. 793, mng. 4)—Two meanings are connected with this root in Aramaic: Hermopolis *nqyh,* Syr. BT *nqyʾ,* "sheep," and Syr. *nqʾ* (*pael*), "to libate," and *AP,* No. 72:15, 16 *nqyh,* Mand. *nʾqwtʾ, nyqyʾ,* "libation(s)." In addition Biblical Hebrew has *m^e^naqqîṯ,* "sacrificial bowl." The verb is certainly the same one which means "pure" in Hebrew, but this use is rare (possibly foreign?) in Aramaic and does not occur in Syriac at all, where the meaning "libate" is at home. Apparently the root is cognate in Aramaic and Akkadian, but the noun "sheep" may well be a borrowing of the Akkadian term in a very limited usage. The origin of Syr. *nqê,* "eager," "prone," remains uncertain as does the meaning in Ahiqar, l. 92 of *wynyqnhy.*[238]

nīru, "yoke"—Common Ar. *nîrâ* and MH and Arabic. There is no convincing evidence that this word is of Sumerian origin or other than cognate in Akkadian and Aramaic. Cf. BH *mnwr,* "part of a loom," and compare the similar Aramaic uses. Con-

orientale II [Paris, 1897] 206 ff.). The name of the Nerab of Aleppo is attested in the seventh-century B.C. Nerab stelae (*KAI,* Nos. 225-26) but was almost certainly an Assyrian name there, though it is very ancient, probably already mentioned by Thutmosis III (see Clermont-Ganneau, *op.cit.).* The topographic situation precludes the interpretation "pass" for the name of this town, so it must have its original meaning of "entrance." This presents a very nice parallel to the Biblical name Lebo-Hamath, the first town of the kingdom of Hamath on the road from the south (cf. Y. Aharoni, *The Land of the Bible* [Philadelphia, 1967] pp. 65 ff.). Modern Nerab is still situated very close to the main road into Aleppo from the east.

235. Muffs, *Studies,* p. 186; *AHw.,* p. 786; von Soden, in *Or.* n.s. XXXVII 261; *KBL* (2d ed.) p. 1097.

236. Z, p. 20; *LS,* p. 429 (Aramaic not cited in *AHw.,* p. 789). This old Sumerian loanword acquires the meaning "possessions" only in Neo-Babylonian. In all periods it appears both with and without a doubled "k."

237. *MD,* p. 284; W. Baumgartner, in *HUCA* XXIII 58.

238. Z, p. 50; *AHw.,* p. 744; *KBL* (2d ed.) p. 540. Cf. W. F. Albright, "The Babylonian Sage Ut-Napišti^{m} Rûqu," *JAOS* XXXVIII (1918) 65. If the Ahiqar form is an example of our verb, it lends further support to the cognate theory, for it occurs in the "western" proverbs (see below, p. 157), in a standard wisdom context (the "two-three" progression).

nections with Heb. *nîr*, "fallow ground," and the related root are uncertian.[239]

* *nishu*, "extract," "copy"—Nab. *nsḥt*; Arab. *nusḫah*; Mand. *nsʾ*, "to copy," *nʾsʾkʾ*, "copyist"; Syr. *nwskʾ*; Medieval Hebrew *nusḥah*.[240]

niṣirtu, "secret"—One of the problems of Mandaic studies is the origin of the Mandeans' name for their sect, *nʾṣwrʾyʾ*, and the abstract *nʾṣyrwtʾ*, and its possible relationship with the equally enigmatic New Testament term *Nazōraîos* and the Syriac and Jewish word for Christian. It has been suggested that the Mandaic terminology, at least in part, was influenced by this not infrequent NB term.[241]

nīšu, "oath"—See below, p. 153.

* *nišû*, "people"; in *nišê bīti*, "household personnel"—*AD*, No. 8:2 *nšy bytn*, "our staff" and No. 9:2 *nšy byth*. This interpretation of the Aramaic was proposed by H. L. Ginsberg. A scribal error for *ʾnšy* is not totally out of the question, but in view of the common LB idiom is very unlikely.[242] Akk. *nišû* is certainly not the source of the Mand., BT form of the word for "person," *ʿnyš*, *ʾynyš*.[243]

* *nubbû*, "to mourn," *munambû*, "mourning priest"—Mand. *nmbʾ*, "to mourn." The only participial form attested in Mandaic is the incorrect *nʾmbʾyʾtʾ*.[244]

239. Z, p. 42; *AHw.*, p. 793; Salonen, *Hippologica Accadica*, p. 99. A. Goetze, "Umma Texts Concerning Reed Mats," *JCS* II (1948) 179 and n. 30, discussing the Akkadian lownword in Sumerian *nirrum*, thought that it is "not impossible" that this is really a reborrowing of an original Sumerian word, an uncertain suggestion which Salonen cites misleadingly.

240. Z, p. 29; *LS*, p. 434; *AHw.*, p. 795; Fraenkel, *Aramäischen Fremdwörter*, p. 251; *AF*, p. 90, n. 7. See Phonology in Chap. IV.

241. Cf. *MD*, p. 286 and the many references given there p. 285, especially H. Zimmern, "Nazoräer (Nazarener)," *ZDMG* LXXIV (1920) 429-38, and Macuch, in Altheim and Stiehl, *Die Araber in der alten Welt* II 94 ff. See also C. Rabin, "Noṣerim," *Textus* V (1966) 49 ff.

242. H. L. Ginsberg, in *ANET* (3d ed.) p. 633, n. 4. For the LB idiom cf. *AHw.*, p. 797 Blc.

243. It was long ago recognized (cf. *MD*, pp. 353 f. and *MG*, p. 151, n. 1) that there was a Proto-North-West-Semitic form *ʾinš* (preserved at least in Arab. *ʾins* and the Heb. pl. *ʾănāšîm*, if not actually in the sing. *ʾîš* < **ʾišš* < *ʾinš*) alongside the form *ʾu/inâš*; thus, its presence in Babylonian Aramaic need not derive from Akkadian influence. The semantic difference between the two terms (the Aramaic is used in the sense of "someone," whereas the Akkadian is the collective "people") is further evidence for independence. It is precisely in this sense of "someone" or "no one" that *ʾyš* is frequently found in Imperial Aramaic and in Palmyran texts and as a Middle Persian logogram (cf. *AD* [abridged] p. 55), hardly a Hebraism. Cf. as well *KAI*, No. 276:10 *ʾynš*.

244. Z, p. 67; *MD*, p. 301.

* *nudunnû*, "dowry"—BT *ndwnyʾ*. In BH (Ezek. 16:33) *ndny*, "a woman's own capital."[245]

* *nuhatimmu*, "baker"—MH, JPA, BT (only B. Bat. 20b?), Syr. *nḥtwm(ʾ)*.[246]

* *pagulu*, "a vessel"—BT *gwlpʾ*.[247]

* **pagumtu*, "bridle"—Syr. *pgwdʾ* (*pḡuddâ*), *pgwdtʾ*; Mand. *pygwdtʾ*, *pʾgʾ/wdtʾ* (and denom. verbs). The Aramaic can only be explained as deriving from an as yet unattested feminine form of *pagūmu*. (For the NB development *-mt* > *-nd* > *dd*, cf. *šalamtu* > *šladdâ*.) The existence of such a feminine form is confirmed by the NB plural *pugudātu*.[248]

* *pahāru*, "potter"—BA, JAr., CPA, Syr. *pḥrʾ*, Mand. *pʾhʾrʾ* > Arab. *faḫḫâr*. JAr., CPA and Mandaic have *pa/eḥrâ*, "clay," "sherd," as well.[249]

* *palgu*, "ditch," "canal"—NB brick *plgʾ*. Though the root *plg* is very common in Aramaic, the common Semitic noun **palg*, "ditch" or "river," which occurs in Akk., Ug., BH, Arab. and Ethiopic, is not attested elsewhere in Aramaic and must be treated as a loan from Akkadian in this text.[250]

paqādu—The wide range of meanings of this verb in the various Semitic languages allows for the possibility of various mutual influences. In Akkadian its basic meaning appears to be "to entrust," which may have been borrowed into Aramaic. The sense "to command" is probably original in Aramaic, oc-

245. Z, p. 46; *AHw.*, p. 800. This is the BT term for the institution known in the Mishnah as *mlwg* (see s.v. *mulūgu*). The terms seem to have been confused in some Akkadian sources, but in his study of *mulūgu*, Baruch Levine (in *JAOS* LXXXVIII 271-85) mentions our term only in passing (p. 278 and n. 37). In the sense of "a woman's private money" it certainly makes sense in Ezek. 16:33 (cf. *KBL*, p. 597, which mistranslates the Akkadian). The medieval Heb. *nāḏān*, "dowry" (whence Yiddish *nadan*) is apparently based on the BH passage.

246. Z, p. 39; *LS*, p. 525; *Additamenta*, p. 278; *AHw.*, p. 801. This word is probably of Sumerian origin; cf. Weisberg, *Guild Structure*, p. 72. The change of vowels in the Aramaic form can be explained either by assimilation to the *qâṭôl* participial formation or else by a series of phonetic changes such as: *nuhatimm* > Ar. *nuḥtîm* > *nuḥtûm* > *naḥtûm* (by dissimilation).

247. Kaufman, in *Leš*. XXXVII 102 f.

248. Cf. J. C. Greenfield and S. Shaked, "Three Iranian Words in the Targum of Job from Qumran," *ZDMG* CXXII (1972) 42, n. 35; von Soden, in *Or.* n.s. XXXVII 263.

249. Z, p. 26; *LS*, p. 563; *AHw.*, p. 810; *KBL*, p. 1112.

250. Cf. G. R. Driver, in *PEQ*, 1945, p. 12; R. Koldewey, *Das wieder erstehende Babylon* (Leipzig, 1913) p. 80. For the Ugaritic cf. *UT Supplement*, p. 555.

curring as a westernism in Akkadian (so too the noun *paqīdu*, "official," "appointee").[251]

* *p/baqāru*, "to claim"—BT (*Aruch*) and Gaonic *pqr*.[252]

* *parakku*, "dais," "sanctuary"—Hat. *prkʾ*, *prykʾ*, Syr. *prkʾ*, Mand. *prykʾ*, "altar," "shrine."[253]

parsu—In Akkadian *parsu* means "part." Contrary to the opinions of early scholars and the modern Biblical dictionaries, there is no cuneiform evidence that *parsu* was ever natively used in the meaning "half-mina," as is Aramaic *prs*, almost certainly a native Aramaic development. To be sure, alphabetic *prš* does occur in the Assyrian lion weights, corresponding to an Assyrian */pars/*; but in light of the lack of cuneiform evidence, this may well have been a short-lived Aramaic loan adaptation in Assyrian. In Aramaic *prs* is a common term for half of anything. In fact the famous *prsyn* of Dan. 5:25 makes more sense as half-shekels than as half-minas. The homograph *prs* in Panammuwa, l. 6 and in Imp. Ar., a grain measure, is to be connected with the grain measure ${}^{gi\check{s}}$PA : *pa-ri-si* found in Hittite, Alalakh Akkadian, and Ugaritic alphabetic and cuneiform texts, which, as the Ugaritic spelling with "ś" indicates, is of foreign, probably Hurrian, origin. Zimmern's suggested connection between Akkadian uses of *parāsu*, "to cut," and West Semitic *prš*, " to make clear," is extremely doubtful.[254]

251. Z, pp. 10, 18 f.; on the Ugaritic, Hebrew and Aramaic, see H. L. Ginsberg, *The Legend of King Keret* (*BASOR* "Supplementary Studies," Nos. 2-3 [New Haven, 1946]) p. 48. This verb merits a full study. An ostracon from Arad (ca. 600 B.C.) already has *hbqyd* (< *hpqyd*) in the sense "assign," "entrust"; cf. Y. Aharoni, "Three Hebrew Ostraca from Arad" *BASOR*, No. 197 (1970) p. 21.

252. E. Y. Kutscher, "On the Terminology of Documents in Talmudic and Gaonic Literature" (Heb.), *Tarbiz* XIX (1947-48) 125 f. Kutscher (in *Tarbiz*) and E. A. Speiser (*Oriental and Biblical Studies*, pp. 128 ff.) have suggested that the standard meaning of MH and JAr. *pqr* (varying in the hiphil with *bqr*, but hardly because of the Akkadian variation, compare *hbqyd* in the Arad ostracon, n. 251): "to be free of controls or ownership" and the related noun *hpqr* are ultimately to be derived from Akkadian as well. This explanation seems somewhat forced in the light of Syr. and Mand. *pqr*, "to run wild," obviously the same word.

253. Z, p. 68; *LS*, p. 597; *AHw.*, p. 827; *DISO*, p. 235.

254. Z, p. 21; *KBL* (2d ed.) p. 1113. In general cf. O. Eissfeldt, "Die menetekel-Inschrift und ihre Deutung," *ZAW* LXIII (1951) 111. The grain measure is listed as *parīsu* in *AHw.*, p. 833, where it is considered to be Akkadian in origin. In spite of the conjectured size given there, "1/2 kor," no conclusive evidence for its actual size in any period has turned up, and assumptions that it must be half of something have resulted in contradictory computations (cf. D. Wiseman, *The Alalakh Tablets* [London, 1953] p. 14, and Kraeling, *Brooklyn Museum*, p. 263). For *prš* cf. Zimmern, in *ZDMG* LXXIV (1920) 434, n. 4, and Z, p. 24.

paršigu, "turban"—Although this is generally connected with Syr. *barzanqâ*, "greave(?)" and Mand. *bwrzynqᵓ*, "turban," all of the phonemes except *r* represent exceptions to the proper phonetic correspondences. The identical meaning of the Akkadian and Mandaic terms suggests some ultimate connection, but it is best to reject any associations with the Syriac, the uncertain BT *bwrzynqᵓ*, and Mand. *pᵓrqsᵓ*, "chain," possibly the same as BT *prsq* (var. *prstqy*), all words of clearly foreign, but hardly Akkadian, etymology.[255]

paruššu, "a sharp prick"—BH *prš* (hiphil), "to sting"; Syr. *piršᵓ*, "barb," BT and Targ. Proph. *piršᵓ*, "goad," "plowshare." *Paruššu* is often assumed to be a Sumerian loanword and hence necessarily a loan into Aramaic, but the Akkadian is so rare as to require commentary in *Ludlul* (*BWL*, p. 44, l. 101), which hardly suggests that it could have served as the model for a loanword.[256]

pašāru, "to loosen," "to solve"—Several scholars have ascribed various Aramaic uses of the verb *pšr* to Akkadian influence. Most commonly cited is the sense "to interpret (a dream)," but the meanings "to break the bonds of enchantment" and "to settle an account" have also come into consideration. Little is certain here.[257]

paššuru, "table"—Common Ar. *ptwr*, Arab. *fâṯûr*. The Akkadian is generally regarded as a loan from Sumerian BAN.ŠUR, an etymology which would require it to be a loanword in Aramaic. This is, however, the only possible Akkadian loanword where Aramaic "*t*" reflects Akkadian "š," an inconsistency which must be explained. It is now known that in the second millennium Akkadian "š" could represent a pronounced [ṯ], but there is no evidence to suggest that late Akkadian preserved this phone.[258] Nor is there any Akkadian evidence that this

255. Z, p. 36; *LS*, p. 96; *AHw.*, p. 836; *Additamenta*, p. 343; G. Widengren, *Iranisch-semitische Kulturbegegnung in parthischer Zeit* (Cologne and Opladen, 1970) pp. 91 f. The best available explanation appears to be to consider the Mandaic as a word of Persian origin, whose original meaning is found in Syriac, altered in meaning under the influence of the old Akkadian word.

256. *LS*, p. 607; cf. *AHw.*, p. 837.

257. Z, p. 68; *LS*, p. 614; A. L. Oppenheim, *The Interpretation of Dreams in the Ancient Near East* ("Transactions of the American Philosophical Society," Vol. XLVI, No. 3 [Philadelphia, 1956]) pp. 217 ff.; Wagner, p. 96; J. C. Greenfield, "The Lexical Status of Mishnaic Hebrew," pp. 89, 220 f. BH *ptr*, "to interpret a dream," an Aramaic type form, only serves to complicate the situation.

258. J. Aro, "Die semitischen Zischlaute (ṯ) š, ś und s und ihre Vertretung im Akkadischen," *Or.* n.s. XXVIII (1959) 333; von Soden and W. Röllig, *Das akkadische Syllabar* (2d ed.; Rome, 1967) p. xix; and see

particular word was ever pronounced with [ṯ], that Sumerian has such a phoneme, or even that the word BAN.ŠUR is originally Sumerian; it does occur already in Old Akkadian. It could be either a very early loan from Akkadian into pre-Aramaic or an old culture word borrowed separately by Akkadian and Sumerian and pre-Aramaic.[259]

pāšu, paštu, "axe"—Syr. *pwstʾ*. Cf. Arab. *faʾs*, "axe," and Leviticus Rabbah *psʾ*, "spade" or "hoe." These words are undoubtedly all etymologically connected, but the exact relationships are obscure.[260]

* *pattu*, "canal"—BT *ptyʾ*.[261]

* *pattû*, "water bucket"—BT *ptyʾ*, "bucket"; Mand. *pʾtyʾ*, "basin(?)."[262]

* *pīhatu*, "governor"—Adon, l. 9, Eg., Behistun, BA *pḥh*, *pḥtʾ*, pl. *pḥwtʾ*, BH *peḥāh*.[263]

pilakku, "spindle"—*Plk*, "spindle," occurs in Ugaritic (*Ugaritica* V 243, l. 22' *pí-lak-ku*), BH, Phoen., JAr. and

Spirantization in Chap. III. This early preservation of ṯ may be the explanation of the West Semitic spellings of the place name Aššur, spelled with "š" in Hebrew and Old Aramaic but with "t" in later Aramaic. That it was no longer preserved in the late Akkadian dialects themselves is evident from all of the transcriptions as well as all of the other loanwords. Cf. the name of the god Aššur, pronounced with [s] as shown by alphabetic spellings of Assyrian names. See Chap. IV, n. 11.

259. Z, p. 33; *LS*, p. 618; *AHw.*, p. 845; Salonen, *Möbel*, p. 176. The word is rare in early Aramaic, occurring once in a late *AP* text, in Uruk and in Hatran, but the Uruk spelling *pa-tu-ú-ri* proves it was a well established Aramaic word, with the phoneme /t/. The suggestion that Sumerian had the sound [ṯ] is an old one; cf. von Soden, "Zur Laut- und Formenlehre des Neuassyrischen," *AfO* XVIII (1957-58) 120.

260. Z, p. 12; *LS*, p. 585. The Arabic and Akkadian are probably cognate, for the Arabic *aleph* must be original. If so, the sibilant should be /š/. The Assyrian pronunciation of the two Akkadian forms should have been [*pās*] and [*pašš*], neither of which easily yields the Syriac form, though the sibilant of the Syriac could be explained on the basis of Babylonian (see p. 140). The hapax Galilean Aramaic form *psʾ* is suspect by reason of both spelling and syntax.

261. S. A. Kaufman, in *Leš*. XXXVI 32 f.

262. *Ibid.*, pp. 31 ff. For the Akkadian, see Salonen, *Hausgeräte* I 264.

263. Z, p. 6; *AHw.*, p. 862; *KBL*, p. 112; see, too, E. Y. Kutscher, "*Pḥwʾ* and Its Cognates," *Tarbiz* XXX (1961) 112-19 (Heb.), though his reading *pḥwʾ* in the Ramat Rahel seals is no longer to be accepted; cf. J. Naveh, *The Development of the Aramaic Script* (Jerusalem, 1970) p. 61. The old reading of this word in the Panammuwa inscription l. 12 *pḥy* was shown to be incorrect by H. L. Ginsberg, "Aramaic Studies Today," *JAOS* LXII (1942) 236, n. 35. In Akkadian this term is usually spelled logographically: ^{lú}NAM.

Arab., certainly as an old culture word of unknown origin. I know of no Akk. form **pilaqqu* meaning "axe," cited by the early scholars as the origin of Syr., Mand. *pelqâ*. The latter has a satisfactory Semitic etymology (*plq*, "to split") but could be a loan from Greek *pelekús*.[264]

* *pilku*, "region," "sub-province"—BH *pelek*, Phoen. *plg*, RH, Targums *plk*, "district."[265]

* *pīqu*, "dumb"—Syr. *pʾqʾ*, "dumb," Mand. *pygʾ*, "dumb," "demon." The Akkadian is an adjective from *piāqu*, *pâqu*, "to be narrow, tight," said especially of the mouth.[266]

pīt pī, "mouth-opening ritual"—A connection with Mand. *pyhtʾ*, "sacrificial bread," is highly doubtful.[267]

* *puhru*, "assembly"—The Akkadian is very probably the origin of Syr. *pwḥrʾ*, Mand. *pwhrʾ*, *pwrʾ*, "banquet" (in Mandaic also "assembly(?)"); for although the noun *pḫr* is not uncommon in Ugaritic (note, too, the alternate form *mpḫrt*, found also in the Yehimilk inscription from Byblos, *KAI*, No. 4), the verb *pahāru*, "to gather," is known only from Akkadian. The Aramaic distribution is also indicative of a loan.[268]

* *purkullu*, "stone or seal cutter"—Syr., Targ. Prophets *ʾrgwblʾ*, "stone mason." Some of the significant phonetic difference between the two forms can be accounted for by assuming assimilation to the semantically similar *ʾardîḵlâ* (see s.v. *arad ekalli*).[269]

264. Z, pp. 28, 9; *LS*, p. 576; *MD*, p. 371. Salonen, *Fussbekleidung*, p. 116, considers this word to be from the Chalcolithic substratum in Sumerian. For the Greek see Émilia Masson, *Recherches sur les plus anciens emprunts sémitiques en Grec* (Paris, 1967) p. 117.

265. Z, p. 9; *KAI* II 26. The "g" of late Phoen. *plg*, if correctly interpreted, is to be considered a late phonetic development. The difficult Karatepe II:6 (*KAI*, No. 26) *plkm* is still best taken as "spindles." The Mand. hapax *ʿtpʾlʾk*, "to be divided," used in a geographical text, should probably be connected with the common verb *plg*, "divide."

266. Z, p. 49; *LS*, p. 588. Cf. H. Holma, *Die assyrisch-babylonischen Personennamen der Form quttulu* (Helsinki, 1914) pp. 81 f. J. Blau, "The Origins of Open and Closed e in Proto-Syriac," *BSOAS* XXXII (1969) 4, n. 33, correctly observes that the Syriac cannot be proven to be from Akkadian merely on morphological grounds; but although the cognate roots *pqq* and *pqpq* occur in Aramaic, Hebrew, and Arabic, the middle weak form is known only in Akkadian (as opposed to the situation with *kên* and *kwn*) and the Aramaic form is attested only in Eastern Aramaic.

267. Z, p. 66; *AF*, p. 231; W. Baumgartner, in *HUCA* XXIII 59, n. 72, and the references in *MD*, p. 370.

268. Z, p. 46; *LS*, p. 563; *AHw.*, p. 876.

269. Z, p. 26; *LS*, p. 46. I assume that the *b* of the second syllable of *ʾrgwblʾ* results from a transposition of the initial labial; see below, p. 138. Though the *purkullu* is best known as a "seal cutter," it

* *purqidam,* "(lying) on the back"—BT *prqdn,* "one lying on his back," *ᵓprqd,* "on the back," *ᵓtprqd,* "to be on the back" (once in Targ. YI Gen. 49:17 but not in Neofiti); Syr. (lex.) *prqd,* "to fall on the back." In spite of the uncertainties raised by the possible Arab. cognate *brqṭ, tbrqṭ* (as indicated in *AHw.*, p. 735, s.v. *naparqudu*) and the Akkadian distribution (limited almost exclusively to divination, a sphere whose connections with Amorite have already been mentioned), I have taken this to be a loan. The similarity of the forms *purqidam* and *prqdn* is highly suggestive of a loan, as is the limitation of the distribution to Eastern Aramaic.[270]

* *pūru,* "lot"—BH *pur,* "lot," to explain the name Purim. Since it is glossed in the Hebrew text, *pur* was still considered a foreign word. Subsequent RH and JAr. usages are certainly based on the BH usage; Syriac translates Purim by *pwryᵓ*; Mand. *pwrᵓ,* "lot" (uncertain). The Akkadian word is derived from *pūru,* "bowl" < Sum. bur. The latter meaning is continued in three Jewish magic bowl texts where *pwrᵓ* means "bowl."[271]

puṣṣû, "to whiten"—Kutscher, in discussing the Eg. *pṣl,* "to clear a claim," correctly connects it with the later Common Ar. (and Arab.) *pṣy,* "to set free." He suggests that the latter is a loan from Akk. *puṣṣû,* "to make white," "to clean," and that this first loan was then used to translate the Akkadian legal term *zukkû,* "to clear a claim," since its basic meaning is also "to make clean." This is extremely unlikely, for *puṣṣû* is not used in any similar legal context in Akka-

is clear that not only did he perform all sorts of stone engraving and carving, but he was probably the most important artisan involved with stone in general, as opposed to precious gems and metals (cf. Weisberg, *Guild Structure*, pp. 58 ff.). A complete analysis and description of the duties of the various artisans who worked in stone has not yet been made, but there appears to be no general Akkadian term that can be translated "stone mason" (cf. *CAD,* Vol. I/J, p. 297).

270. The comparison with Aramaic was made as soon as the Akkadian was first isolated; see W. von Soden, "Zum akkadischen Wörterbuch," *Or.* n.s. XV (1946) 430, for previous literature and most recently E. Y. Kutscher, in *Leš*. XXXI 114, who points out the limited distribution of the Aramaic (and Babylonian Rabbinic Hebrew) and the similarity of forms, and J. Jacobovitz, "LeInyan 'prqd,'" *Les*. XXXI (1967) 240. Might the Arabic ultimately derive from Greek *prōktos,* "posterior," as was long ago suggested for the Aramaic? The phonetics certainly favor that explanation. For the significance of the Targ. YI occurrence see below, p. 163.

271. *AHw.*, p. 881. In general cf. J. Lewy, "Old Assyrian *puruᵓum* and *pūrum*," *RHA* XXXVI (1938) 117, n. 2, and 188 f., though, as indicated, his etymology from *parāᵓu,* "to cut," cannot be accepted. For the magic bowls cf. Montgomery, *Aramaic Incantation Texts from Nippur*, pp. 162, 228, and J. N. Epstein, *REJ* LXXIV (1922) 46.

dian, nor is it preserved in Aramaic in any non-legal sense. Of greatest significance, however, is the fact that the Akk. term *zukkû* itself, though frequent in Middle-Assyrian and the peripheral dialects, was no longer current in Neo-Babylonian (where the Aramaic loanword *murruqu* was the corresponding term) and occurred only sporadically in Neo-Assyrian.[272]

* *pūtu*, "forehead"—Mand., BT *pwtʾ*, Syr. (lex.) *ʾpwtʾ*.[273]

qabuttu (LB), "stall"—For semantic reasons, Syr. *qʾbwtʾ*, Mand. *qʾbwtʾ*, *qwbytʾ*, "box," "chest," would not appear to be developments of this late Akkadian term; nor should Syr. *qeḇyâ*, "cistern," be connected with *qabû*, "poultry stall."[274]

qarbatu, "field"—Early scholars compared the Eastern Aramaic verb *krb* (Syr., BT, Mand., and Arab.), "to plow," with a form **kirubû*, which they translated "field," relating it to *qarbatu*. The former is now properly read *kišubbû*, a Sumerian loanword meaning "wasteland" (*AHw.*, p. 493). Any connection between *krb* and *qarbatu*, whose initial consonant is definitely /q/, is unlikely.[275]

qātu, "hand"—The relations between this common word and Syr., BT, Mand. *qattâ*, RH *qnt*, *qt*, YT *qntʾ*, "handle" (verb *qtt* in Syriac, "to stick in," in Mandaic, "to be fixed"), are uncertain at best. The Akkadian form is never used in any similar way; the correct word for handle is *šikru*.[276]

272. E. Y. Kutscher, in *JAOS* LXXIV 240; *idem*, in *Tarbiz* XIX 53. His suggestion that *pṣh l-* > *pṣl* is reasonable. Others have suggested a contamination of *pṣh* by *nṣl* (cf. *DISO*, p. 233). It may just be a dialectal assimilation of the roots *pṣh* and *pṣl*, both of which mean "to split."

273. The BT form is cited as *ʾpwtʾ* in the lexicons, although the variants imply a reading *ʾ-pwtʾ*, "on the forehead," for some of the examples. Nevertheless, the legitimacy of the unusual form *ʾpwtʾ* is confirmed by the Syriac lexicographers.

274. *LS*, p. 645. The similarity between the Syriac form and Greek *kibōtós* can hardly be coincidental.

275. Z, p. 40; *LS*, p. 342. Suggested similar etymologies for the land measure *grybʾ* (cf. *LS*, p. 130) are also ruled out. But what is the etymology of *krb*? One distant possibility is to consider it somehow cognate to Akk. *karābu*, "to bless" (cf. ESA *mkrb*, "priest"), for connections between terms of the "cult" and "cultivation" are well known outside of this familiar Latin example. Compare Ar. *plḥ*. I would prefer, however, to relate it to the Akk. term *nukaribbu*, "gardener," whose supposed etymological connections with Sum. nu-kiri$_6$ are tenuous (cf. most recently D. O. Edzard, "Sumerische Komposita mit dem nominal Präfix nu-," *ZA* n.f. XXI [1963] 92 f., and C. J. Gadd, "Ebeḫ-il and His Basket-seat," *RA* LXIII [1969] 2). In light of the Aramaic root, it would appear that the Akkadian term is, in origin, a D participle of a root **krb* : **mukarribu*, with the change of the initial nasal due to dissimilation of labials and/or assimilation to the Sumerian form.

276. Z, p. 35; *LS*, p. 704.

qinnāzu, qi(n)nanzu, "whip"—Syr. (hapax lex.) *qnztᵓ*. The etymology is unknown.[277]

qištu, "forest"—Syr., JAr., CPA, Mand.(?) *qysᵓ*, "wood," "tree"; BT (Mand.?) *qynsᵓ*, "chip."[278]

**qudādu* (*AHw. k/gudādu*), "weak," "crippled(?)"—Not to be read in the Uruk Incantation, l. 11 (cf. *DISO*, p. 250, s.v. *qdd*); read *[d]i-da-qé-e* or *[d]a-da-qé-e*, the predecessor of the common Mand., BT word for child, *drdqᵓ*.[279]

* *qudāšu,* "earring"—JAr., Syr. *qdšᵓ*.[280]

qullû, "food dish," "bowl" only NA, LB—JAr. *qwlᵓ*, "bowl"; JAr., Syr. *qwltᵓ*, "pitcher." Compare the older Akk. *gullu,* BH *gullāh*.[281]

* *quppu,* "collection box"—MH *qwph,* "money box," "common fund"; Syr. *qwptᵓ*, "purse"; Mand. *qwpᵓ*, *qwptᵓ*(?).[282] This is the only meaning of this word where Akkadian influence seems probable. There is little reason to maintain that in their basic meanings *quppu,* "reed chest," and Ar., Arab. *qupp/ff,* "large basket," are anything but cognate (or an early loan into Akkadian[?]; note that almost all the early examples are from Mari or Amarna). The profusion of Jewish Aramaic and Hebrew forms supports this (i.e. *qwph, qwpᵓ, qwptᵓ, qpyph, qpwph, kpyph*). The famous Mesopotamian basket boat, Arab. *quffah,* is possibly attested in Mand. *qwptᵓ*, but there is no evidence that its precursor was ever called *quppu* in Akkadian.[283]

277. Z, p. 42; *LS*, p. 676; Salonen, *Hippologica Accadica*, p. 154.

278. Z, p. 53; *LS*, p. 665; on the Syr. see J. Blau, in *BSOAS* XXXII 3.

279. Thus, the interpretation "child" for Ugaritic *kdd* no longer finds support in Akkadian or Aramaic. Though Landsberger suggested the incorrect identification of the expression in the Uruk incantation, he himself realized that the reading *da-da-qé-e* was perhaps to be preferred, especially in l. 36; cf. "Zu den aramäischen Beschwörungen in Keilschrift," *AfO* XII (1937-39) 257, n. 48. Another possibility for the origin of the form *drdq* is to view it as an amalgam of two old Amorite words for child: *da/irku* and *daqqu* (for which see *CAD*, Vol. D, pp. 107, 115, and 160). The scarcity and use of these terms in Akkadian indicates an almost certain West Semitic origin. (Cf. also Geᵓez *daqîq*, "children.")

280. Z, p. 38; *LS*, p. 649; B. Meissner, "Lexikographische Studien," *OLZ* XXV (1922) 244 f. A derivation of Syr. *qldᵓ*, "nose ring" (cf. *LS*, p. 677) from the feminine form of this word is possible but far from certain: *qudāštu* > *qudāl(t)* > *qulâd* by metathesis (to avoid homonymy with the word for "neck"?).

281. *AHw.*, p. 926.

282. A. L. Oppenheim, "A Fiscal Practice of the Ancient Near East," *JNES* VI (1947) 116-20; most recently Weisberg, *Guild Structure*, p. 61, and B. Levine, in *JAOS* LXXXVIII 279 f.

283. Z, p. 34; Salonen, *Hausgeräte* I 203. The difficult word *qwp* in

* *qurqurru*, "a large ship"—Syr. *qwrqwrʾ* > Arab. *qurqûr*, "long or big ship."[284]

rabīku, "flour pulp"—MH, Targ. *rbykh/ʾ*. Although the verb *rbk* does not definitely occur in Aramaic, it is found in BH and in Arabic.[285]

* *rabû*, "great"—The term GAL, usually in the plural GAL. MEŠ, is used in late Akkadian for "officers," "officials" and is generally read *rabûti*, of which the singular would be *rabû*. This Akkadian term must be the origin of the strange form *rby*, "officer," in the Ahiqar narrative. On the other hand, the construct form *rab*, "chief," in Akkadian is almost certainly of Amorite origin. In OB it occurs only in the expression GAL. MAR.TU, "chief of the Amorites."[286] Later it is common in the western peripheral dialects and in Assyrian. Thus, the Heb. and Ar. term *ra<u>b</u>* is a native West Semitic development.[287]

rakābu, "to ride," "to be on top of"—Although no Akkadian antecedents are actually attested, Syr. *rqpʾ*, Targ. Proph. *rkptʾ*, "joined timber" may have an Akkadian etymology. Compare *rikbu*, "a top part of a plow," but note as well the many uses of the II stem of *rkb* in Arabic.[288]

rakāsu, "to bind"—Any direct connections with BH *rᵉ<u>k</u>ûš*, "property," BH and Common Ar. *rkš*, "horse," are unlikely. Note that the verb *rks* does not otherwise occur in Aramaic, but for some reason became *rkš*. The Akkadian nominal forms cited by Zimmern are now known to be misinterpreted or misread.[289]

* *rapāqu*, "to dig," "to hoe"—BT *rpq*, "to hoe."[290]

Kraeling, *Brooklyn Museum*, No. 7:17, may be one of the words discussed here, though the long vowel makes that very unlikely. Salonen, *Wasserfahrzeuge*, pp. 72 ff., makes an effort to associate this word with pictorial and descriptive evidence of the early basket boat, yet his only adduced lexical connection is the reed *quppu* (clearly an enclosed box) of the Sargon legend, in which the babe Sargon was sent floating down the river.

284. Salonen, *Wasserfahrzeuge*, p. 51, n. 2.

285. Z, p. 49. In Aramaic *rbk* may occur in the broken *AG*, No. 2:2.

286. *Rabû* is actually given as the "Amorite" equivalent of Akk. *rubû* in the lexical list Explicit *Malku-Šarru* I 35; see A. D. Kilmer, "The First Tablet of *malku* = *šarru* Together with Its Explicit Version," *JAOS* LXXXIII (1963) 433.

287. Z, p. 6; *AP*, p. 229; Rosenthal, *An Aramaic Handbook*, Vol. I, Part 2, p. 14.

288. Z, p. 26; *LS*, p. 744.

289. Z, p. 41; still cited in *KBL* (2d ed.) p. 892. **Rukūšu*, "herd," is now read *rukūbu*, "mount." For **rakisu*, cf. Salonen, *Hippologica Accadica*, p. 97.

290. Z, p. 41. Interestingly, the meaning "hoe" for this root is confined to the Babylonian dialects of both Akkadian and Aramaic.

* *rapšu*, "shovel for winnowing grain"—Syr. *rap̄šâ*, Arab. *rafš*.[291]

raqqatu (late SB, LB), "swamp"—MH *rqq*; JAr., Syr. *rqtʾ*; Mand. *rʾ/yqʾtʾ*. The limited distribution of the Akkadian suggests that it is a loan from Aramaic.[292]

* *rāšû*, NB "creditor"—Targ. Onk., Targ. Prophets, BT *ršyʾ*, "creditor," *ršy* (peal), "to lend," *ršwtʾ*, "loan"; Mand. *ršʾ*, "to lend." There can be little doubt that this is a loan. This meaning of the Aramaic root is of extremely limited distribution, whereas the Neo-Babylonian meaning derives easily from the known Akkadian usages of the verb *rašû*, "to have," "to acquire."[293] Still not fully determined, however, is the extent of the influence attributable to Assyrian or Babylonian legal formulation on the use of the verb *ršy* and its virtual synonym *gry* at Elephantine. The usage of these two terms and their Akkadian cognates *rašû* and *gerû* has been carefully analyzed by Muffs adding to the more general, but important observations made by Kutscher.[294]

Gerû, *gry* is easier to analyze. Its meaning in BH, RH, JAr., and Syr. (all piel, pael) is "to provoke," obviously the same as Akkadian "to begin hostilities" (and Arab. *ǧrʾ*, "to dare," though the *hamza* is unexpected in light of the BH form); no doubt it could be used quite naturally in juridical as well as martial contexts (see Prov. 15:18, 28:25, 29:22). But in view of the long history of the Akkadian formulaic use of the verb in the sense "to initiate a lawsuit" and the virtual identity between the late Akkadian and Egyptian Aramaic phraseology, Akkadian influence here cannot be discounted.[295] On the other hand, there is little reason to assume that any of the other Aramaic usages of this verb have been influenced by the Akkadian formulaic expression.

291. R. Borger, "Der Gerätname *rapšu*," *AfO* XVIII (1957-58) 128.

292. Perles, in *OLZ* XXI 70; *LS*, p. 743.

293. Suggested in Z, p. 17, but of course to be separated from BH *nšh*. For NB *rāšû*, see A. Ungnad, *Neubabylonische Rechts- und Verwaltungsurkunden, Glossar* (Leipzig, 1937) p. 135 (hereafter cited as Ungnad, *Glossar*); H. Petschow, *Neubabylonisches Pfandrecht*, p. 19, n. 40, pp. 71 f. Mand. *rʾšywtʾ* is from Arab. *ršw*, "to bribe," not Aramaic. The YT examples of *ršwt* cited by Jastrow, *Dictionary*, are of doubtful legitimacy; I know of no other western occurrences.

294. Muffs, *Studies*, p. 31, n. 2, pp. 196 ff.; Kutscher, in *JAOS* LXXIV 238 f.; cf. *idem*, "On the Terminology of Documents in Talmudic and Gaonic Literature," *Tarbiz* XVII (1946) 125.

295. Muffs, *Studies*, p. 197, emphasizes the difference between Eg. and NA in the use of the personal object and suggests a late NB component here. I would suggest, rather, that the NB was influenced by Aramaic and that the usage in the papyri merely reflects native Aramaic syntax.

The relationship between *rašû* and Eg. *ršy* is more difficult to analyze. Its basic meaning in Old Aramaic, well attested in later Aramaic and in Hebrew, is "to have control, authority, right," in the derived stems "to grant authority,"[296] again clearly cognate to Akkadian, "to have, get possession." The Egyptian Aramaic meaning "to bring suit" to my knowledge is found elsewhere only in Syr. *ršʾ*, "to accuse," "to find fault." What is the origin of this usage? It almost certainly did not develop from the Neo-Babylonian form "creditor," especially since different verbs are used in the Babylonian equivalents of the Egyptian Aramiac formulae which use *ršy*. *Rašû* does occur in similar contexts in Akkadian, though much earlier and even then only sporadically,[297] but perhaps that is where one must look for the origin of the Egyptian Aramaic usage.

rāṭu, "watercourse," "pipe"—Targ. Onk. (so in good MSS), Iraqi Arabic *râṭ*; BH, RH, Syr., *rhṭ(ʾ)*; Mand. *r(ʾ)hʾṭʾ*. Since the Akkadian form is attested as early as Old Babylonian, this word is apparently not to be connected with the Aramaic root *rhṭ*, "run" < *rh/wẓ*. Although the *h* is preserved in Mandaic, the form *râṭâ* is the expected Babylonian Aramaic reflex of *râhṭâ* and could be a Babylonian form in Onkelos. Alternatively, the targumic (and Arabic) form could preserve the Akkadian pronunciation.[298]

redû, "to follow," "to drive"—Three meanings, possibly derived from different original roots, are associated with the verb *rdʾ* in the Aramaic dialects: "to chastise," "to plow," and "to move," "to journey." The last is found only in Syriac and Mandaic but as a common verb and, though possibly continuing a native Aramaic meaning, may owe some influence to Akkadian. Compare Akk. *mardītu,* "course," "cult procession," and the common Ar. *mardîṯâ,* "course," "journey."[299]

296. In Old Aramaic the verb occurs in Sefire III 9 and Hadad ll. 27, 28 (and in Phoenician, Karatepe A III 6 *ršʾt*); cf. Fitzmyer, *Sefîre*, p. 112, and Muffs, *Studies*, p. 208. The Sefire example might be an aphel: "you shall not control me nor (have to) grant me permission concerning it." Could the "l" of *ltršh* be asseverative: "rather you shall grant me permission . . ."? The context of Hadad is broken, but it may even be more like Akkadian "to acquire."

297. On OB with *awatam,* see *CAD,* Vol. A, Part II, p. 39*b*; in the MA laws and in MB with *rugummê,* "claim"; cf. F. R. Kraus, "Ein mittelbabylonischer Rechtsterminus," in *Symbolae Martino David* I (Leiden, 1968) 10, note c.

298. *LS,* p. 717; *AHw.,* p. 963; cf. T. Nöldeke, "Einige Bemerkungen über die Sprache der alten Araber," *ZA* XII (1897) 187.

299. Z, p. 42; *AHw.,* p. 645. The meaning "to plow" is certainly a native Aramaic development.

* *riqītu*, "part of the stomach of a ruminant"—Targ. Y Dt. 18:3 *rqyth*.[300]

rubê, NA "interest"—The verb *rabû* and related noun forms are used in several Akkadian dialects to refer to interest, but there is no reason to regard any of them as other than cognate with similar Aramaic terminology. In Aramaic *rby* is the only root commonly used here, whereas Akkadian has other words which are much more frequent (*ṣiptu, hubullu*). Specific formulaic uses of the Aramaic may, however, have Akkadian models.[301]

saddinnu, see n. 324.

sāhertu, sahhertu—Syr. *sḥrtʾ*, Mand. *sʾhrʾ* means "walled enclosure" or "palace." Since the verb *sḥr* (common elsewhere in Aramaic as "to go around") is not otherwise used in those dialects except in the meaning "to go around peddling," one suspects a loan here. Possibly related Akkadian forms may be found in the rare *sāhertu* 4 translated "Ummauerung" by von Soden, and in the lexical equation bàd-nigin : *sahhirat dūri*, whose meaning is uncertain.[302]

* *sāhiru*, "magician"—Mand. *sʾhrʾ*, "demon"; Arab. *sâḥir*, "magician." The Mandaic is not definitely derived from this word, but Arabic *ḥ* (not *ḫ*) suggests an Aramaic intermediary.[303]

samīdu, "fine flour"—Syr., Targ. Y, BT *smydʾ*, Mand. *symʾd*, Arab. *samîd*. Compare Ug. *smd*, a food of some sort. The evidence for an Akkadian origin is the verb *samādu*, "to grind fine," found only in Akkadian. If it is a loanword, however, the consonants of the Aramaic form (*s* with *m*) indicate a very early date for the borrowing.[304]

s/zamītu, "corner"—BH, MH *zwyt*; Common Ar. *zâwîṯâ*, ESA *ʾzyym* (pl. indefinite); Arab. *zâwiyah*. The origin of this

300. The correct form occurs only in Neofiti; cf. W. L. Moran, "Some Akkadian Names of the Stomachs of Ruminants," *JCS* XXI (1967) 178. There must be some relationship between *riqītu* and Syr. *mrqqʾ*, "the upper part of the belly." Cf. *LS*, p. 743, and Holma (cited there).

301. Z, p. 18; Muffs, *Studies*, p. 185.

302. Z, p. 14; *AHw.*, pp. 1008-9; *CAD*, Vol. D, p. 192*a*. Sum. bàd-nigín occurs in literary contexts (see A. W. Sjöberg and E. Bergmann, *The Collection of the Sumerian Temple Hymns* [texts from Cuneiform Sources," Vol. III (Locust Valley, N.Y., 1969)] p. 51), where the meaning "outer city wall" is possible but not certain.

303. Z, p. 67. For the Akkadian see *AHw.*, pp. 1009 and 1008 (s.v. *sahertu*).

304. *LS*, p. 479; B. Landsberger, "Zur Mehlbereitung im Altertum," *OLZ* XXV (1922) 337 ff. If borrowed from Babylonian one would expect to find *w* (for *m*) in Aramaic, whereas the preservation of *s* indicates that it could not come from Assyrian.

word remains uncertain. The Akkadian term, known only from first-millennium texts, has no Akkadian etymology, nor is there any indication that the second consonant was ever anything but /w/.[305]

sihharu (*AHw. sahharru*), "kind of bowl"—Probably the same as Persepolis *sḥr*, "plate," "shallow bowl." The word is clearly Semitic but not definitely of Akkadian origin.[306]

sikiltu, "hoard"—See s.v. *suk/gullu*.

* *sikkānu*, "rudder"—Syr. *swknʾ*, Mand. *swkʾnʾ* > Arab. *sukkân, sikkân*.[307]

* *sikkatu*, "peg," "nail," (NB) "plowshare"—JAr. (primarily Targ. Onk., Proph., BT), Sam., CPA, Syr., Mand. *sikkâ/ṯâ*, pl. *sikkîn*, "peg," "nail," "plowshare" > Arab. *sakk*, "nail."[308]

sikkūru, "bolt," "lock"; *sikru*, "dam"—Syr., Mand. *sukkrâ*, "bolt," "bar"; JPA *swkrʾ*, "bolt," "dam." The root *skr* is common in both Aramaic and Akkadian; thus, the difference in the noun forms suggests that the terms are only cognate.[309]

* *simānu*, "set time"—Common Ar. *zmn* (Syr. *zbn*); late BH, MH z^{e}*mān*; Arab. *zaman, zamân*; Ethiopic *zaman*; Pehlevi *zamân*.

305. Z, p. 31; *LS*, p. 190; *KBL* (3d ed.) p. 256; Wagner, p. 48; von Soden, "Zum akkadischen Wörterbuch," *Or.* n.s. XVI (1947) 448 f. There is no reason to consider this word separate etymologically from *zamû* (cf. *CAD*, Vol. Z, p. 41*a*), although they are probably not synonymous. An Akkadian pronunciation *zam/wītu* is indicated by spellings with the sign ZA (hardly to be read *sà*); cf. *CAD*, Vol. D, p. 192*a*, lex. section.

306. Cf. *Persepolis*, p. 49; Salonen, *Hausgeräte* II 112 f.; *AHw.*, p. 1008. This connection was not made by Bowman. Note that the Akkadian, found often in NA and lexical lists, does occur once in LB.

307. Z, p. 45; *LS*, p. 464; *AHw.*, p. 1041; Salonen, *Wasserfahrzeuge*, p. 8.

308. Z, p. 35; *LS*, p. 472; *AHw.*, p. 1041; for the meaning "plowshare," see Salonen, *Agricultura*, p. 92. This is to be separated from Ar. *sikk*, derived from *śikk*, BH *śēḵ*, "thorn" (confused in JAr. sources with *syrtʾ*, "thorn," and *swkʾ*, "bush"). In *KBL*, p. 921, BH *śēḵ* is incorrectly compared with the Akkadian, cited as *šikkatu*. It belongs rather with BH *śakkîn*, Ar. *sakkîn*, "knife," and neither is from Akkadian (cf. Wagner, p. 366, n. 5).

Jastrow's translation of *sktʾ* in Targ. Deut. 23:14 as "spade" is misleading (*Dictionary*, p. 993). The word merely translates BH *ytd*, normally "peg," whatever it may actually mean in that context. Arab. *sikkah*, BT *sktʾ*, Syr. (lex.) *sktʾ dṭbʿ* (see Payne Smith, *Thesaurus Syriacus*, p. 2622), "minting die," represents a development of this word, but the place of origin of this usage is uncertain.

309. Z, p. 30; *LS*, p. 475. J. Barth (*Die Nominalbildung in den semitischen Sprache* [Leipzig, 1894] p. 23) suggests that *swkrʾ* is a loan from Akkadian because of its unusual form.

Iranologists are convinced that the word is of Iranian origin, while Assyriologists propose an Akkadian etymology from *(w)asāmu*, "to be appropriate." The recently discovered occurrences of this otherwise late word in Old Babylonian texts conclusively refute the position of Iranologists.[310] The Aramaic could not have been borrowed from Babylonian, however, where it was pronounced, as shown by the Aramaic month name, [siwān]; but an Assyrian pronunciation [zimān] is quite possible (see Phonology, Sibilants, in Chap. IV).[311]

* *simmiltu*, "staircase"—Eastern Neo-Ar. *semmilta*, Syr. *sblt*ʾ, Mand. *swmbylt*ʾ, "ladder." See *hūqu*.[312]

sippu, "doorsill"—There is little evidence that would suggest that *sippu* is anything but cognate to Common Ar. *sippâ*, Heb. *sap̄*, and Phoen. *sp*.[313]

sipru, "border," "shore(?)"—MH, Targ. Onk., Syr., CPA *spr*. In light of the common Arabic forms *šufr* and *šafîr*, which show the original sibilant to be *ś*, the rare late Akkadian term, if correctly interpreted, must be an Aramaism.[314]

310. Cf. J. J. Finkelstein, "The Edict of Ammiṣaduqa: A New Text," *RA* LXIII (1969) 56 ff.; *ARMT* XIII, No. 39:12 (cf. J. T. Luke, "Observations on *ARMT* XIII 39," *JCS* XXIV [1971] 22). The meaning of the thrice-repeated *simānî* in the OB Atrahasis myth remains uncertain, however (cf. W. G. Lambert and A. R. Millard, *Atra-ḫasīs* [Oxford, 1969] p. 155).

311. Z, p. 63; *LS*, p. 187*b*; H. S. Nyberg, *Hilfsbuch des Pehlevi* II (Uppsala, 1931) 253; J. Markwart, "Np. *ādīna* 'Freitag,'" *Ungarische Jahrbücher* VII (1927) 91; S. Telegdi, "Essai sur la phonétique des emprunts iranien en Araméen talmudique," *JA* CCXXVI (1935) 242; Nöldeke, *Neue Beiträge*, p. 44; Widengren, *Iranisch-semitische Kulturbegegnung*, p. 106; *KBL* (3d ed.) p. 91 and additional bibliography in Wagner, p. 49 (*AHw*., p. 1044, does not adduce the non-Akkadian forms!). The proposed Akkadian etymology is discussed by Landsberger, "Jahreszeiten im Sumerisch-akkadischen," *JNES* VIII (1949) 256, nn. 44f. Note that he is surprised to find that none of the logograms for *simānu* contain me-te, the Sum. correspondent to Akk. *wsm*. The possibility of an Egyptian etymology, based on a rare verb of conjectured meaning (cf. Nöldeke; *KBL* [3d ed.]; A. Erman and H. Grapow, *Wörterbuch der aegyptischen Sprache* [Leipzig, 1940-55] III 453 *smn*, "jemanden weilen lassen? sich verweilen") should be discounted.

312. *AHw*., p. 1045.

313. Z, p. 31; *LS*, p. 489; Salonen, *Türen*, p. 62. The only evidence for a non-cognate relationship is the sign ZIG, which also has the value ZÍB, translated in one lexical text by Akk. *ziqqu*, which in turn is matched in a synonym list with *sippu* (cf. *CAD*, Vol. Z, p. 129*a*, s.v. *ziqqu* C). On this slim, indirect evidence, Salonen claims that *sippu* is a Sumerian loanword from ZÍB.

314. For *sipru* see A. Boissier, *Documents assyriens relatifs aux présages* (Paris, 1894-99) pp. 225 ff., No. 35 r. and especially No. 42 r., *si-ip-ra šá māti Adad iraḫḫiṣ*^iṣ^ (note the different interpretation in *AHw*., p. 1049). L. Ginzberg, "Beiträge zur Lexikographie des Jüdisch-Aramäischen. II," *MGWJ* LXXVIII (1934) 29 f., and J. N. Epstein, *Prolego-*

suk/gullu, "herd," *sikiltu*, "hoard," "accumulated property"—Ug. *sglt* (broken context), BH *s^e^gullāh*, "accumulated property," "treasure"; Targ. YII *sgwlʾ*, "property" and derived verbs in RH and late JAr. There is little reason to regard the Ugaritic and Hebrew as loans from Akkadian in any period. The JAr. forms are clearly secondary derivations from the Hebrew.[315]

* *sunqu*, "hunger," "need"—Syr. *swnqʾ*, "need" and derived verbs in Syr. and Mand. (cf. Geʿez *šnq*, "provisions(?)"). The limited distribution of the Aramaic indicates a loan here. On the other hand, there is no reason to regard the Common Ar. *šnq*, "to choke," as a loan from Akkadian. The hapax occurrence of *tašnīqu*, "choking," in Akkadian is certainly a loan from Aramaic.[316]

supinnu, "trowel(?)," "spindle point(?)"—MH, Targ. Onk. and Proph., BT, Syr. *šwpyn(ʾ)*, "file"; JAr. *swpynʾ*, "spear butt," "spike." The Akkadian is late, primarily in lexical texts, and the origin of the word (or words) is uncertain.[317]

* *suqāqu*, "alley"—Palm. *šqq*, Syr. *šqqʾ*, *ʾšqqʾ*, "alley";

mena, p. 214, suggest that Ar. *spr* is derived from Akk. *supūru* (cited by them as *supāru*), previously translated "surrounding wall" but now known to mean "(animal) stall." Although the etymology of the Akkadian term is uncertain, it surely is not the origin of Ar. *spr*.

315. Thoroughly discussed most recently by M. Held, "A Faithful Lover in an Old Babylonian Dialogue," *JCS* XV (1961) 11 f.; cf. also M. Weinfeld, "The Covenant of Grant in the Old Testament and in the Ancient Near East," *JAOS* XC (1970) 195, n. 103. The following additional observations are relevant: The occurrence of *sglt* in Ugaritic (*UT* 2060:7, 12 meaning "treasure"?) and *su-gul-la-ti*, "accumulation," in a text of Egyptian origin found at Boghazkoy (*KUB* III, No. 57:4-6) show that the form **sugullat* was already current in the West at that time, certainly quite different in form from Akk. *sikiltu*, and some type of cognate relationship is thus most likely. But there are still difficulties. The Akk. *suk/gullu*, "herd," "cattle," can hardly be separated from this group of words (Held suggests possible coincidental homonymy), nor can the Ar. form *sgwl*, "cluster of grapes," for the otherwise common West Semitic **ʾiṯkāl*. In all these words the idea of "collection" is primary.

316. For *snq*, Z, p. 47; *LS*, p. 485; F. Perles, "Lexikalisches Allerlei," *MGWJ* LXXVI (1932) 294; von Soden, in *Or*. n.s. XXXVII 265. For *šnq*, Z, p. 49; *LS*, p. 791; von Soden, in *Or*. n.s. XXXVII 268. Note *sanāqu* II, "bedürfen," in LB (*AHw*., p. 1022), apparently reborrowed from Aramaic.

317. *AHw*., p. 1060. When spelled with the logogram ^giš^BA, *supinnu* is something which can be part of a spindle (*pilakku*, cf. Hh.IV 36, 50); I suggest "point" on the basis of the JAr. word *swpynʾ*. The meaning "file" seems to have a connection with the Aramaic root *šwp*, "to make smooth," but the ending *-yn* is problematic on a native Aramaic word (see below, n. 324).

JPA *šqqʾ, šwqqʾ*, "alley," "street," > Arab. *zuqâq*. An Akkadian etymology for this word and for its more common relative *sūqu* (Eg. and Common Ar., Heb.) *šūq* > Arab. *sûq*, "street" > "market," was recently rejected by Landsberger, his sole criterion being the sibilant shift Assyrian *s* > Aramaic *š*, which he believed not possible.[318] The evidence fails to support his position, however (see Phonology, in Chap. IV), and his argument must be rejected. But, he quite correctly observed that the sibilant difference does not preclude the possibility of a cognate relationship.[319] Nevertheless, an etymology is available only in Akkadian: Common Semitic *ḍyq*, "to be narrow, strait," which correctly becomes *siāqu* in Akkadian by Geer's Law.[320] That this is the correct eytmology is demonstrated by the place name Suqāqu, whose topographical location correctly fits the meaning "narrows."[321] The word *suqāqu* is a diminutive whose form has parallels in Akkadian.[322] The early meaning of *šûq* in Aramaic, Hebrew, and Arabic was "street." Later this developed into "market," at which time *š(u)qâq* probably assumed part of the former semantic range of *šûq* in JPA.[323]

* *sūqu*, see s.v. *suqāqu*.

* *susapinnu*, "best man"—MH *šwšbyn*, JAr., Syr. *šwšbynʾ*, Mand. *šwšbʾnʾ*. Although this word may well originally have been of foreign origin, the phonetic correspondences indicate that it was borrowed by Aramaic from the Assyrian dialect.[324]

318. B. Landsberger, in Suppl. *VT* XVI 185, though he does recognize that Assyrian /š/ is rendered by Aramaic "s" (see p. 199).

319. For examples of unusual Akkadian reflexes of Proto-Semitic sibilants see J. Aro, in *Or*. n.s. XXVIII 330 f.

320. Cf. *GAG Ergänz.*, § 51*e*; *AHw.*, p. 1039.

321. See W. W. Hallo, "The Road to Emar," *JCS* XVIII (1964) 70.

322. Cf. *GAG Ergänz.*, p. 9**: *buqāqu*, "little gnat," and the examples cited by F. R. Kraus, "Ein Sittenkanon in Omenform," *ZA* XLIII (1936) 112, for *purās* as a diminutive, though admittedly none of these is precisely like our word where the originally single final consonant is reduplicated.

323. Z, p. 43; *LS*, pp. 766, 798. *Sūqu* is common in Akkadian. The earliest occurrence I know of *suqāqu* is in a lexical text from Boghazköy, *KBo* I 40, but a by-form *sūqēnu* occurs already in OA (cf. von Soden, *GAG Erganz.* § 132*g*, but read *sukinnu* in *AHw.*!). LB forms with "š" are clearly reborrowings from Aramaic.

324. Z, p. 46; *LS*, p. 766; *AHw.*, p. 1063. Cf. most recently C. Wilcke, "ku-li," *ZA* XXV (1969) 76; S. Greengus, "Old Babylonian Marriage Ceremonies and Rites," *JCS* XX (1966) 68 ff., and *BWL*, pp. 339 f. No etymology is yet known. The *-innu* ending (as opposed to *-ennu*, *-ēnu* < *-ānu* on good Semitic words like *qutrennu*, "incense"; cf. *GAG* § 56*r*) points to a northern, possibly Anatolian, origin; cf. *GAG* § 58*b*; E. Bilgiç, "Die Ortsnamen der 'kappodokischen' Urkunden im Rahmen der alten Sprachen Anatoliens," *AfO* XV (1945-51) 17, n. 123. A similar history is probable for another *-innu* culture word, *saddinnu* (*AHw.* *s/šaddinu*), "a piece of

ṣabātu—The Aramaic root *ṣbt,* found in the pael in Palmyran and Syriac meaning "to ornament," in the Mand. noun *ṣʾwtʾ,* "ornament," and probably in the BT root *ṣbt,* meaning "to arrange," "to offer," is connected by Brockelmann (*LS,* p. 620) with Akk. *ṣibūtu,* "dyed fabric"; but this Akkadian word is now known to be a rare lexical term, and the meaning "to paint," "to dye" for the verb *ṣabû* is not even certain (*CAD,* Vol. S, p. 46*a*). Greenfield has suggested that the Aramaic is rather a loan from Akk. *ṣabātu,* "to seize," found in the D stative in two Neo-Assyrian texts in the apparent meaning "adorned."[325] A similar semantic development is more commonly found in the D stem of its synonym *ahāzu,* "to seize," *uhhuzu,* "to mount in precious metal." But a direct borrowing of this verb would be unexpected (see below, p. 161), especially in light of the rarity of this meaning. One should not omit from consideration the Akkadian word for "garment," *ṣubātu,* common in the older dialects, a noun which probably does not derive from *ṣabātu.*[326] In addition, NB has *ṣibtu,* a garment used primarily for clothing sacred images, identical in shape to the basic noun of the Syriac complex, *ṣeḇtâ,* "ornament." Definite conclusions cannot be reached, however, for the problems with this root are manifold, and any assumption that only one Proto-Semitic root (*ḍbṯ*) is involved and that all variations from the expected reflexes are due to borrowings from Akkadian leads only to further confusion. Much more, including dialect borrowing, assimilation, and root contamination, is clearly involved. In Ugaritic one finds *mṣbṯm,* "tongs," but *ṣbt* means the same in Mishnaic Hebrew. *Ṣbtym,* "grain bundles," occurs in Biblical Hebrew, certainly a related form. As a verb, *ṣbt* occurs in MH and JPA meaning "to join," certainly related to the common Eastern Aramaic *ṣawtâ,* "group." There is also the common Western Aramaic *ṣmt,* "to join," "to press together," to heap up," which is almost certainly Proto—West-Semitic.[327] As a provisional analysis one might posit that Akk. *ṣubātu* and Syr. etc. *ṣbt*

cloth," "garment," first attested in texts from Nuzi, occurring as BH, MH, and JAr. *sdyn* (> Arab. *sadîn*(?); cf. Fraenkel, *Aramäischen Fremdwörter,* p. 48). Syr. *sdwnʾ* is either a direct development of this word or a borrowing from Greek *sindōn,* which itself is probably related to *saddinnu.* (Z, p. 36; A. L. Oppenheim, in *JCS* XXI 249 and n. 73. A Sumerian etymology is out of the question, contra Ellenbogen, *Foreign Words,* p. 121)

325. J. C. Greenfield, in *JAOS* LXXXII 292 ff. The examples can be found in *CAD,* Vol. S, p. 37*a* under paragraph 3'.

326. It is almost certainly cognate with Egyptian *ḏbꜣ,* "garment."

327. Ras Shamra Akk. *ṣmt,* used in the stative, said of a sold object "transferred" to someone; Arab. *ṣmt,* "to be silent," IV "to become hardened," "render solid"; and BH, Ug. *ṣmt,* "to destroy," are all probably the same root whose basic meaning is "to press together."

are related—perhaps the Aramaic is a loan from the Akkadian through Amorite—and that NB *ṣibtu* and NA *ṣubbutu* are Aramaisms.

The restored word *[ṣb]y(?)t ʿzqh,* "seal-bearer," in Ahiqar is also usually derived from Akk. *ṣabātu,* but since no known Akkadian term for seal-bearer involves that verb and only the final consonant of the Aramaic is certain, the equation remains dubious.[328]

ṣerru, "door pivot"—BH and MH *ṣîr,* JAr. *ṣyrʾ ṣyrtʾ,* Syr. *ṣyrtʾ* (*ṣâyartâ*!); Arab. *ṣîr*. There is no good reason to regard the West Semitic forms as loans. Sum. za-ra is now considered a loan from Akkadian.[329]

* *ṣītu,* "expenditure" (Bab.)—BA, Eg., Palm., Nab., Syr. *npqtʾ*; BT *npqwtʾ*; > Arab. *nafaqah*. This is taken to be a loan-translation because of its long Akkadian history dating back to Sumerian economic usage and because this does not seem to be a normal semantic development from the verb "to go out" in Semitic. MH *yṣyʾh* is probably a calque from Aramaic. On the other hand, the MH form *hwṣʾh* from the causative stem could well be an independent development.[330]

* *ṣumbu,* "wagon"—BH *ṣb*; Targ. Proph. *ṣyb* as a royal conveyance. Though the etymology of the Akkadian is unknown, the scarcity of the Aramaic attestations makes a loan probable.[331]

ša—As I have shown elsewhere, the standard interpretation of the first "š" in the Nerab inscriptions as this genitive particle is incorrect.[332]

šaddaqdim OB, *šaddaqad* LB, *šaddagg/diš* NA, "previous year"—Syr. *ʾštqd(y)*, BT, YT *ʾštqd*. Since the Akkadian is almost certainly a loan from Amorite and the late Akkadian forms differ considerably from those of Aramaic, the Aramaic and

328. Cf. *AP*, p. 226, and Greenfield, in *JAOS* LXXXII 292 ff. The Akkadian term for "seal-bearer" is the Sum. loanword *kišibgallu* (or perhaps, as a loan-translation, **nāš kunukki*); *ṣābit kunukki* occurs in *YOS* I, No. 37:30, but apparently in the meaning "possessor of the document" (cf. *CAD*, Vol. Ṣ, p. 18*b*).

329. Z, p. 30; *LS*, p. 627; Salonen, *Turen*, p. 66.

330. B. Landsberger, "Bemerkungen zur altbabylonischen Briefliteratur," *ZDMG* LXIX (1915) 506. *Npqtʾ* was probably an official term in Imperial Aramaic.

331. Z, p. 42; *KBL*, p. 790. The BH term (if correctly vocalized) could be cognate, for the Akkadian seems to go back to a similar form (cf. Salonen, *Landfahrzeuge*, p. 62), but note NB *ṣabbu*. The targumic form with "y" probably derives from the Akkadian *u*.

332. S. Kaufman, "'Siʾgabbar, Priest of Sahr in Nerab,'" *JAOS* XC (1970) 270-71.

Akkadian are probably separate developments from Amorite. The initial *aleph* of the Aramaic form is prothetic, not a development from an Akkadian *ina š-*.[333]

* *šadû*, "east"—BT *šdyʾ*, "east wind."[334]

* *ša ekalli*, "queen"—BH *šēgāl*, BA pl. *šglṯʾ*. In spite of phonetic difficulties, a loan is almost certain here. As demonstrated by Landsberger, the reading *ša ekalli* for SAL.É.GAL cannot be doubted, and the identity in meaning between the Akkadian and BH and BA could not be coincidental.[335]

* *šaknu*, "prefect"—BH, BA, *DEA*, No. 70:1, Persepolis, Eg. *sgn*, "prefect," MH, JAr., "viceroy," "adjutant." The Babylonian docket proves that *sgn* is *šaknu* and further shows that the Assyrian pronunciation was standard for this word even in Babylonia, as does the LB form *sagānu*. The Amarna period precursor of the Assyrian form served as the model for the Ug., Phoen. and Heb. title *skn*, studied most thoroughly by Alt,[336]

333. Perles, in *OLZ* XXI 67 f.; *LS*, p. 53; D. O. Edzard, "Mari und Aramäer?" *ZA* XXII (1964) 147. For the Akkadian forms see *GAG* § 72*c*. The Amorite origin of *šaddaqdim* is shown by its frequent occurrences (and the frequent occurrences of forms of *qdm*) at Mari (cf. *CAD*, Vol. A, Part II, s.v. *aqdamatu*) and the phonetic difficulties involved were it an original Akkadian word (cf. Edzard).

334. Z, p. 45. J. N. Epstein, "Zum magischen Texte," *JAOS* XXXIII (1913) 280, n. 1, suggested that Aramaic *gbl*, "south," may derive from a loan-translation of *šadû*, but in spite of the interpretation in *Aruch* of *šdyʾ* as south wind (s.v. *ʾstnʾ*), there is no indication that *šadû* was ever anything but east (or northeast?).

335. R. Borger, review of *CAD*, Vol. E, *Bi.Or.* XVIII (1961) 152; B. Landsberger, in Suppl. *VT* XVI 198 ff. The Akkadian term occurs in at least one Achaemenid text (cf. Landsberger, p. 200), and therefore it is possible that the loan was from the Babylonian pronunciation of the word, borrowed from NA, where a partial Babylonization of the pronunciation has occurred ([š] for [s] but maintaining the Assyrian [g] in *ekalli*; cf. *sgn* for *šaknu* in Babylonian Mesopotamian Aramaic). The alternative explanations suggested by A. R. Millard, "Fša Ekalli -ŠGL- Dsagale," *UF* IV (1972) 162, cannot be accepted. The BH verb *šgl*, with no other known cognates, can hardly be anything but a denominative from *šēgāl*; but one cannot be forced to regard the loan as early merely because this verb seems attested in otherwise pre-Exilic BH texts. It may even be that the Masoretic substitution of Qre *škb* for written *šgl* actually reflects an earlier substitution in reverse, when *šgl* was felt to be the euphemistic form.

F. Perles, in *OLZ* XXI 68, suggested that BT *dbyt*, "wife," was formed under the influence of *ša ekalli*. One might be more correct to say under the influence of noun forms with *ša*, such as *ša ekalli* and *ša rēši*, frequent in the late dialects; but the still unexplained suffixed form *dbythw*, "his wife," adds an element of uncertainty to the origin of the BT term.

336. A. Alt, "Hohe Beamte in Ugarit," *Studia Orientalia Ionni Pedersen Dicata* (Havniae, 1953) pp. 1-11.

found in Aramaic only in one of the early bricks from Hama (*KAI*, No. 203).[337]

* *ša la*, "without"—In Eastern Aramaic and, sporadically, in Western Aramaic, *d-lā̂* is used to mean "without."[338] NB *ša la* is similarly used, and even developed into a secondary preposition, *šalānu-*.[339] Since, as shown by Rimalt, the Akkadian can be viewed as the result of a long development,[340] and since the form *b-lā̂* appears to be the Common Aramaic expression for "without,"[341] the likelihood of Akkadian influence here is great.

* *šalamtu*, "corpse"—Syr. *šldʾ*; Mand. *šlʾndʾ, šʾldʾ*; BT *šldʾ*, RH (in BT) *šld*, (in Lam. Rabbah) pl. *šldwt*.[342]

šalāṭu, "to rule," "to have control over"—The root *šlṭ* is much more common in Aramaic than is its cognate in Akka-

337. Z, p. 6; *KBL*, pp. 649, 1103; *Persepolis*, pp. 25 ff.; von Soden, in *Or.* n.s. XXXVII 265. For the NA *šaknu* cf. R. A. Henshaw, "The Office of *šaknu* in Neo-Assyrian Times," *JAOS* LXXXVII (1967) 517 ff., LXXXVIII (1968) 461 ff. The Assyrian form of this word was probably always *šaknu*, but the construct form *šakin* (*māt* X) was probably the model for the early Canaanite borrowing, hence Heb. *sôḵēn*. For Bab. *šakkanakku* as a reborrowing of an early Sumerian loanword from an Akkadian form like *šākinu* cf. Edzard, in *ZA* n.f. XXI 94 ff., contra A. Goetze, "Šakkanakkus of the Ur III Empire," *JCS* XVII (1963) 7, n. 90; previously W. W. Hallo, *Early Mesopotamian Royal Titles* (New Haven, 1957) pp. 106 f.

338. It occurs in BA, 11QtgJob (25:1), Targ. Onk. Ex. 21:11, and Targ. Amos 2:16 and several times in the late targums as well as in Samaritan (see Z. Ben-Hayyim, in F. Rosenthal, ed., *An Aramaic Handbook*, Vol. II (Wiesbaden, 1967) s.v. *lʾ*). I know of no occurrences in Targ. Y., JPA, or CPA.

339. Cf. *AHw.*, p. 521*a* bottom. Lexical entries can be found s.v. *balu* in *CAD*, Vol. B.

340. Rimalt, in *WZKM* XXXIX 114 ff. He tried to find its origin in expressions of the negative of the infinitive such as *ša lā ragāmim*, "of non-claiming," but of course in such constructions *lā ragāmim* is to be considered a single unit. More recently another frequent usage has come to light, translated "ohne den Willen" by von Soden (*AHw.*, p. 521*a*). The interpretation "except for," "apart from" also fits many of the cases, and is now attested in the OB Atrahasis story (Lambert and Millard, *Atra-ḫasīs*, III vi 14 [= Gilgamesh XI, l. 175]). Given this background, there is little reason to regard the common LB preposition as an Aramaism (as in *AHw.*, p. 521*a*). As Rimalt points out (p. 114), NB did borrow the native Aramaic form for "without" as *ina lā*.

341. This was borrowed into NB and the Akkadian of Mari as *ina lā* (see n. 340 and I. J. Gelb, *Language* XXXIII [1957] 203) and into late BH as *bᵉʾēn*.

342. Z, p. 48; *LS*, p. 779. For the sound change cf. *GAG* § 31*f* and below, p. 138. The occurrence of this otherwise eastern word in Lamentations Rabbah, thought to be an early Palestinian Midrash, is worthy of note.

dian. Accordingly, the rare NA and common NB and LB use of this verb in legal formulae is probably modeled after Aramaic usage, not the reverse.[343]

* *šamāhu,* "to sprout"—Syr. *šwḥ,* Targ. Proverbs *šwwḥ,* "to sprout"; MH, BT *šbḥ,* "to increase naturally."[344]

* *šamallû,* "apprentice"—BT *šwlyʾ,* Mand. *(ʾ)šwʾlyʾ.*[345]

* *šambaliltu,* "fenugreek"—BT *šblwlytʾ, šblyltʾ.* Syr.

343. Muffs, *Studies,* p. 178, correctly shows that *šalāṭu* in such formulae is only a late substitution for several earlier verbs. Nevertheless, he insists (pp. 153, n. 4, 177) that the Aramaic is modeled on the Neo- and Late Babylonian form. There is no evidence to support such a position. The Aramaic verb was borrowed into late BH as well (Wagner, p. 114).

344. Z, p. 70; *LS,* p. 762. The ingenious proposal to connect *šwḥ* with MH, BT *šbḥ* was made by Kutscher (orally); he also pointed out a possible connection with MH *bt šwḥ,* a kind of plant. The suggestion is based on the well known alternation between *waw* and *bet rafe* in MH. Greenfield, in his excellent study of the verb *śmḫ* and its relatives ("Lexicographical Notes II," *HUCA* XXX [1959] 141-51), considers the relationship between the Aramaic and Akkadian to be uncertain (p. 142, n. 10). His objection to the pronunciation of *šamāhu* as [šawaḫ] is incorrect, however, for the loan must be from Babylonian, and Babylonian intervocalic /m/ certainly was pronounced [w], no matter what the phonetics underlying Assyrian spellings with ʾ (see Nasals in Chap. IV).

345. Z, p. 16; for the OB use of the term *šamallû* see W. F. Leemans, *The Old-Babylonian Merchant* (Leiden, 1950) pp. 22 ff. The meaning "apprentice" in NB is proven conclusively by two apprenticeship contracts: E. and V. Revillout, "A Contract of Apprenticeship from Sippara," *Babylonian and Oriental Record* II (1898) 119-27, and T. G. Pinches, "Tablet Referring to the Apprenticeship of Slaves at Babylon," *Babylonian and Oriental Record* I (1887) 81-85, No. 2. In the former (ll. 3 ff.) the apprentice-to-be is handed over to a baker *ana šamallûtu nuhatimmūtu,* "for the apprenticeship of the baking trade," which is exactly paralleled in the other text by *ana lamādu nuhatimmūtu,* "to learn the baking trade." Though correctly interpreted by the original editors of the text, this *šamallûtu* was misunderstood by M. San Nicolò, *Der neubabylonische Lehrvertrag in rechtsvergleichende Betrachtung* (Munich, 1950) p. 5, n. 6, who translates uncertainly "Krämerei" on the basis of the OB meaning. He is followed in this interpretation by Weisberg, *Guild Structure,* pp. 99 f.

N. H. Tur-Sinai, *The Language and the Book* II (Jerusalem, 1950) 275 ff., attempts to demonstrate that the Akkadian word is native, deriving from an older form **ša mala,* equivalent to OA *ša kīma,* "substitute," which itself, he claims, was borrowed into early Canaanite in the form *sml,* which he translates "substitute." The latter portion of his suggestion is intriguing, but since **ša mala* is hypothetical and the Sum. šaman-lá is attested, its probablility is low. (For the Sumerian etymology see W. W. Hallo, "A Mercantile Agreement from the Reign of Gungunum of Larsa," *AS,* No. 16 [Chicago, 1965] p. 199, n. 5*a*). In the course of his argument, Tur-Sinai proposes and then rejects (certainly with good reason) the possibility that *sml* in Ezek. 8:3, 5 is our word in its older sense of "merchant's representative."

plîltâ reflects the original form to which, in Akkadian, the generic term *šammu*, "plant," has been added.[346]

šammu, "plant," "herb," "drug"—Common Ar. (MH) *sm*, pl. *smmnyn*, "drug," "poison," "pigment"; BH *sammîm*, "fragrant herbs"; Arab. *samm*, "poison." The Aramaic form is the correct reflex of the Proto-Semitic word **śamm*, but it may have been influenced semantically by the Akkadian in medicinal usage. The Biblical Hebrew is probably native, though the spelling with "s" is Aramaized. The Arabic form is certainly an Aramaic loanword.[347]

* *šanû* in *ṭēmu šanû*, "to loose one's senses"—BH *šnh ṭᶜm*; Syr. *šnyᵓ*, "crazy"; Mand. *šᵓnywtᵓ*, "madness."[348]

šanûma, "again"—See below, p. 153.

šaqālu, "hang," "weigh," "pay" (cf. *šiqlu*, p. 29)—In Eastern Aramaic *šql* is the common word for "to lift up," "to take" (also in Genesis Apocryphon and the Palmyran tariff, *CIS* II 3913). In light of its distribution an Akkadian origin certainly seems probable, but one would have to posit such chains of semantic development as "pay" > "pay for" > "buy" > "take" and "hang" > "lift up." An alternative and reasonable non-Akkadian etymology is offered by Brockelmann, *LS*, p. 798. As another possiblity the writer somewhat hesitantly offers the observation that the common perfect of *leqû*, "take," in Neo-Assyrian is *isseqe* [*iššeqe*]. The latter, with the direct object marker *l-*, would yield *šql*. (Compare Syr. *ntl*, "give" < *ntn l-*.)

* *ša rēši*, "eunuch"—Sefire I B 45, III 5 *srs*; Imp. Ar. *srs*, *srys*; BH, MH; Common Ar. *srîsâ* > Arab. *sarîs*; derived verbs in MH, JAr., CPA, Syr., and Mand.[349]

346. Z, p. 56; R. Campbell-Thompson, *A Dictionary of Assyrian Botany* (London, 1949) p. 65.

347. Z, p. 56; *LS*, p. 479. The cognate forms, Eg. *smw*, "plant," and Arab. *šamm*, "smell," "perfume," prove that the original form was **śamm*. With *KBL* (2d ed.) p. 661 (following Löw) one might read a verbal form from this root in II Kings 9:30. A. Goetze, "The Akkadian Masculine Plural in -ānū/ī and Its Semitic Background," *Language* XXII (1946) 123, n. 10, based on an uncertain reading, suggests that the Semitic word might be a loan from Sumerian. Cf. Joshua Blau, *On Pseudo-Corrections in Some Semitic Languages*, p. 119.

348. Z, p. 48; for the Akkadian, very frequent in medical and magical texts, see *BWL*, p. 325. The earliest occurrence I know of is Atrahasis III iii 25. Although Jastrow (*Dictionary*, p. 1606) cites a meaning "to act strangely" for the verb, the only JAr. references I know that may derive from this meaning are *šnyᵓ* and *šnw* in Targ. Prophets for BH *mhtlwt* and *šᶜrwrh*.

349. Z, p. 6; *LS*, p. 500; *KBL*, p. 668. This is a very old compar-

* *šāru*, "wind," "direction"—Mand. *šʾrʾ* (also *šyrʾ*?), "direction," "side."[350]

* *šatammu*, "steward"—Mand. *šʾtʾmʾ* (var. *šʾṭʾmʾ*), "a temple functionary(?)"; BT *ʾštymʾ*, "an official"; Syr. *ʾštymʾ*, Arab. *ʾštymʾ*, "ship captain," "supercargo."[351]

* *šaṭāru*, NB "document"—Babylonian dockets, Nerab tablets, *AP*, No. 81, Nab., Palm., Murabbaᶜat, JAr., MH, Syr. *šṭr*; Mand. *šʾṭʾrʾ*(?).[352]

* **šē bābi*, "neighbor"—Palm. *šbb*, Targ. Onk., Proph., YI, BT *š(y)bbʾ*, Mand. *šybʾbʾ*, Syr. *šbbʾ*. The masculine singular form of this compound is not yet attested in our Akkadian sources, but the Aramaic attestations indicate that it was the common word for "neighbor" in late Akkadian.[353]

* *šēdu*, "demon"—BH *šēḏ*; Paik. 960; Palm.(?); MH and JAr. *š(y)d*; Syr. *šʾdʾ*; Mand. *šydʾ*. The Akk. *šēdu* is generally a good demon, while in Aramaic it is usually malevolent.[354]

ison (cf. *BDB*, p. 710), but the Akkadian reading itself was not proven correct until recently (see B. Landsberger, in Suppl. *VT* XVI 199 and n. 1, and an OB example of the plural in *YOS* X, No. 59 r. 5).

350. Previously unrecognized. Certainly not from *mšʾrʾ*.

351. Fraenkel, *Aramäischen Fremdwörter*, pp. 222, 293; *LS*, p. 812; *Additamenta*, p. 71; F. Rundgren, "Semitische Wortstudien," *Orientalia Suecana* X (1961) 100 ff. For the Akkadian see B. Landsberger, *Brief des Bischofs von Esagila an König Asarhaddon* (Amsterdam, 1965) pp. 58 ff. The semantic development from steward of a temple or household to supervisor of a ship is not unreasonable, but the explanation of the sound changes proposed by Rundgren is far from convincing; while the form of Mand. *šʾtʾmʾ*, with "a" in the first syllable, is certainly a proper reflex (see Chap. IV, n. 39). The Mand. form *ʾštyymʾ*, cited by Fraenkel, is not in *MD*.

352. Z, p. 92; *LS*, p. 773; Muffs, *Studies*, p. 188. Note that although *šṭr* is already common in Babylonian Aramaic texts of the NB period, the only Egyptian example is from the late text *AP*, No. 81. The entry $šṭr_1$ in *DISO* (p. 295) is incorrect. The verb *sṭrw* in *AD*, No. 7:7, if correctly read, can scarcely be the proper reflex of the Babylonian verb *šaṭāru*, for it should have "š" like the noun. Nor is Driver's comparison with Syr. *sṭr* satisfactory. The latter is related to *seṭrâ*, "side" < *šṭr*, and were the derived verb to occur this early it would be spelled with "š". Further speculation on the basis of this uncertain reading is unwarranted. The Punic and JAr. forms cited in *DISO* are to be connected with BH *šôṭēr*, *mišṭār* which is not, as often claimed (cf. *KBL*, p. 964), a loan from Akkadian. There is no reason to regard the Canaanite, Akkadian, and ESA and Arabic *šṭr* as anything but cognates; cf. I. J. Gelb, "Standard Operating Procedure for the Assyrian Dictionary," (mimeograph; Chicago, 1954) pp. 6 and 22 ff.

353. Kaufman, in *Leš*. XXXVII 103 f.

354. Z, p. 69; *LS*, p. 748; *KBL*, p. 949. For the Akkadian see A. L. Oppenheim, *Ancient Mesopotamia: Portrait of a Dead Civilization* (Chicago, 1964) pp. 199 ff.; W. von Soden, "Die Schutzgenien Lamassu und Schedu in

šemiru, "bracelet"—BH pl. *šrwt*; MH, Common Ar. *šyr*, Mand. pl. *šʾyryʾ*; Arab. *siwâr*. These are all cognate, as shown by the older Akk. form *šewiru*.[355]

šiddu, "side"—Targumic *šydʾ*, used to translate BH *yrk*, and Mand. *šydʾ* (hapax in this sense) do not mean "side" but rather "base," as does Syr. *šdtʾ*, pl. *šddʾ*, probably related to Akk. *išdu*, Heb. *št*, Syr. *(ʾ)št*, but certainly not a loan from the Akkadian word for "side." The Akkadian feminine form *šiddatu* seems to mean "chest," "box" in one Neo-Babylonian text, but is probably an Aramaism rather than the source of BH(?), MH *šiddā*, BT *šydtʾ*, and Mand. *šydʾ*(?).[356]

* *šiknu*, "mud," "slime"—Syr. *šknʾ*, Mand. *šyknʾ*, Gaonic Ar. *šwknʾ*.[357]

* *šillatu*, "vulgarity," "blasphemy"—BA (Dan. 3:29) *šlh* (Qrē, *šālû*), "blasphemy."[358]

šindu (< *šimtu*), "mark," "brand," *šamātu*, "to brand" NB—*AD šntʾ*, "mark," Eg. *šnytʾ*, "mark," *mšnt*, "to mark," *šnyt*, "marked"; MH *šntwt*, "marks." Although these Akkadian and Aramaic words are quite obviously related, neither the precise connection between them nor their etymology is clear. The most reasonable explanation seems to be to connect the Akkadian with the common Arabic root *wsm*, "to brand," presumably from a Semitic root **wšm*[359] yielding the regular ver-

der babylonisch-assyrischen Literatur," *Baghdader Mitteilungen* III (1964) 148 ff. Since the *šēdu* is a protective demon, the word may derive from the root *šʿd* as in Arab. *sʿd*, "to have good luck," if that can be separated from Arab., Heb., and Ar. *sʿd*, "to help," which, but for the sibilant, would provide a perfect etymology itself.

355. Z, p. 38; *LS*, p. 749. Perles, in *OLZ* XXI 70, suggests that the Akkadian word is the origin of the rare RH *šwmyrh*, which he translates "ring." His suggestion must be rejected on phonetic grounds, for Akkadian "m" represents [w] here.

356. Z, p. 32. The NB text is *YBT* VII, No. 185:21; cf. Salonen, *Hausgeräte* I 204.

357. *LS*, p. 776. For the Akkadian see R. Campbell-Thompson, *Dictionary of Assyrian Chemistry and Geology*, pp. 20 ff. and A. L. Oppenheim and L. F. Hartman, *On Beer and Brewing Techniques in Ancient Mesopotamia* (*JAOS* Suppl. X [New Haven, 1950]) n. 70. The Gaonic example was discovered by J. N. Epstein, "Notes on Post-Talmudic-Aramaic Lexicography," *Jewish Quarterly Review* XII (1922) 367, n. 70. The "w" in the latter form is probably an error for "y."

358. Perles, in *OLZ* XXI 71; *KBL*, p. 1127. It can certainly be no coincidence that precisely where the context demands "insolence" or "blasphemy" and not "negligence," the *ktîb* has *šlh* instead of the usual *šlw*; read *šillâ*. The correct Babylonian form is *šillatu*, not *sillatu*, as in *KBL* (cf. *GAG* § 30e).

359. Thus, to be separated from *wsm*, "to be beauiful," Akk. *wasāmu*, "to be fitting, proper."

bal noun **šimt*. The *n* of Aramaic *šnt* would thus be due to the NB form *šindu*, showing the normal NB pattern *-mt* > *-nd*, but the preservation of *t* instead of *d* in the Aramaic forms remains unexplained (compare *šalamtu*). Talmudic *šmt*, "to place under the ban," may represent a late survival of this word.[360]

* *šinepû*, "two-thirds"—Samalian, Nineveh Lion Weight (*CIS* II 7) *snb*; Bauer and Meissner 7 *šnby*(?).[361]

* *šiptu*, "incantation"—Mand. *šʾptʾ*, "scroll."[362]

šūbulu, "to send," "to have carry away"—BA *mswblyn*, "laid" or "raised," said of foundations, is often considered to be a loan from this causative of *(w)abālu*, but the Akkadian verb never means anything even similar to the Biblical Aramaic usage. Etymologists would do well to look elsewhere for an explanation of the Biblical Aramaic form, perhaps to Aramaic itself.[363]

* *šukkallu*, "vizier"—Aššur tablet, l. 4 *skl*.[364]

360. *AD* (abridged) p. 66; *DISO*, p. 314; E. W. Moore, *Neo-Babylonian Documents in the University of Michigan Collection* (Ann Arbor, 1939) p. 301. For the finite use of *šamātu* see *YOS* VII, No. 66:3 (cited in *CAD*, Vol. Z, p. 30*a*).

361. Z, p. 65; *DISO*, p. 195; the Samalian is to be read *snb*, not *ʾsnb*; see H. L. Ginsberg, in *JAOS* LXII 236. This is an official unit of weight, probably two-thirds mina. For etymological suggestions and comparisons with Hebrew, cf. E. A. Speiser, "Of Shoes and Shekels," *Oriental and Biblical Studies*, pp. 156 ff.; A. Goetze, "Number Idioms in Old Babylonian," *JNES* V (1946) 202, n. 81; F. Rundgren, "Parallelen zu Akk. šinēpūm '2/3,'" *JCS* IX (1955) 29 f.; R. B. Y. Scott, "The Shekel Sign on Stone Weights," *BASOR*, No. 153 (1959) p. 34. Ug. *šnpt*, previously interpreted as "two-thirds," is to be translated "wave-offering"; see D. R. Hillers, "Ugaritic šnpt, 'Wave-Offering,'" *BASOR*, No. 198 (1970) p. 42.

362. *MD*, p. 444.

363. Cf. *KBL* (2d ed.) pp. 1080, 1102; Rosenthal, *Grammar*, pp. 49, 58; H. L. Ginsberg, in Franz Rosenthal, ed., *An Aramaic Handbook*, Vol. I, Part 2, p. 32. In Aramaic the causative forms of *ybl* and several forms of *sbl* are much closer in meaning to the BA than is the Akkadian. The initial *s* is certainly no cause to look outside of North West Semitic (see Shaphel in Chap. III).

364. As indicated by the Aramaic spelling with "s," the correct NA form is *šukkallu*, as in OB (not *sukkalu*); cf. *AHw*. s.v. and *GAG Ergänz*. § 30*e*. The sibilant shift *š* > *s* in the transliteration is correct; see below, p. 140. Contrary to the view of M. Lidzbarski, *Altaramäische Urkunden aus Assur* ("Wissenschaftliche Veröffentlichungen der Deutschen Orient-Gesellschaft," Vol. XXXVIII [Leipzig, 1921]) p. 17, the representation of Akkadian *š* in Aššur tablet 4 is not inconsistent. The Aramaic text has *s* for Akkadian *š* in the following forms: *rsl* (l. 2), *skl* (l. 9) *srsrd* (l. 11) and the second element of *šlmʾsr* (l. 8). *šmšdlh* (l. 14) is obviously an Aramaic name, hence the use of *š*. The other apparent inconsistencies are in *šlmʾsr* (l. 8) and *šrnʾd* (ll. 1, 4). The first is easily

šuklulu, "to complete"—The Akkadian was possibly of some influence on Common Ar. *škll,* "to complete," "to perfect," "to decorate," especially when said of buildings, but there is no compelling reason to treat the Aramaic as a loanword.[365]

šunṣû, NA "to bring about"—*AD,* No. 5:7 *šnṣyw,* "they succeeded," "they were able," is most probably not to be connected with Aramaic *šyṣy(ʾ)* (see s.v. *šuṣû*) but is rather a form from the root *mṣy,* "to be able." Inasmuch as a meaning corresponding to the Aramaic usage does not actually occur in the Akkadian causatives of this verb, the attested Aramaic form is probably the result of a Babylonianized pronunciation (with *mṣ* > *nṣ*) of a native Ar. form **šmṣy.*[366]

* *šuplu* in *šupal šēpē,* "footstool"—Syr. (lex.) *šwplʾ.*[367]

šusuppu, šasuppu, "sheet," "tablecloth"—Targums, Leviticus Rabbah *šwš(y)pʾ,* "cloak," "sheet"; Syr. *šwšpʾ,* "towel," "veil," "robe." This is probably of foreign origin in both languages. Another reflex of this word may occur in Targ. Onk. BT, Mand. *twtbʾ,* "sheet," "dress," "shirt."[368]

šuṣû, "to make leave," "to deliver"—BA *šyṣyʾ,* "to finish," JPA, Sam., CPA *šyṣy,* "to finish," common in the targums also in the meaning "to be finished," "to be destroyed," "to destroy." This Aramaic verb is usually connected with the Akkadian causative of *(w)aṣû,* since the original form of the root meaning "to go out" is *wḍʾ,* which occurs correctly in Aramaic as *yʿʾ.* The ê of the first syllable also points to an Akkadian origin, as in *šyzb* < *šūzubu.* But the situation is far from clear. The Akkadian never means anything at all similar to "to finish," "to complete" or "to destroy." BA (*ktîḇ*) still preserves the final /ʾ/, which shows that at most there is only an assimilation of a West Semitic root to the Akkadian form; but why such assimilation to a form so differ-

explained, for we now know that the common form of this root in Akkadian is *salāmu,* not *šalāmu* (cf. *AHw.,* s.v.). The second is merely misread. The correct reading is not *šrnʾd* : *šar-naʾid* but *šnnʾd* : *Sin-naʾid,* with Aramaic *š* corresponding to Akkadian *s* as in the above example (*šlm*) and in *ʾdšy* (l. 10) (cf. Chap. IV, n. 13). This reading is confirmed by the new reading *ḥzn* in l. 2 (see s.v. *hazannu*), for in two Harper letters *Sin-naʾid* is the *hazannu* of Aššur (*HABL,* Nos. 150, 812). The spelling with double *n* is unusual, however.

365. Z, p. 70; *LS,* p. 327; see C. Rabin, "The Nature and Origin of the Šafʿel in Hebrew and Aramaic," *Eretz Israel* IX (1969) 150, and below, Shaphel in Chap. III.

366. *AD* (abridged) p. 54; *DISO,* p. 314; Rabin, in *Eretz Israel* IX 150.

367. Z, p. 34; Salonen, *Möbel,* p. 33.

368. Z, p. 36; Salonen, *Möbel,* p. 202; A. Van Selms, "The Best Man and Bride—From Sumer to St. John," *JNES* IX (1950) 72 ff.

ent in meaning? Initial *ê* in the causatives of primae *y* (< *w*) verbs is not unknown; see e.g., BA *hybl*; furthermore, the verb *šyṣy* is found only in the West, either representing a limited survival of an Imperial Aramaic term or indicating that the verb was always only native to the West. I favor the latter possibility. A loan from some other North West Semitic language where *ḍ* > *ṣ* (and which also had shaphel, such as Ugaritic) seems more probable than Akkadian influence here.[369]

* *šuššu*, "one-sixth" or "sixty"—Mand. *šwšʾ*, a unit of time, probably one-sixth of an hour.[370]

* *šutappu*, "partner" M/NB—Palm. *šwtpwt*, "partnership," and derived verb; Common Ar. *šwtp*, "partner" and derived verbs > Ethiopic.[371]

* *šūtu*, "south"—BT, Syr. (lex.), Mand. *šwtʾ*, "south wind."[372]

* *šūzubu* (preterite *ušēzib*), "to rescue"—Ahiqar narrative, *AP*, No. 38 *šzb*; BA, Nab., JAr. *šyzb*; Syr., Sam. JPA, Mand. *šwzb*.[373]

tab/palu, rare SB "tambourine"—Syr., BT, Targ. Hagiographa (once YT), Mand. *ṭab̲lâ*; Arab. *ṭabl*. Origin unknown.[374]

tahūmu, "boundary"—Common Ar., MH *tḥwm*; Mand. *tʾwmʾ*; Arab. *taḫûm*, *taḫûmah*. In Akkadian the word is primarily confined to Assyrian, occurring, to my knowledge, no earlier than

369. Z, p. 70; *KBL* (2d ed.) p. 1129; Rabin, in *Eretz Israel* IX 150. Mand. *šwṣ*, occurring only in the participle and only in one late magical text, is tentatively translated "to drive out," "to consume" in *MD*. Since two out of its three occurrences are connected with verbs meaning "to excite," "to enrage," I suggest that this verb is not from Western Aramaic *šyṣy* but rather Arab. *šyṣ*, "to chastise (I and II)," *šiyâṣ*, "temper," "anger." Mand. *mʾštwṣyʾ*, "monsters(?)," may be related; cf. OA and OB *šutēṣû*, "to fight with one another."

370. Z, p. 65; *MG*, p. xxviii and n. 2. According to earlier scholars this word means "1/12 hour," but the reason for such a translation is unclear. Nöldeke's explanation and the passage he cites to prove the point make little sense. I find the Greek word *sôssos*, cited in Z, *MG*, and *MD*, only attested lexically as some kind of measuring device or distance.

371. Z, p. 46; *LS*, p. 767; Rosenthal, *Sprache*, p. 90. The Akkadian (for an example see *CAD*, Vol. A, Part II, p. 513*b*, bottom) derives from the verb *šuta(p)pû* (for an MB example see *PBS*, Vol. I, Part 2, No. 61:13) itself a denominative verb from *tappu*, the original word for "partner," borrowed from Sumerian.

372. Z, p. 45; *LS*, p. 767.

373. Z, pp. 69 f.; *LS*, p. 762; *AHw.*, p. 268; *KBL*, p. 1129. In light of the common development in all other late dialects to *šwzb*, the unvarying JAr. *šyzb* may represent scribal assimilation to the BA form.

374. Z, p. 30; *LS*, p. 266. I know of the Akkadian only from *Shurpu* III 89 ff. and once in *TCL*, Vol. III (see *LS*).

the Middle Assyrian period. Since no good etymology is known and Arabic has /ḫ/ as Akkadian does (and thus was not borrowed through Aramaic, though see *kimahhu*), there is little reason to suggest an Akkadian origin.[375]

* *tajjāru,* "merciful"—Palm. *tyrʾ.* This and the possible loan translation *rḥmnʾ* represent the Palmyran equivalents of the Akkadian divine epithets *rêmēnu, tajjāru,* "merciful," "forgiving." The Akkadian form itself, however, may be a calque from Aramaic as found in Syr. *tybʾ* and Mand. *tʾyʾbʾ* (and Arab. *tawwâb*).[376]

takālu, "to trust in"—Eg., Hermopolis, Syr., Mand., Targ. Hagiographa (once YT), *tkl.* In this meaning the *t*-form of the verb *wkl* is Common Semitic, found also in Arabic and Geʾez; thus, it is possible that the Aramaic and Akkadian are only cognate. But because the development of primae *t* verbs from verbs originally primae *w* is far more common in Akkadian than in Aramaic, and, in addition, the Aramaic is of very limited distribution, Akkadian influence cannot be ruled out.[377]

talīmu, "brother" (rare and literary)—Sam. (frequent) *tlym,* "brother"; Targ. Y (Gen. 49:5) *tl(ʾ)myn* (Neofiti *tlymyn*), "twins"; CPA *tlym,* "own brother(?)." The root may be *lʾm* (Arab. *liʾm,* "equal," "alike"). The forms are probably cognate.[378]

375. Z, p. 9; *LS,* p. 820; Fraenkel, *Aramäischen Fremdwörter,* p. 282. A connection with Heb. *ḥômāh,* "wall," and the root *ḥmy,* "to defend," has been suggested; if so the Akkadian would almost certainly be a loan from pre-Aramaic (and the Arabic, which has *ḫ,* a loan from Aramaic). Note C. Bezold, *Babylonisch-assyrisches Glossar* (Heidelberg, 1926) p. 292, "wests. LW.?"

376. M. Lidzbarski, *Handbuch der nordsemitischen Epigraphik* (Weimar, 1898) p. 153, n. 5; Rosenthal, *Sprache,* p. 89; J. Cantineau, *Grammaire du Palmyrénien épigraphique* (Cairo, 1935) p. 153.

377. Perles, in *OLZ* XXI 71. The form *wkl* is found in Akkadian only in the noun *wāklu,* "overseer." In favor of a cognate relationship is the fact that the verbal nouns, Akk. *tukultu* and Ar. *tuklânâ,* are too different from each other to be a loan but too similar not to be related. For primae *w/t* cf. *GAG* § 103*d,* C. Brockelmann, *Grundriss der vergleichenden Grammatik der semitischen Sprachen* I (Berlin, 1908) 597, and K. Tsereteli, "Über die Reflexivstämme in den modernen aramäischen Dialekten," *RSO* XXXIX (1964) 125-32.

378. Z, p. 46; M. Jastrow, "On Assyrian and Samaritan," *JAOS* XIII (1889) 148. Could the targumic *aleph* be consonantal? The specific meaning of the Akkadian appears to be "brother of equal status." If *talīmu* is indeed from *lʾm,* it would be another "Personenbezeichnung" of the *taqtīl* formation (cf. *talmīdu*), which lends support to the possibility of a loan.

* *talmīdu*, "apprentice"—BH, MH, JAr., Syr., CPA *talmîḏ*, Sam. *tlmwd*, "student," "disciple" > Arab. *tilmîḏ*; Mand. *tʾrmydʾ*, "priest." Akkadian attestations are surprisingly rare, but *talmīdu* was apparently the Assyrian word for apprentice, student. As noted long ago, it is only in Akkadian (and only Assyrian(?), see *GAG*, p. 68) that the noun form *taprīs* is a "Personenbezeichnung."[379]

* *tamkaru*, "merchant"—Palm., MH, JAr., CPA, Sam., Syr. *tgr(ʾ)*, Mand. *tʾngʾrʾ* > Arab. *tâǧir*. Not unexpectedly the denominative verbs in the various languages were easily confused with forms of *ʾgr*. There is, however, no reason to suggest that this confusion accounts for the *g* of the Aramaic form, for original /mk/ was pronounced and often written "ng" in NB (see Phonology, in Chap. IV).[380]

* *tarbaṣu*, "court"—Eg. *trbṣ*, "courtyard," Imp. Ar. "official residence"; BT, Targ. Chronicles, RH *trb(y)ṣ(ʾ)*; Syr. *trbṣʾ*; Mand. *tʾrbʾṣʾ*, "court," "forecourt," "hall." The Akkadian is attested in this sense only in Assyrian and the peripheral dialects.[381]

targumānu, "interpreter," "dragoman"—BH *mtrgm*, "interpreted"; Common Ar. *targmânâ*, *turgmânâ*, etc., Arab. *tarǧa/umân*, *turǧumân* > dragoman. This word was recently the object of an extensive study by I. J. Gelb. As he has shown, there is little reason to relate *targumānu* to the root *rgm*, "to speak," or to consider it of Akkadian origin. Although it is almost certainly foreign, perhaps Hittite, in origin, the word could have entered Aramaic through Akkadian but may not have. The *-ān* nominalizing suffix is at home in both Akkadian and West Semitic.[382]

379. Z, p. 29; *LS*, p. 367; Wagner, p. 119. Note that in Zimmern's time the existence of the Akkadian was still uncertain. The earliest attestation I know of is a broken passage in an OB lexical list: lú KAB-zu-zu : *ta-a[l-m]i-[du]* (*MSL* XII 195, l. 14). In Hittite the logogram *kab-zu-zu* occurs frequently in the meaning "student" or "apprentice."

380. Z, p. 16; *LS*, p. 876; B. Landsberger, in Suppl. *VT* XVI (1967) 176 ff. For *mk* > *ng* see *GAG* § 31*f* and such NB spellings as *d/tam-ga-ar* (Ungnad, *Glossar*, p. 162).

381. Z, p. 42; *LS*, p. 710. In Ugaritic *trbṣ* is "stable," and Ras Shamra Akkadian gives the equation É-*tum* : *tar-ba-ṣi* (*MRS* VI 92, RS 16. 189:17), cf. *CAD*, Vol. B, p. 283*a*), that is, "house." Since the correct Aramaic reflex of this root is *rbᶜ*, the Aramaic form must be the result of either Akkadian or Canaanite influence. The evidence of distribution, as well as the lack of a suitable meaning in Canaanite, points clearly to an Akkadian origin.

382. Z, p. 7; *LS*, p. 834; Wagner, p. 81; I. J. Gelb, "The Word for Dragoman in the Ancient Near East," *Glossa* II (1968) 93-104. Gelb suggests, without expressing his reasons for doing so, that the Aramaic word did come through Akkadian (p. 102).

* *tarlugallu*, "cock"—Phrah. viii 1 *trngwl*, MH *trnwgl*, *trngwl*, JAr. *trngwl*, *trnglʾ*, Syr. *trnglʾ*, *trnwglʾ*, Mand. *tʾrnʾwlʾ*.[383]

* *tibûtu*, "attack," "invasion"—Mand. *tybʾ*, *tyʾbwtʾ*(?), "invasion."[384]

tillu, "mound," "ruin heap"—Heb., Ar., Arab. *till*, *tell*. Suggested Akkadian etymologies from various weak roots are very uncertain, and the origin of this word remains obscure. Sum. dul is probably an independent development of this ancient culture word.[385]

tinūru, "oven"—BH, MH, CPA, Syr., Mand. (in JAr. only in the Targums for BH *tnwr*), Arab. *tannûr*. The first Akkadian occurrence of this vocable is in MB Alalakh. Although the word seems Semitic, an Akkadian origin is unlikely.[386]

* *titurru*, "bridge"—BT *tytwrʾ*, Syr. *ttwrʾ*, *twtrʾ*, Mand. *tʾtwrʾ(qʾ)*. The Akkadian assumes the meaning "bridge" fairly late; in Old Babylonian it is a kind of swampy ground. It is interesting to note that Akkadian has two words for "bridge," and both were borrowed, though the other (*gišru*) is more widespread in Aramaic.[387]

* *tubalû*, "a device for climbing the palm tree"—BT *twblyʾ* > Arab. *tubalyâ*, *tablyâ*.[388]

tumru, "ashes"; in *akal tumri*, "bread baked in ashes"—Syr. *ṭmîrtâ* (from *ṭmr*, "to bury") means the same but, in light of the difference in form and initial consonant, is probably cognate rather than a loan (Akk. *temēru* means "to bury in ashes").[389]

383. Z, p. 51; *LS*, p. 836. The Akkadian is from Sum. dar-lugal. For MH *trnwgl* see MS Kaufmann, Ab.Zar. I 5.

384. *MD*, p. 484. The contextual meaning of *tybʾ* is quite certain, but that of *tyʾbwtʾ* is not clear.

385. Z, p. 14; *LS*, p. 824; *KBL* (2d ed.) p. 1029; D. O. Edzard, review of *MAD*, No. 3, *ZA* LIV (1961) 263.

386. Z, p. 32; *LS*, p. 829; Salonen, in *Baghdader Mitteilungen* III 101 ff. The rare late Sumerian lexical list forms *ti-nu-ur* and *tu-nu-ur* are certainly artificial creations of the scribes, but the legitimate forms durun and dilina (see *MSL* VII 195) suggest that this is an old culture word.

387. Z, p. 44; *LS*, p. 839*b*. The meaning "bridge" first occurs in MB *kudurru*'s. For OB, see *CAD*, Vol. E, s.v. *edurû* end.

388. Z, p. 54; *Additamenta*, p. 407; B. Landsberger, *Date Palm*, p. 38 and nn. 132 ff. Landsberger expresses uncertainty about the standard Sumerian etymology ^{giš}tuba$_{x}$(TUG)-lá, but no other etymology seems possible.

389. Z, p. 38; *LS*, p. 280*b*; F. Hrozny, *Das Getreide im alten Babylonien* (Wien, 1913) p. 131. The synonym *ṭa/urmûs* (also in Arabic) probably has a different origin. For some Akkadian attestations see *CAD*, Vol. A, Part 1, p. 239*a*.

* *ṭēmu*, "order," "decree"—Eg., *AD*, BA, BH *ṭʿm*, "order," "decree." The word *ṭʿm* itself, in the meaning "taste" or "reason," is, of course, cognate, but the meaning "order" in Aramaic (and Hebrew) occurs only during the Imperial Aramaic period and must derive from Akkadian where such a meaning is already frequent in Old Babylonian. The use of this word in the sense "matter" (Hermopolis 1:12, *AP*, No. 41:7) may be either a loan from similar Akkadian usage or an Aramaic development.[390]

* *ummānu*, "artisan"—*AD*, Nab., Palm., Sam. *ʾmn*; BH *ʾommān*, *ʾāmôn*; MH, JAr., CPA, Syr. *ʾwmn*; Mand. *ʿwmʾnʾ*.[391]

urû, late and rare "stall"—Late BH *ʾrwt*, *ʾrywt*; Syr. *ʾwryʾ*; BT, Targ. Proph., and Hagiog. *ʾwryʾ*, *ʾwrwwʾ*; Arab. *ʾiry*, *ʾârîyah*; a late culture word of non-Mesopotamian origin.[392]

* *urubātu*, (Lex.) "a kind of brick construction"—BT *ʾwrby*.[393]

* *uṣurtu*, "figure," "circle"—Mand. *ṣwrtʾ*, "circle," "halo." There is little reason to accept the frequent suggestion that Common Ar. (and BH) *ṣûrâ/tâ*, "picture," "form," is a loan from Akk. *uṣurtu* except for their phonetic similarity, but there are several reasons for rejecting this suggestion. Although both Hebrew and Akkadian have the verb *yṣr*, "to form," it

390. Z, p. 10; *KBL*, p. 1079; Wagner, p. 61. The BA title *bʿl ṭʿm*, "commander," is probably modeled after Persian and not Akkadian; for the Persian form see H. H. Schaeder, *Iranische Beiträge* I: *Schriften der Königsberger Gelehrten Gesellschaft* (Halle, 1930) p. 67. The expression *bēl ṭēmi* does occur in Akkadian (*HABL*, No. 555:5; E. Klauber, *Politisch-religiöse Texte aus der Sargonidenzeit* [Leipzig, 1913] *passim*; Moore, *Neo-Babylonian Documents*, 89:4), but it refers to someone who delivers orders as an intermediary, not to someone who makes them. The correct NA equivalent of the BA expression is rather *šākin ṭēmi*. On Hermopolis 1:12, see E. Bresciani and M. Kamil, *Le Lettere aramaiche di Hermopoli* (*AANL*, "Memorie," Scienze Morali, Series VIII, Vol. XII [Rome, 1966]) p. 381, and B. Porten and J. C. Greenfield, in *ZAW* LXXX 229.

391. Z, p. 25; *LS*, p. 25; Wagner, p. 25. The Akkadian form derives from Sum. um-mi-a. J. Barth, *Etymologische Studien* (Leipzig, 1893) p. 60, suggested that *ʾwmnwt* in MH B.Batra 9:4 *npl lʾwmnwt hmlk*, "was summoned to governmental service," is from the Akkadian homonym *ummānu*, "army." This is uncertain, but the Mishnaic usage is difficult to explain otherwise.

392. Z, p. 42; *LS*, p. 48; *KBL* (3d ed.) p. 82; Salonen, *Hippologica Accadica*, p. 177; C. Rabin, in *Sefer Shmuel Yeivin*, p. 473. The Sumerian form found in the late lexical lists is certainly artificial. The OA hapax *arû* is perhaps to be connected (as in *CAD*, Vol. A, Part II, p. 313a) with the late synonym list term *arû*, "granary," but certainly not with *urû*. For the meaning "granary" see JAr. *ʾwryʾ*, "storehouse," apparently of Mediterranean origin.

393. Meissner, in *OLZ* XXV 241 f.; J. N. Epstein, *Prolegomena*, p. 195.

does not otherwise exist in Aramaic, and there is every reason to believe that the verb *ṣwr*, "to form," occurring in the peal with a great many associated noun forms, is the Aramaic reflex of this root. Further, the aphaeresis of the initial vowel cannot be explained either as an Akkadian or an early Aramaic development.[394] Nevertheless, the influence of *uṣurtu* can be found in Aramaic. The most certain example is Mand. *ṣwrtʾ* II, "circle" or "halo around a heavenly body," which, though ostensibly connected with the root *ṣrr*, "to enclose," certainly bears the influence of the Akkadian word, used often in magical and astronomical contexts in precisely these meanings.[395]

* *ušallu*, "marsh"—Syr. *ʾwslʾ*.[396]

* *uššu*, "foundation"—BA *ʾš*; CPA, RH, Targ. *ʾwš*, *ʾš*; Sam. *ʾrš*; > Arab. *ʾuss*. See *asītu*.[397]

* *utūnu, atūnu*, "kiln," "furnace"—BA, Targums, BT, Syr., Mand. *ʾtwn* > Arab. *ʾattûn*, Ethiopic *ʾettôn*. This is an old, probably pre-Sumerian, culture word.[398]

wuššuru, "to let loose"; in OB, Amarna (and LB?) also "to send"—Aššur Ostracon and Eg. *hwšr*, "to send"; cf. 11QtgJob XXXII:3 *twšr* for BH *t^ešallaḥnah*. The distribution of the meaning "send" in Akkadian is strongly suggestive of a western origin; but in light of the strong semantic connection between "release" and "send" in many languages, the extent and nature of the possible influences here must remain uncertain.[399]

394. This is common, especially with initial *a-* in foreign words in Akkadian, but almost never occurs in native words (cf. *GAG* § 14). No other loanword shows such a loss, nor would we expect to find it as a native development in the early period attested in BH.

395. For the Mandaic see E. S. Drower, *The Book of the Zodiac* (London, 1949) p. 127, n. 5; Baumgartner, in *HUCA* XXIII 58. In general, Z, p. 27; *LS*, p. 624.

396. Z, p. 43; *LS*, p. 35. *Ušallu* is a loan from Sum. ú-sal; cf. *CAD*, Vol. A, Part I, p. 91*b*.

397. Z, p. 31; *KBL*, p. 1054. The Akkadian is borrowed from Sumerian; see A. Falkenstein, "Sumerische Bauausdrücke," *Or.* n.s. XXXV (1966) 229 ff. Note the derived verbs in CPA, Arab., and, rarely, JAr. Syr. *ʾeštâ*, a byform of *šeṯ*, has nothing to do with *uššu*. For the Samaritan see Z. Ben-Hayyim, *The Literary and Oral Tradition of Hebrew and Aramaic amongst the Samaritans*, Vol. III, Part 2 (Jerusalem, 1967) p. 96.

398. Z, p. 32; *LS*, p. 55; A. Salonen, in *Baghdader Mitteilungen* III 114 ff., *Fussbekleidung*, p. 116; *KBL*, p. 1055. The confusion in the initial vowel goes back to Sumerian.

399. Cf. *AD* (abridged) p. 45; Koopmans, *Aramäische Chrestomathie*, p. 82; Kraeling, *Brooklyn Museum*, p. 288, *KAI* II 284. Akk. *wuššuru* is an extremely problematic verb. Von soden, *GAG* § 103*p*, claims that in later

* *zabbilu*, "basket"—BT *zbylʾ*, Syr. *zn/bbylʾ* > Arab. *zabîl*, *zibbîl*. W. von Soden and A. Salonen consider the Akkadian to be a loan from Aramaic (see also *CAD*, s.v.), but the Aramaic cognate of Akk. *zabālu*, "to carry," is *sbl*, not *zbl*; thus, *zbylʾ* must be a loan from Akkadian.[400] Moreover, it is difficult to explain MH *sblnt* and Syr. *sblwnʾ*, "betrothal gifts" (BT *sabbel*, "to send betrothal gifts"), as calques from Akk. *zubbullû*, for the latter term is limited to the OB and MA periods.[401]

zabbu, "ecstatic"—Mand. *zʾbʾ*, "a kind of priest." The meaning of the Mandaic is uncertain, and an alternative etymology from *dʾbʾ*, "slaughterer," is quite possible. If, however, the parallel word *ʾdydyʾ* means "oracle tellers," the semantic similarity would suggest that *zʾbʾ* is indeed Akk. *zabbu*.[402]

zakāru, "to speak"—Syr. *zkwrʾ*, JAr. *zkwrw*, RH *zkwr*, "necromantic spirit," "necromancer(?)," and the related verb *zkr* in Syr. (and Mand.?). It is by no means certain that *zkwrʾ* is related to the root *ḏkr* and hence was necessarily borrowed from a language where *ḏ* > *z*. In addition it must be noted that the Akkadian verb has no significant magical connotations.[403]

Babylonian this verb split into two forms: *uššuru*, "to let loose," and *muššuru*, "to send." A confirmation of this position must await the publication of the "U/W" volumes of the two dictionaries, but the frequent examples of *mussuru* meaning "to let loose," "to leave," "to abandon to," such as in J. Aro, *Glossar zu den mittelbabylonischen Grammatik* (*St.Or.* XXII [Helsinki, 1957]) pp. 64 ff. (MB) and Ungnad, *Glossar*, pp. 99 f. (NB) with no examples meaning "to send" and *uššuru*, "to send," at Amarna, leave cause for doubt. The etymology of the verb itself is uncertain. It would seem to be the result of a metathesis of the root *šrw*, "to let loose," common in Aramaic, a metathesis perhaps occasioned by the similarity of the root *yšr*, "straight," used in the causative in the sense "to make go straight," "to direct." In Akkadian these two roots form a kind of suppletive paradigm. (Note that *ešēru* < *yšr* occurs only in stems I and III whereas *wuššuru* is found only in II [cf. *CAD*, Vol. A, Part II, s.v. *ašāru* C].) In support of this theory note the synonymous use in the Amarna documents of *(w)uššuru*, *šutēšuru* and *šūšuru* in this meaning.

400. Z, p. 34; *LS*, p. 187; *CAD*, Vol. Z, p. 7*a*; von Soden, in *Or.* n. s. XXXVII 269; Salonen, *Hausgeräte* I 249.

401. Contra M. Held, "The root *ZBL/SBL* in Akkadian, Ugaritic and Biblical Hebrew," *JAOS* LXXXVIII (1968) 90 f. and n. 19. The difference in the sibilant, the *n* affix of the Aramaic and Hebrew forms of the noun, and the limited use of the Akkadian indicate cognate terminology here, though a very early calque cannot be ruled out.

402. Baumgartner, in *HUCA* XXIII 58; *MD*, p. 156.

403. Z, p. 67; *LS*, p. 196. Nöldeke's comparison with Arab. *zukrah*, "wine skin," resulting in a perfect parallel with Heb. *ʾôḇ*, is worthy of consideration.

zakû, "to be clear," "to be clean," "to be free of claims"—Common Ar. *zky*, "to be innocent," "to be victorious," as opposed to *dky*, "to be pure," the correct reflex of Proto-Semitic *ḏky*, is generally thought to be a loan. But there can be little certainty that Akkadian was the donor. In juridical use the Akkadian term means only "to be free of claims" and, in the D stem, "to clear of claims." Although the requisite semantic development is not impossible, it is far from probable. Furthermore, the juridical use of *zukkû* disappeared in the late Akkadian dialects (see s.v. *puṣṣû*). Since the sense "to be righteous" for the verb *zkh* already occurs in BH (Ps. 51:6, Micah 6:11), Canaanite is a much better candidate for the origin of the Aramaic than is Akkadian.[404]

Similarly, the Aramaic word for the "clear" substance par excellence, glass, *zgwgytʾ* (BH *zkwkyt*, BT also *zwgytʾ*, *zwgʾ*, Mand. *zgʾgytʾ*, *zgʾwytʾ*, etc. > Arab. *zuǧâǧ*) can hardly be a native Aramaic term; but here, too, a western origin must be given primary consideration, for the rare Akk. *zakakatu* seems to be an Aramaic loanword, and the more common *zukû* is only a kind of intermediary in the glassmaking process.[405] The latter could conceivably be the forerunner of the unusual BT variant *zwgʾ*, however.

* *zaqīpu*, "stake"—Syr. *zqypʾ*, "cross," BT and Targ. Hagiog. *zqypt*, *zyqpʾ*, "stake," "gallows," Mand. *zyqpʾ*, "pillory," and derived verbs in the sense to "impale," "hang," or "crucify" in BA(?), CPA, Syr., BT, and Targ. Hagiog. This particular usage of this otherwise cognate root almost certainly derives from the Assyrians and their notorious practice of impalement.[406]

**zāzu*—The Mandaic magic bowl hapax *zʾzyʾ* was connected with an Akk. form *zāzu*, supposedly meaning "abundance," by earlier scholars. The Akkadian word does not exist.[407]

* *zibānītu*, "scales"—Mand. *z(ʾ)bʾnytʾ*. Akkadian must also be the ultimate origin of the Arabic star name *zubâniyâ* and

404. Z, p. 25; *LS*, p. 195; *KBL* (2d ed.) p. 1071; Rosenthal, *Grammar*, p. 16; E. Y. Kutscher, in *Tarbiz* XIX 125.

405. Cf. A. Leo Oppenheim, *Glass and Glassmaking in Ancient Mesopotamia* (Corning, 1970) pp. 17 f.

406. Z, p. 13; *LS*, p. 204; R. Kittel, "ʾzdqp = *úpsothênai* = gekreuzigt werden," *ZNW* XXXV (1936) 282 ff. This usage is clearly eastern, but *slb* is the equivalent in the West.

407. Cf. *MD*, p. 158. The rejection of this word can be found in *CAD*, Vol. Z, p. 76. The origin of this understandable error was the mistaken equation of two different eponyms of the NA period, HÉ.NUN-*a-a* (703 B.C.) and *za-za-a-a* (692 B.C.), HÉ.NUN meaning "abundance" and so given in the lexical lists.

the Qurʾânic *zabâniyah*, but the intermediary is unknown. As is frequently remarked, there must be some connection between this word and the common word for "to buy" in Aramaic, *zbn*. What is almost certainly involved is an old culture word of uncertain origin, *zbn* (zibana?), meaning "weight," for which there is evidence from Akkadian, Hittite, and Egyptian.[408]

* *zīmu*, "appearance," "luster," "glow"—BA, JAr., MH, Syr., Sam., Mand. *zywʾ*, "appearance," "splendor."[409]

* *zīpu*, "mold," "impression," "cast coin"—Targ. Onk. Ex. 32:4 *zypʾ*, "mold"; Syr. (lex.) *zybʾ*, "envelope(?)"; Syr. and Mand. *zypʾ*, "falsity" and denominative verbs "to falsify" in Syr., MH, and BT; Arab. *zîf*, "false coin."[410]

* *ziqpu*, "zenith," "culminating star or constellation"—Mand. *zyqpʾ*, "a type of star or constellation."

ziqtu, "sting," "barb," *zaqatu*, "to sting"—Targ. Prophets, Hagiographa, BT, *zyqtʾ*, Syr. *zqtʾ*, "prick," "goad"; Syr. *zqt*, "to prick," "to goad." While there is no proof of a loan here, the limited distribution suggests one.[411]

ziqtu, zīqu, "torch" NA—The connections, if any, between

408. Z, pp. 16, 62; *MD*, p. 156. See also Mand. *zbʾnytʾ* 2, "a horned creature." For *zbn* cf. *CAD*, Vol. Z, p. 100, and add the common Egyptian word *dbn*, "weight," "part of a scale." There may be some ultimate connection with Ug. *mznm*, Heb. *mô(ʾ)znayim*, Arab. *mîzân*, etc., but it remains obscure.

409. Z, p. 47; *LS*, p. 195; *KBL*, p. 1071. The origin must be Babylonian, for the Akkadian definitely has original /m/. Thus, I find it difficult to see how this late borrowing could be the correct etymology of the BH month name *zîw* (cf. *KBL* [3d ed.] p. 255, and Chap. IV, n. 77).

410. Z, p. 27; *LS*, pp. 194-95; *CAD*, Vol. Z, p. 87*b*. The semantic development "(coin) mold" > "false coin" > "false" is perfectly paralleled by the development of the English word "bogus": an apparatus for coining money > counterfeit money > anything not genuine, a development which is said to have taken place in the course of a mere twenty-five years (H. L. Mencken, *The American Language* [New York, 1965] p. 558; *Supplement* I [New York, 1966] p. 232). A further parallel is English "fabricate."

To my knowledge no one has previously interpreted *zypʾ* in the Targum Onkelos passage as "mold" (but see *Aruch* III 311). This interpretation is proven correct by the translation of BH *ḥrṭ* in our passage given in Targ. Y II and Neofiti, *ṭwpsʾ*, and the medieval dictionaries of Ben-Janach, *dpws*, and David ben Abraham al-Fāsī, "mold" (for which see C. C. Torrey, "The Foundry of the Second Temple at Jerusalem," *JBL* LV [1936] 259 f.). *Phrah.* XV/2 *zbʾ*, "tablet," is interesting if correctly interpreted, because this meaning is attested in Akkadian only for the OB period, for which see now F. R. Kraus, "Altbabylonisch *zeʾpum*," *Bi.Or.* XXIV (1967) 12 ff., and J. J. Finkelstein, in *YOS* XIII 4 ff.

411. Z, p. 42; *LS*, p. 204; Salonen, *Hippologica Accadica*, p. 159.

this word and Ar. *zîqâ,* "shooting star," are unclear. Syriac also has the form *zyqtʾ* for "shooting star," so perhaps the Aramaic is related to the preceding entry.[412]

zīqu, "wind," "breath"—Is Common Ar. *zîqâ,* "storm," cognate or a loan? The verb *zâqu,* "to blow," is known only in Akkadian.[413]

zukû, see *zakû.*

* *zuruqqu,* "irrigation hose"—BT *zrnwqʾ, zrwnqʾ,* Mand. *zʾrnwqʾ* > Arab. *zurnûq.*[414]

* *zūzu,* "half-shekel," "half-sila"—Eg., Hermopolis, Palm., Murabbaʿat, MH, JAr., CPA, Syr., Mand. *zwz,* "a small coin," "small measure."[415]

MONTH NAMES

The actual pronunciation of the Akkadian month names in the late periods is often difficult to determine because of the almost universal use of logograms. For several of the names one must rely entirely upon the evidence of a few (SB) lexical lists and what can be determined from the shape of the equivalent Aramaic or Hebrew forms. The Imperial Aramaic names are clearly derived from the NB/LB calendar. In the list that follows, the probable NB (NA for *kanūnu*) forms are given, followed by the Imperial Aramaic consonantal spelling and the Hebrew and Syriac traditional vocalizations.

abu—ʾb, Heb., Syr. *ʾâḇ.*

addaru—ʾdr, Heb. *ʾăḏār, ʾāḏār, ʾaddār,* Syr. *ʾâḏâr.*[416]

a/ijjaru—ʾyr, Heb., Syr. *ʾiyyâr.*[417]

412. Z, p. 12. Other related terms are BH *ziqqîm,* "fire arrows," RH *zyqwq,* "spark," "dart." These are probably from *zqq,* "to forge."

413. Z, p. 45; *LS,* p. 195.

414. *CAD,* Vol. Z, p. 167; Salonen, *Hausgeräte* I 266. The root *zrq,* "to sprinkle," is common, but this strange Aramaic form must be related to the Akkadian, and if so, *zrwnqʾ* (*zŭrunqâ*) would appear to be the correct original Aramaic form; see below, Chap. IV, n. 29.

415. Z, p. 21; *LS,* p. 191; *CAD,* Vol. Z, p. 170. For *zwz* in Eg. cf. R. Yaron, "'ksp zwz' in the Elephantine Documents," *Leš.* XXXI (1967) 287 f., and "Minutiae Aramaicae," *JSS* XIII (1968) 202 f.

416. For the Hebrew (Yemenite) vocalization with a *dagesh,* see E. Y. Kutscher, in Suppl. *VT* XVI 168.

417. Ug. *ḫyr* is the Hurrian month name *hiari.* Note the SB spelling IA-*e-ru* (*CAD,* Vol. A, Part I, p. 230*b*).

arahšamnu (phonetically probably *[mar(a)ḫšawan])—*mrḥšwn*, Heb. *marḥešwān*, Mand. *mᵓšr(ᵓ)wᵓn*.[418]

e/ilūlu—*ᵓlwl*, Heb. *ᵓĕlûl*, Syr. *ᵓêlûl*.[419]

kanūnu—Hat. *knwn*, Syr. *kânô/ûnâ*.

kislimu—*kslw*, Heb. *kislēw*.

nisannu—*nysn*, Heb. and Syr. *nîsân*.

simānu—*sywn*, Heb. *sīwān*.

šabāṭu—*šbṭ*, Heb., Syr. *šḇâṭ*.

**tammūzu*—*tmwz*, Heb. *tammûz*, Syr. *tâmûz*.[420]

tešrītu—*tšry*, Heb. *tišrî*, Syr. *tešrî*, *tešrîn*.[421]

ṭebētu—*ṭbt*, Heb. *ṭēḇēṯ*.

418. For the initial *m* see Phonology in Chap. III. I transcribe the Akkadian with *š* rather than traditional *s* because of the Aramaic form and on the basis of a clear NA vocalization with [s] deriving necessarily from historic /š/ (Aššur tablet 5, *yrḥh smnh*; this tablet has proper Assyrian representation of the sibilants in every other case; note the two separate words, for this is not a normal Assyrian month). Landsberger's explanation of the Aramaic "š" (in Suppl. *VT* XVI 185) as the result of syllable-final position is not applicable to early Imperial Aramaic, where there is little reason to assume that it indeed was already syllable-final. Forms with "š" also occur in OA (see *GAG*, p. 91, and Karl Hecker, *Grammatik der Kültepe-Texte* [*An.Or.*, Vol. XLIV (Rome, 1968)] § 68*b*). Note the metathesis in Mandaic after the loss of *h*.

419. *AHw.*, p. 210. The original initial vowel is /e/. The often cited *ulūlu* is the Assyrian form resulting from vowel harmony.

420. There is no native evidence for the NB pronunciation (see *AHw.*, s.v. *Duᵓūzu*), but **tammūz* is almost certainly the only possible form which could produce the resulting Aramaic; cf. Chap. IV, n. 34.

421. Imp. Ar. *tšry* is the absolute form. The final /t/ of the Akkadian was understood as the feminine ending (correctly, for the root is *šry*); contrast the preservation of the *t* in *ṭebētu*. It is possible that *tšry* is actually an old Aramaic month name adopted by the Babylonians, for the root is a common one in Aramaic but not in Akkadian (cf. S. Langdon, *Babylonian Menologies and the Semitic Calendars* [London, 1935] p. 29). In fact the rare root may be a loan from Aramaic in Akkadian (cf. s.v. *wuššuru*). The unexpected final "n" of the Syriac (from Arabic?) and Arabic is perhaps to be explained as a plural, since there are two months called *tešrîn*.

III

THE NON-LEXICAL INFLUENCES

Aside from differences in the lexical stock, many of the non-lexical differences between the older and younger forms of Aramaic and among the contemporary younger dialects have been explained as the result of Akkadian influence. As noted above, the dialects of Eastern Aramaic can be distinguished by several grammatical divergences from Old Aramaic, Imperial Aramaic, and later Western Aramaic;[1] and one might rightfully expect some of these peculiarities to be the result of the Akkadian substratum. These influences, as well as those non-lexical Akkadian influences found in the other dialects, will be studied in this chapter. Discussed here as well are those grammatical characteristics that previous scholars have suggested are due to Akkadian influence but are to be considered uncertain or even improbable. The final two topics *kî* and *mî* in the section on syntax, which might well be considered lexical items, are included here because of their syntactic nature.

PHONOLOGY

Spirantization of Postvocalic Stops

The date and place of origin of this phonetic principle common to the traditional vocalizations of Aramaic and Hebrew have long been in doubt, although there is now some general consensus that in Hebrew it is due to Aramaic influence.[2] The possibility of a similar alternation in the pronunciation of the stops in Akkadian, at least in some dialects, has often

1. See p. 11.

2. For convenient summaries and bibliographies see E. E. Knudsen, "Spirantization of Velars in Akkadian," *Lišān mitḫurti* (*AOAT*, Vol. I [Neukirchen-Vluyn, 1969]) pp. 150 f., and Wagner, p. 129. The argument, based on Greek and Latin transcriptions, that Aramaic and Canaanite long knew only the spirantized pronunciation of the *bgdkpt* series and another that views spirantization as a Masoretic innovation in Hebrew have been most concisely refuted by E. Y. Kutscher in "Contemporary Studies in North-Western Semitic," *JSS* X (1965) 24 ff. See, too, J. Barr, "St. Jerome and the Sounds of Hebrew," *JSS* XII (1967) 9 ff., and E. Brønno, "Samaritan Hebrew and Origen's Secunda," *JSS* XIII (1968) 195 ff. I fail to understand the reasoning that insists that the interchange *b/p* in Old Hebrew and Canaanite texts presupposes spirantization at that early date; cf. Y. Aharoni, "Three Hebrew Ostraca from Arad," *BASOR*, No. 197 (1970) p. 20, n. 13.

been proposed. Recently a great deal of attention has been paid to this subject, and the Akkadian evidence has been gathered by von Soden, E. Knudsen, and other scholars.[3] It has even been suggested that Akkadian might now be considered the origin of this feature of the Aramaic morphophonemic system.[4]

There can be no objection to this hypothesis on chronological grounds. The internal Aramaic evidence points to the period 700-400 B.C. for the development of this feature into a systematic characteristic of Aramaic. Although sporadic spirantization may well have occurred earlier, as a systematic phenomenon, whatever its ultimate origin, it cannot be separated from the merging of the Proto-Semitic stops *d*, *t*, and *ṭ* with their spirantized counterparts *ḏ*, *ṯ*, and *ṯ̣* (*ẓ*),[5] a merger which is clearly to be dated sometime between the end of Old Aramaic and early Elephantine Aramaic. Spirantization could not have been operative in Old Aramaic,[6] whereas the appearance of at least traces of it in all of the later Aramaic dialects indicates that it must have been a feature of Imperial Aramaic.

Objections on other than chronological grounds are numerous, however. The only stops that have been subjected to a complete study are the velars *k* and *g*, and with good reason.[7] Knudsen has shown conclusively that in many words a spelled "k" alternates with "h." He concludes that, at least in our written sources, the alternation is free, but he claims that the phonetic environment necessary for this alternation is either a preceding vowel (even of a preceding word, as in Masoretic Biblical Hebrew and Aramaic) or the presence of

3. Knudsen, in *Lišān mitḫurti,* pp. 147 ff., W. von Soden, "Die Spirantisierung von Verschlusslauten im Akkadischen," *JNES* XXVII (1968) 214 ff., *GAG Ergänz.*, pp. 4** f., and von Soden and Röllig, *Das akkadische Syllabar* (2d ed.; Rome, 1967) pp. xix f., and bibliography there.

4. Knudsen, in *Lišān mitḫurti,* p. 155.

5. This observation of Schaeder's (*Iranische Beiträge* I [Halle, 1930] 244, and see n. 6 below) has received less recognition than is rightfully due it.

6. Once one accepts the inescapable conclusion that Old Aramaic (and old Mesopotamian Aramaic) used the graphemes for the sibilants to represent the Proto-Semitic spirants for which the Canaanite alphabet had no symbols, it is obvious that a spirantized pronunciation of the stops could not have occurred in Old Aramaic, for if spirantization had occurred, *d*, *t*, and *ṭ* would have been confused with the corresponding spirants, still separate graphemes, in the orthography. For bibliography and a list (not without errors) of the early spellings see F. Altheim and R. Stiehl, *Die Araber in der alten Welt* I (Berlin, 1964) 213 ff., though their conclusion that the phonology of Old Aramaic is due to Canaanite influence, cannot be accepted, as has been demonstrated by E. Y. Kutscher, *A History of Aramaic* (Jerusalem, 1972-73) p. 15, among others.

7. Knudsen, in *Lišān mitḫurti*.

another identical velar. Unfortunately, the sound laws he proposes bear little relationship to his examples, and a complete re-analysis of the material is in order. Certainly of greater significance in the Old Babylonian examples of *k/h* interchange is the presence of an unvoiced sibilant in the vicinity of the velar.[8] There is no significant evidence for the alternation *g/h* except for the Neo-Babylonian spelling of Aramaic /ḥ/ as "g" in a syllable *ḥuL* (*L* = labial).[9] Knudsen does note correctly that double /kk/ is never spelled "hh."

There is also evidence for an alternation *t/š* (only in cases where [ṯ] is meant?), which is of limited occurrence, restricted to certain words and primarily found in Old Babylonian.[10] There is no significant evidence for a spirantized *d*, and the evidence for the labials is restricted to the use of signs that bear a labial stop to represent the phoneme /w/, foreign to Sumerian.

It is regretable that von Soden, in his latest statement on the problem, apparently based on Knudsen's conclusions, has given the impression that postvocalic position is a precondition for spirantization in Akkadian.[11] There is no support for such a statement. His previous position, that whatever general rules there might be remain undiscovered but are clearly different from those of Aramaic, is to be preferred.[12] Thus, for the present at least, there exists no convincing evidence that there was ever any systematic spirantization of any of the stops in any Akkadian dialect.[13]

8. Cf. J. Renger, "Überlegungen zum akkadischen Syllabar," *ZA* LXI (1971) 30.

9. Discussed by von Soden, "Aramäisches *ḥ* erscheint im Spätbabylonischen vor *m* auch als *g*," *AfO* XIX (1959-60) 149; see also von Soden, "Aramäische Wörter in neuassyrischen und neu- und spätbabylonischen Texten. Ein Vorbericht," *Or*. n.s. XXXVII (1968) 271.

10. See von Soden and Röllig, *Syllabar* (2d ed.) pp. xix f. There is reason to believe that there is no conditional or free alternation here but merely spelling variations to represent constant [t].

11. *GAG Ergänz.*, p. 4**.

12. *Syllabar* (2d ed.) p. xx; *JNES* XXVII 214.

13. All students of the problem claim that cuneiform spelling conventions mask the phonetic realization of the various phonemes, and that spirantization must have been more extensive. This is certainly true. It is also true that our modern multiplication of syllabic values for the cuneiform signs has tended to obscure phonetic realities. Nevertheless, at present there is only a small amount of evidence for a minimal amount of insignificant variation, differing in each of the various dialects. If /d/ were spirantized in Old Babylonian, for example, one would expect to find it varying orthographically with "z," just as both "z" and "d" signs are used for Proto-Semitic /ḏ/ in Amorite (cf. J. C. Greenfield, "Amurrite, Ugaritic, and Canaanite," *Proceedings*, p. 94, n. 9, p. 95, n. 13).

Surprisingly overlooked by most of these scholars has been the analogous situation of Neo-Babylonian /m/ where the evidence overwhelmingly indicates that every non-lengthened /m/ in intervocalic position was pronounced [w] (see Phonology in Chap. IV). This same evidence, that of Aramaic loanwords and transcriptions, gives no indication of any other spirantization of Akkadian phonemes and in fact proves that Akkadian could not have been the origin of Aramaic spirantization.[14]

The theory of an Akkadian origin for spirantization must be rejected.

The Loss of Laryngeals

In the course of their development, many of the Semitic languages lost some of their distinctive laryngeal phonemes. As an element of the general trend toward simplification of the phonemic inventory, most of the losses may be regarded as a natural linguistic development; but in certain cases this weakening or loss must be attributed to foreign influence, almost always in the form of a substratum.

It is generally assumed, no doubt correctly, that the early loss of the laryngeals in Akkadian is due, at least in part, to the Sumerian substratum. It is reasonable to suppose that if in a similar fashion a large enough Akkadian-speaking group formed the basic population of a new Aramaic dialect area, that Aramaic dialect should in time give evidence of a weakening of laryngeals.

Although there is confusion or weakening of some of the laryngeals in most Aramaic dialects, it is precisely in Mandaic and Babylonian Talmudic that this condition is most pronounced, a situation which must result from the earlier Akkadian-speaking substratum in southern Mesopotamia.[15] There is, on the other hand, no reason to regard the weakening of the laryngeals in some of the Palestinian dialects as due to Akkadian influence. Greek influence, however, may be partly responsible.[16]

14. One must also ask if the Akkadian loanwords in Aramaic give any indications or counterindications of spirantization in Aramaic but not in Akkadian; see Spirantization in Chap. IV. B. Batto, "DINGIR.IŠ.HI and Spirantization in Hebrew," *JSS* XVI (1971) 33-34, has shown that the Akkadian transliteration of the theophoric element ^{D}IS.HI in personal names, long read as ^{D}*mil-hi* (i.e., West Semitic *milki*) and taken to indicate spirantization of the *k*, is now to be read ^{D}*Iš-šar*.

15. Cf. E. Y. Kutscher, *The Language and Linguistic Background of the Isaiah Scroll* (Jerusalem, 1959) p. 402. The weakening does not at first sight appear to be as severe in BT as in Mandaic, but this is almost certainly due to the more conservative spellings of the Jewish scribes.

16. All the evidence has been carefully collected by Kutscher, *Isaiah Scroll*, pp. 42 ff., 57 ff., and especially 402 f., who suggests a

In a limited number of Mandaic words, /a/ before original /ᶜ/ or /h/ changes to /e/. Naturally, this cannot be due to the influence of Akkadian, for, although a similar sound shift occurred there, it was millennia earlier than the shift in Mandaic.[17] Mandaic forms of originally third guttural verbs that have a final î vowel are formed by analogy to verbs IIIy.

Nasalization

A significant feature of several of the Aramaic dialects is the dissimilation of a geminated consonant by initial nasalization, expressed orthographically by "n." Though occurring elsewhere in the Semitic and Indo-European language families,[18] it is a salient feature of the Babylonian dialect of Akkadian, found occasionally in Old Babylonian and reaching full development in Middle Babylonian.[19] The origin of this feature is unknown, however, and it may well be a phonetic feature common to a group of languages around Babylonia including Amorite and the early southeastern dialects of Aramaic.[20]

The distribution of this feature in Aramaic is distinctive. It is totally absent from Old Aramaic, occurring first in Imperial Aramaic.[21] Even etymological /n/, which is as-

Greek origin. Since neither Imperial Aramaic nor Syriac shows any significant indication of this phenomenon, it cannot be considered a general Aramaic tendency, and thus, where it occurs outside of BT and Mandaic, cannot be assigned to Akkadian or Persian influence (contra S. Morag, review, *Kiryat Sepher* XXXVI [1951] 27). The limited confusion of laryngeals in the local Aramaic dialects of Assyria may rightfully be considered the result of Akkadian influence (cf. W. Baumgartner, "Zur Mandäerfrage," *HUCA* XXIII [1950-51] 47.)

17. Contra Rimalt, "Wechselbeziehungen zwischen dem Aramäischen und dem Neubabylonischen," *WZKM* XXXIX (1932) 100. See *MG*, p. 16.

18. C. Brockelmann, *Grundriss der vergleichenden Grammatik der semitischen Sprachen* (Berlin, 1908) § 90. Cf. Kutscher, in *JSS* X 38.

19. The best analysis of this feature in Babylonian is J. Aro, *Studien zur mittelbabylonischen Grammatik* (*St.Or.* XX [Helsinki, 1955]) p. 37.

20. The Mesopotamian Amorite personal names in cuneiform sources of the second millennium present a picture which can only be described as free variation. Original /n/ is found both assimilated and non-assimilated, and nasalization of a doubled consonant may or may not occur. (Cf. I. J. Gelb, "La lingua degli Amoriti," *AANL, Rendiconti*, Classe. . . Morali, Series VIII, Vol. XIII [1958] p. 151, and H. Huffmon, *Amorite Personal Names in the Mari Texts: A Structural and Lexical Study* [Baltimore, 1965] p. 301) Assimilation appears to be more frequent. We also find non-assimilation of original /n/ in verbal forms in the West Semitic names from Palestine in the Amarna period (see W. F. Albright, "An Archaic Hebrew Proverb in an Amarna Letter from Central Palestine," *BASOR*, No. 89 (1943) p. 31, n. 17.

21. It must be remembered that a distinctive feature of Imperial

similated in Old Aramaic, appears unassimilated again in Imperial Aramaic.[22] The other dialect where this feature is frequent is Mandaic. Attempts to deduce western origins for the Mandeans on this basis have not been productive.[23] In Mandaic as in Imperial Aramaic it is almost certainly of Babylonian origin (at least in the geographic sense of "Babylonian"). In the other later dialects where less frequent dissimilation occurs (Qumran, Targums, Nabatean, Hatran, Palmyran, Syriac, loans in Armenian),[24] it is certainly only an orthographic remnant of Imperial Aramaic.[25]

Dissimilation of Emphatics

Another characteristic of Mandaic that has been linked to the West by some scholars is the dissimilation of /q/ to /k/ when preceding /ṣ/ or /ṭ/, best known in Mandaic in the important word *kušṭâ*.[26] The first occurrence of such dissimilation in Aramaic is in the BR-RKB inscription (*KAI*, No. 216) from Samʾal, *kyṣʾ*, "summer." It occurs in one of the Nerab inscriptions (the verb *qṭl* > *kṭl*) and is frequent in the proverbs of Ahiqar.[27] Of the later dialects, only Man-

Aramaic dissimilation is that of /ᶜᶜ/ in forms of the root *ᶜll*, which could hardly be of Akkadian origin.

22. Note that the preservation of /n/ and nasalization are prevalent in the Ahiqar proverbs but absent in the Hermopolis letters; cf. J. C. Greenfield, "Dialect Traits in Early Aramaic," *Leš*. XXXII (1968) 365 ff.; E. Y. Kutscher, "The Hermopolis Papyri," *IOS* I (1971) 106.

23. Most recently discussed by R. Macuch in "Anfänge der Mandäer," in Altheim and Stiehl, *Die Araber in der Alten Welt* II (Berlin, 1965) 84 ff. The suggestion of Spitaler, decisively refuted there by Macuch, that the "n" is only a spelling convention to indicate consonantal length, no longer needs to be seriously considered. The evidence suggests, however, that precisely the reverse may be true, that nasalization was always present but often, just as in Old Persian cuneiform, not written. Note the Aramaic spelling *ḥbš* for (Assyrian!) cuneiform *ha-am-bu-su* (*DEA*, No. 12).

24. Targ. Onkelos only once; cf. G. Dalman, *Grammatik des judisch-palästinischen Aramäisch* (reprint; Darmstadt, 1960) p. 102. For Armenian see Brockelmann, *Grundriss* I 245. Nasalization is also found rarely in the Pehlevi logograms; cf. E. Ebeling, *Das aramäisch-mittelpersische Glossar Frahang-i-Pahlavik im Lichte der assyriologischen Forschung* (*MAOG*, Vol. XIV, 1 [Leipzig, 1941]) p. 111.

25. The occurrences and supposed occurrences have been discussed by Kutscher in "The Language of the 'Genesis Apocryphon': A Preliminary Study," *Scripta Hierosolymitana* IV (1965) 19 f., and *JSS* X 37 ff. Note his important observation that the rare attestations of this phenomenon in Galilean Aramaic are in non-Galilean Aramaic contexts.

26. For the argument see *AF*, p. 245, and Macuch, in Altheim and Stiehl, *Die Araber in der alten Welt* II 103 f. For the phonetic feature see *HM*, pp. 74 f., and *MG* § 42.

27. P. Leander, *Laut- und Formenlehre des Ägyptisch-Aramäischen* (Goteborg, 1928) p. 17.

daic has it as a regular feature of the language.[28] Not surprisingly, Akkadian origins for this morphophonemic feature have been suggested, but there is little to support this position.[29]

According to the well known rule of the incompatibility of root consonants in Akkadian, two different emphatics cannot occur in the same verbal root, the so-called Geer's Law.[30] But there are several reasons why this Akkadian sound change was probably not the cause of the Aramaic change. In Akkadian it is a law of root formation alone and was probably no longer functioning as part of the language in the first millennium. This is demonstrated by examples of assimilation of non-emphatic consonants to emphatics such as in *iqtabi* > *iqṭabi*.[31] Furthermore, there is an order of precedence in Akkadian: /q/ becomes /k/ before /ṣ/ but /ṭ/ becomes /t/ in the presence of /q/ (or /ṣ/), whereas in the Aramaic examples it is only initial /q/ that dissimilates, even before /ṭ/, the reverse of the Akkadian change. Thus, one must discount the possibility of Akkadian origins for this trait in Aramaic in general. The extent of its preservation in Mandaic, however, may be partly due to the Akkadian-speaking substratum.

MORPHOLOGY

There is no lack of disagreement among linguists over the processes by which grammatical features may be borrowed by one language from another.[32] In general the evidence suggests that in cases where there is significant bilingualism such transference can occur. Where contact is more limited, morphological and syntactic borrowings are quite rare and almost certainly can occur on the morphological level only when a number of words with the same foreign morpheme are borrowed from which the meaning of the individual morpheme can be abstracted. Similarly on the syntactic level, influence is often assumed to be found only when several similarly constructed two- or three-word semantic units are borrowed, with

28. In the later dialects, aside from the well known occurrence of *kšṭ* in Eastern Neo-Aramaic, traces of this dissimilation occur in Galilean Aramaic (cf. E. Y. Kutscher, "Studies in Galilean Aramaic I," *Tarbiz* XXI [1951] 202) and in BT (see above, s.v. *kamāṣu*).

29. H. L. Ginsberg, "Aramaic Dialect Problems II," *AJSL* LII (1936) 96.

30. Cf. *GAG* § 51*e*, and Chap. II, s.v. *suqāqu*.

31. *GAG* §§ 26*e*, 90*g*

32. Cf. Els Oksaar, "Bilingualism," in *Current Trends in Linguistics* IX (The Hague, 1972) 492.

the obvious exception, of course, of the case of translation language.[33]

Shaphel

In spite of the discovery of Ugaritic, a North West Semitic language which uses the shaphel as the common causative conjugation, and the fact that only a small number of the verbs with shaphel forms in Aramaic could possibly be related to Akkadian, claims that the use of the shaphel in Aramaic results from Akkadian influence and even such statements as "Most Aramaic causatives with *š*-prefix seem to be loan-words from Akkadian. . ." are still to be found in the literature.[34]

A complete study of the shaphel in Aramaic (and Hebrew) was recently published by C. Rabin.[35] Unfortunately he chose to omit from his study those few Aramaic verbs with initial *s* rather than *š*, but even the most cursory perusal of his contribution should suffice to convince anyone that no Akkadian influence is to be sought after here. In any case, it would seem that there are far too few borrowed Akkadian shaphels in Aramaic to have served as the basis for a morphological borrowing.[36]

As pointed out by Rabin, many of the shaphel forms in Aramaic and Hebrew lack a corresponding non-prefixed form of the root;[37] that is to say they are not used as functioning causative stems in the language and that accordingly one must not think in terms of two inherited causative formations in Aramaic. He proposed that all shaphel forms not borrowed from Akkadian were borrowed from another North West Semitic language, which he thinks is probably Amorite. The reasoning behind his argument is fundamentally sound; it is, however,

33. L. Bloomfield, *Language* (London, 1935) p. 454; C. F. Hockett, *A Course in Modern Linguistics* (New York, 1958) pp. 409, 414 f.; L. Deroy, *L'Emprunt linguistique* (Paris, 1956) pp. 102 ff., 109 ff. On the morphological level, at least, this rule does not seem to hold true for the modern European languages, witness the many colloquial American English morphemes which have their origin in one word alone such as -ade, -cade, -teria (cf. H. L. Mencken, *The American Language, Supplement* I [New York, 1966] 352 ff.). Even in English, however, the great majority of borrowed productive morphemes are based on more than one word, and the exceptions may well be accounted for by the nature of modern-day communications.

34. K. Deller with M. Dahood, review of Moscati, *Comparative Grammar*, *Or.* n.s. XXXIV (1965) 41.

35. "The Nature and Origin of the Šafᶜel in Hebrew and Aramaic," *Eretz Israel* IX (1969) 148-58.

36. Rabin (*ibid.*) considers only *šyzb* and *šyṣy* to be certain Akkadianisms. As discussed above, the loanword status of the latter is subject to doubt as well (see s.v. *šuṣû*).

37. *Ibid.*, p. 157.

very unlikely that Mesopotamian Amorite was the source of these shaphel forms, for the usual causative conjugation there was the haphel, as in Aramaic.[38] But the spread of the shaphel forms into the standard Aramaic dialects and Hebrew from other North West Semitic languages which used the shaphel as the causative (Ugaritic and other as yet unknown early dialects) is quite probable.[39]

The *l/n* Imperfect Prefix

One of the characteristics of Eastern Aramaic is the use of *l* or *n* in the prefix of the third person imperfect verbal forms (instead of *y*), a feature frequently attributed to the influence of Akkadian *lū*, used in asseverative and jussive verbal constructions.[40] In his discussion of this, H. L. Ginsberg concluded that "Accadian influence was at most only a contributing factor in the evolution of this feature."[41] His main argument is that the prefix *l-* was already used in the jussive sense in Samalian and in the Aššur Ostracon with syncope of the *y-*,[42] and that thus only its use without jussive force is peculiar to Eastern Aramaic, and even in this latter usage the Aramaic and Akkadian forms correspond only roughly.[43]

A restatement of the data seems appropriate here. Akkadian has a jussive verbal construction known as the precative in which the optative particle *lū* combines with preterite

38. While there are a few Amorite names that seem to yield to interpretation best as shaphels, the common causative is certainly haphel (cf. Huffmon, *Amorite Personal Names*, p. 68; Gelb, in *AANL, Rendiconti* XIII 159.

39. Two tentative pictures of this process can be imagined. Either all shaphels (and saphels) in Aramaic are the result of outside influence, or among those that had been borrowed (from all sources) there were enough with attested verbal cognates in Aramaic to have allowed the realization that this was indeed a kind of causative conjugation and thus to have served as the model for the formation of a new "causative" form.

40. *AF*, pp. 104, 173; C. Gordon, "Šamši-Adad's Military Texts from Mari," *Ar.Or.* XVIII (1950) 201, n. 6; E. Y. Kutscher, "The Language of the Hebrew and Aramaic Letters of Bar-Koseva and His Contemporaries; A. The Aramaic Letters," *Leš.* XXV (1960-61) 128.

41. H. L. Ginsberg, "Aramaic Studies Today," *JAOS* LXII (1942) 234, n. 26.

42. This construction is now known from Aramaic personal names in cuneiform transliteration as well; cf. W. von Soden, "Das akkadische *t*-Perfekt und sumerische Verbalformen mit *ba-*, *imma-*, und *u-*," *AS*, No. 16 (Chicago, 1965) p. 104, n. 2.

43. Ginsberg's other arguments are not as significant: He admits the uncertain nature of his second point, the use of *l-* with *hwy* in BA, to which Kutscher has given a completely different interpretation (see below, n. 46.).

verbs yielding forms like *liprus*, "let him cut," certainly quite similar in shape to the Aramaic jussive construction mentioned above. There is an asseverative particle *lū*, which can be used with any verbal form, but which does not regularly enter into crasis with the initial vowel of the following verb. This asseverative is found commonly only in royal inscriptions.[44]

In Aramaic, in addition to the examples of the jussive in Samalian and the Aššur Ostracon, *l-* is used in BA and Qumran Aramaic both in the jussive and in the indicative of the verb *hwy*.[45] The usual explanation, that this is an intentional scribal change in order to prevent orthographic and/or phonetic similarity to the ineffable divine name, is probably correct. Even so, Kutscher has argued that this practice could only have developed in an area where the use of an *l-* imperfect prefix of some sort was known, that is, in Eastern Aramaic, since but for the old Samalian dialect, there is no other evidence of *l-*, even with the jussive, in Western Aramaic.[46]

A more precise statement of the distribution of this feature in Eastern Aramaic is also desirable. No relevant forms occur in the Uruk incantation. In Hatran the imperfect prefix is consistently *l-*, but in the contemporary Old Syriac texts, which are from farther west, *y-* is still used. We first find *n-* in the middle of the third century A.D. and then generally in Syriac, where there is no trace of *l-*.[47] In Mandaic *n-* is also the most usual form, but *l-* occurs in the earlier texts, alternating with *n-* in both jussive and non-jussive forms.[48]

44. *GAG* § 81*f*. Crasis does occur, but apparently only when the initial vowel of the verb is *u*. The optative particle *lū* is also found commonly with stative verbs but also often in nominal sentences (cf. *GAG* § 121*c*).

45. In Qumran: 4Q Mes.Ar., 1Q 21 and 11QTgJob.

46. E. Y. Kutscher, in *Leš*. XXV 128. The examples adduced from Galilean Aramaic by Dalman, *Grammatik*, p. 264, are certainly corruptions from BT. Their limitation primarily to modal usages is not indicative of authenticity, for this is precisely the correct usage of the imperfect in late Aramaic; see n. 51.

47. See Klaus Beyer, "Der reichsaramäische Einschlag in der ältesten syrischen Literatur," *ZDMG* CXVI (1966) 243. Note that *l-* is used in the Jewish Aramaic text No. 151 from Dura dating from 200 A.D.; cf. J. T. Milik, "Parchemin judéo-araméen de Doura-Europos, an 200 AP. J.-C.," *Syria* XLV (1968) 97 ff., l. 18. As pointed out to me by E. Y. Kutscher, these early texts are of a legal nature and, as in such texts elsewhere, the use of *y-* may be a formulaic archaism.

48. *MG*, pp. 215 ff.; E. Yamauchi, *Mandaic Incantation Texts* (New Haven, 1967) p. 116, suggests that *l-* is jussive and *n-* indicative, but this is not obviously the case. They occur together only in one text (No. 31), and there they are used interchangeably. The example of a *y-* prefix in No. 22:94 is unique in Mandaic. In No. 30:30 read *ḏ* ⟨*lʾ*⟩ *lyštryʾ*.

In Babylonian Talmudic *l-* is the most common form, though *n-* occurs as well. There is some indication that the dialect of the early Babylonian Amoraim may have *y-*, but the possibilities of western influence exist here.[49] Imperial Aramaic influence or formulaic archaism is possible in the Jewish Aramaic magic bowls, which usually have *y-* and sometimes *n-* but never *l-*.[50]

This entire phenomenon cannot be separated from the restructuring of the tense system in the late Aramaic dialects. With the development of a new indicative present-future tense (i.e., the old participle), the old distinctions between jussive and imperfect were lost, and the single resulting form was used in modal, non-indicative functions (jussive, subjunctive).[51] As indicated by the preservation of *l-* as well as by the forms of the pronominal suffixes discussed below, Eastern Aramaic used the old jussive forms to accomplish this function, whereas in Western Aramaic the indicative forms were used. Thus, it would appear that, prior to this restructuring, third person masculine jussives with *l-* or *n-* were the norm, at least in Mesopotamian Aramaic.[52] In spite of the anciently attested, authentic Aramaic jussive prefix *l-*, the replacement of the simple non-*l-* jussive by composite *l-* forms may well have been influenced by the Akkadian precative construction, which is the only way that the jussive idea can be expressed by prefixed verbal forms in that language.

The Loss of the *n*-Bearing Pronominal Suffixes

In Old Aramaic and Imperial Aramaic the pronominal suffixes of the indicative imperfect (as opposed to the jussive and imperative) are preceded by *-(i)nn-*, but in Eastern Aramaic this does not occur, except for the (usually independent) third

49. See J. N. Epstein, *Grammar of Babylonian Aramaic* (Tel Aviv, 1960) pp. 13 ff.

50. Epstein (*ibid.*) claims that the Pehlevi logograms use *n* as well as *y* and that once in the Sassanian logograms one finds *l-* with *hwy*, just as in BA, but I have been unable to locate his source.

51. Cf. Kutscher, "Samaritan Aramaic," *Tarbiz* XXXVII (1967-68) 402. Note that the earliest examples of the *l-* prefix in Hatran are all with jussive and subjunctive verbs (texts 23, 53, 74, 79, 101).

52. Why did *l-* become *n-* in some dialects? This difficult problem is not solved merely by the observation that initial *l* and *n* alternate quite freely in Babylonian Aramaic. Note that BT has *nḥmʾ* and *nqṭ* corresponding to *lʾhmʾ* and *lqṭ* in Mandaic (the *l* is original; cf. *HM*, p. 51), but in the verbal prefix *l-* is most frequent in BT and *n-* in Mandaic. Syriac, which otherwise knows only the shift [n] > [l] (T. Nöldeke, *Compendious Syriac Grammar*, J. A. Chrichton, trans. [London, 1904] § 31*b*) has only the prefix *n-*. In the final analysis it may be that the shift to *n-* was prompted merely by the fact that *n-* was already familiar as the imperfect prefix of the first person plural.

person plural object pronoun.[53] Ginsberg considers this "surely due to the Accadian influence."[54] There is little if any reason to suspect such Akkadian influence here, however, for as described above this merely represents the preference for the old jussive form for the new non-indicative function of the prefixed verb. In Western Aramiac, on the other hand, the forms used for this function are uniformly those of the old indicative.

The Plural Determined Suffix -ê

The ending -ê on the plural determined noun, a third distinguishing characteristic of Eastern Aramaic, is also frequently attributed to the influence of Akkadian, in which, during the first millennium, the common plural ending was -ē in all cases.[55] In contrast to the *l/n* prefix, this was an early and widespread feature in Aramaic. Its first isolated occurrence is the form *ᶜmmᵓ* in Ahiqar. It occurs in the Uruk incantation and the early Eastern texts (Hatran and Old Syriac) and even, infrequently, in Palmyran and in targumic texts.[56] The objections raised to the view that this feature must be from Akkadian are that -ê could be a Common Semitic abstract ending, that it might possibly be the result of a natural phonetic development,[57] or, more likely, that it developed on

53. Compare, however, the Mandaic second person plural suffix *-nkwn* after all verbs, though this is probably modeled after the third person plural suffix. In fifth-century Syriac, traces of *-inn-* are still to be found; cf. K. Beyer, in *ZDMG* CXVI 250, where he attributes it to "Reichs- oder westaramaischer Einschlag."

54. *JAOS* LXII 234, n. 26.

55. There is hardly any uniformity of opinion, however. Cf. Ginsberg, in *AJSL* LII 101, n. 6, and *AF*, pp. 173 f.; K. Beyer, in *ZDMG* CXVI 247, n. 10; J. Blau, "The Origins of Open and Closed e in Proto-Syriac," *BSOAS* XXXII (1969) 8. Ginsberg's suggestion that the Akkadian morpheme could be from Aramaic is quite improbable, for in the early Assyrian dialects -ē was already the ending of the oblique plural (cf. *GAG* paradigm 1).

56. Franz Rosenthal, *Die Sprache der palmyrenischen Inschriften und ihre Stellung innerhalb des Aramäischen* (*MVAG*, Vol. XLI [Leipzig, 1936]) p. 76. A. Tal, "The Language of the Targum of the Former Prophets and Its Position within the Aramaic Dialects" (Diss.; Hebrew University, 1971) pp. 90 ff., has scrutinized the evidence of the occurrence of -ê in Targum Jonathan and has shown that those occurrences which cannot be explained as either errors in scribal transmission or assimilations to nearby construct forms are limited to specific sets of nouns, primarily the terms *ᶜzy*, *twry* and *gyty* as collectives (as opposed to regular plural forms used when an actual plural is required) and the frequent *byt ᵓsyry*, which he considers an eastern loan. The observation that in these texts the semantic value of the morpheme -ê differs from that of the regular plural affix certainly merits further research.

57. The second possibility seems much more probable than the first, whose difficulties were discussed by Rosenthal, *Sprache*, p. 76, n. 6.

the analogy of the *-ê* ending of plural determined gentilic forms.[58] Indeed, I would tend to view the latter as the ultimate origin of the *-ê* ending, but the preservation of this morpheme as a characteristic only of Eastern Aramaic might be partly due to Akkadian.

The Infinitive of the Derived Conjugations

In Babylonian Talmudic, Mandaic, and Neo-Syriac, the infinitives of the derived conjugations end in *-ôCê*, for example the pael *(m)parrôqê*. The similarity between this Aramaic form of limited distribution and the Akkadian infinitive *purrusu* (or even closer, the Assyrian form *parrusu*) was noted by Barth,[59] though I know of no suggestion that Akkadian influence was responsible here. The final *-ê* of the Aramaic forms is difficult to explain in any case,[60] as is the long vowel of the second syllable. The Neo-Syriac peal infinitive *prâqâ*, instead of the Common Aramaic *mipraq*, is likewise similar, in fact identical, to the Akkadian infinitive of the simple stem *parāsu*; but this is also the original Hebrew infinitive absolute form and is quite common as an abstract verbal noun in the other Aramaic dialects.[61]

The Plural Ending *-ân(în)*

In Old Aramaic, the Aššur Ostracon and dockets, and Imperial Aramaic texts from Egypt, the plural masculine absolute suffix is almost always spelled *-n* rather than *-yn*. This fact led Ginsberg to speculate that since the latter two groups of texts almost always expressed internal *î* or *û* in other cases with a vowel letter, this is not merely an historical spelling for *-în* but represents the ending *-ân*.[62] Rosenthal refuted this position with what Ginsberg himself terms a "devasting

58. The gentilic form *-âyê(âʾê)* is certainly a natural Aramaic development, a simplification of the overly cumbersome **-ayayyâ*. From there, the analogy *kaśdây* : *kaśdâyâ* : *kaśdâyê* with *bîš* : *bîšâ* : X is solved, of course, only by *bîšê*. The Ahiqar form *ʿmmʾ* offers an indirect proof of this explanation. Analogy frequently operates where semantic association is strong, and here we see that it is precisely in the word "peoples" that this ending, developed from the proper names of peoples, first occurs.

59. J. Barth, *Die Nominalbildung in den semitischen Sprachen* (Leipzig, 1894) pp. 153 f.

60. Discussed by Barth, *ibid.*

61. *Ibid.*, pp. 59 f., and Nöldeke, *Compendious Syriac Grammar*, p. 70. Peal infinitives without initial *m-* are known from Old Aramaic (cf. *lśgb*, Sefire IB 32) and Imperial Aramaic (*lʾmr*, frequent in the Aššur Ostracon and in Egyptian Aramaic).

62. Ginsberg, in *AJSL* LII 99 ff.

critique."[63] Not only is *-yn* found in Egyptian Aramaic in the same texts with *-n*, but in one text even the same word, "fish" (pl.), is spelled both *nwnn* and *nwnyn*.[64] Ginsberg still maintains, however, that at least in some cases "this view still deserves the serious consideration of sane men."[65]

Whether or not the masculine plural ending *-ân* is concealed in the spellings discussed above, the ending certainly existed, found in Aramaic in the double plural *-ânîn*, limited to certain types of nouns.[66] The plural ending *-ānu/i* (*-ānu/ī*) is frequent in Akkadian as well, indicating, according to the generally accepted view, a plural of individual units.[67] In light of the occurrence of *-ân* as the common plural ending in Geʾez and the remnants of *-ân* in Arabic, Aramaic, and Hebrew,[68] any suggestion that this ending might be other than Common Semitic is very dubious. Nevertheless, since the ending in question is highly productive in the Neo-Babylonian period[69] and is especially frequent in the modern Eastern Aramaic dialects,[70] an Akkadian influence affecting the frequency of use of this plural morpheme cannot be excluded.[71]

The Imperial Aramaic Passive

Another characteristic of Imperial Aramaic is the preservation of the internal passive verbs, limited almost exclusive-

63. Ginsberg, in *JAOS* LXII 237. Further (and to my mind, conclusive) evidence against Ginsberg's position has been collected by Kutscher, *A History of Aramaic*, p. 67 n.

64. *AP*, No. 45.

65. In *JAOS* LXII 237.

66. See Nöldeke, *Compendious Syriac Grammar*, § 74; Brockelmann, *Grundriss* I 451. In addition to the lists of such nouns found in the grammars, see I. Löw, "Lexikalische Miszellen," in *Festschrift zum siebzigsten Geburtstage David Hoffman's* (Berlin, 1914) pp. 135 ff.

67. First stated by A. Goetze, "The Akkadian Masculine Plural in -ānū/ī and Its Semitic Background," *Language* XXII (1946) 121-30; cf. *GAG* § 61*i*; I. M. Diakonoff, *Semito-Hamitic Languages* (Moscow, 1965) pp. 63 f.; Sabatino Moscati, *et al.*, *An Introduction to the Comparative Grammar of the Semitic Languages* (Wiesbaden, 1964) par. 12.42.

68. Brockelmann, *Grundriss*, pp. 450 f.; for Afro-Asiatic cf. I. M. Diakonoff, *Semito-Hamitic Languages*, pp. 63 f.

69. Note that it is the accepted plural ending on foreign titles; cf. W. Eilers, *Iranische Beamtennamen in der keilschriftlichen Überlieferung* I (*AbKM*, Vol. XXV 5 [Leipzig, 1940]) 9, n. 1.

70. The normal plural ending in modern Mandaic is *-âna* (*HM*, p. 225), while in the Neo-Syriac dialects *-ânê* is far more frequent than it is in the earlier dialects (see the partial list of nouns in A. J. Maclean, *Grammar of the Dialects of Vernacular Syriac* [Cambridge, 1895] p. 46 f.).

71. Cf. Ginsberg, in *AJSL* LII 101. Ginsberg's alternative suggestion, that the Akkadian ending was borrowed from West Semitic, can no longer be maintained in light of the occurrence of *-ānu* in OA and OB (cf. *GAG* § 61*i*).

ly to the perfect and participle.[72] Ginsberg has also suggested Akkadian influence here. Indeed, the similarity between the Imperial Aramaic internal passive and the Akkadian permansive does seem "too striking to be accidental."[73] The gradual disappearance of the internal passive in Aramaic and its replacement by the reflexive forms was a general Aramaic development which had already begun prior to the earliest inscriptions, but the pattern of the preservation in Imperial Aramaic, especially the assimilation of the passive perfect of the simple conjugation to the passive participle, could well be due to Akkadian influence.

SYNTAX

The Genitive Construction

In all of the Aramaic dialects, except for Old Aramaic,[74] the relative pronoun *dî/d-* is also used as a genitive particle in place of the construct chain.[75] Since the first examples of this usage come from Mesopotamian Aramaic, where they are, in fact, nothing more than direct translations of Akkadian *ša*,[76] possible Akkadian influence in the development of this feature has been suggested.[77]

The intimate relationship between relative and genitive constructions in all of the Semitic languages suggests that both of these uses of the so-called determinative pronoun *dū/šū* were known in Proto-Semitic; accordingly, the absence of the genitive expansion in Old Aramaic must be taken to indicate only its comparative rarity in that dialect.[78] Nevertheless, in light of the ubiquitous use of genitive *zy* in Mesopotamian

72. F. Rosenthal, *A Grammar of Biblical Aramaic* (Wiesbaden, 1963) p. 44, states that "No passive forms of the imperfect happen to occur in BA," but in view of the fact that in all of Imperial Aramaic only one possible example of an imperfect passive is known (Hermopolis *ybl/ywbl*) and that in contrast Old Aramaic commonly uses the imperfect passive but not the perfect, the non-occurrence of the imperfect internal passive in BA is certainly more than just coincidental.

73. Ginsberg, in *AJSL* LII 99.

74. The one exception generally cited is Sefire III 7-8 *kl mlkyʾ zy sḥrty*, "all the kings of my vicinity." Comparison with the frequent Hebrew construction *ʾăšer sᵉḇîḇôt* strongly suggests, however, that *zy* functions as a relative in this case as well.

75. Cf. F. A. Pennacchietti, *Studi sui pronomi determinativi semitici* (Naples, 1968) pp. 11 f.

76. *Passim* in Assyrian weights, the Aššur Ostracon, and Assyrian and Babylonian tablets.

77. M. Z. Kaddari, "Construct State and *dī*- Phrases in Imperial Aramaic," *Proceedings*, p. 104; Kutscher, *A History of Aramaic*, pp. 104 ff.

78. Indeed, genitive *d-* is relatively rare in Ugaritic as well.

texts and in the Behistun inscription,[79] the rapid development of this feature in Aramaic must be ascribed to the influence of Akkadian. From there it became a fundamental feature of Imperial Aramaic "high style" (see below, p. 160).[80] Its presence in all of the later dialects would thus seem to be the result of a combination of natural development and influence of the literary language.[81]

A related issue is the common anticipatory genitive construction *brh zy/dy X*, "the son of X," corresponding to Akkadian *māršu ša* X. In Akkadian this construction is found not infrequently in OB and rarely in some of the other dialects, but it is most common in western texts (e.g. Ras Shamra) and NB/LB.[82] Especially in the latter it is often attributed to Aramaic influence.[83] Others consider the Akkadian construction to be an internal Akkadian development and the Aramaic to be under the influence of Akkadian.[84]

Since, as has been demonstrated, even the simple genitive use of *zy* was at best extremely rare in Old Aramaic, Aramaic influence on this Akkadian feature would seem to be out of the question. (Note that the anticipatory construction is not yet attested in Mesopotamian Aramaic.) Yet the frequency of the anticipatory suffix in NB/LB may well be the result of immanent development. It is generally recognized that the use of this type of genitive construction indicates a high degree of definiteness of the ruling noun. As in the case of similar constructions in Ethiopic,[85] the natural place for such a syntactic development would be in a language such as Akkadian, which lacks a definitizing morpheme.[86] Thus, it

79. For references see n. 77.

80. Note especially the difference in the frequency of this usage between the proverbs of Ahiqar and the framework story according to Kaddari, in *Proceedings*, p. 103. See below, p. 157.

81. Kaddari's conclusion (*ibid.*, p. 115)—that only the case where one of the members is determined and/or part of a syntagmatic structure was influenced by Akkadian, whereas "in the undeterminated type of B, where an original predication of identity can be re-established (as in the *genitivus materiae*, or *genitivus partitivus* relations), an immanent development can be assumed"—is probably on the right track. Further studies such as Kaddari's (and that of A. Goetze, review of Ravn, *Relative Clauses, JCS* I [1947] 75 f.), concentrating on Old Aramaic, Mesopotamian Aramaic, and Neo-Babylonian, should be helpful in shedding further light on this problem.

82. *GAG* § 138*j-l*.

83. *Ibid*. Cf. *AF*, pp. 38 f.

84. E. Y. Kutscher, review of Rosenthal, *Die aramäistische Forschung, Kiryat Sepher* XIX (1942-43) 178 f.

85. Cf. A. Dillmann, *Grammatik der äthiopischen Sprache* (Leipzig, 1899) § 172.

86. In light of the preponderance of the anticipatory construction

would seem that the development of this feature in Aramaic is to be ascribed at least partially to Babylonian influence.[87]

Word Order

In the Old Aramaic of Syria, the word order in the verbal sentence is the expected ancient Semitic type, in most cases verb-subject-object, with the order variable for purposes of emphasis. In Eastern Aramaic, beginning with the earliest Mesopotamian Aramaic texts and including Syriac, Mandaic, and Babylonian Talmudic, word order is much more free. Several scholars have noted that, except for certain important exceptions, Imperial Aramaic texts also have this free word order, whereas Western Aramaic is generally similar to Old Aramaic.[88]

Naturally, Akkadian is the most obvious possibility for the origin of this characteristic,[89] for, because of the strong influence of Sumerian, the verb-final position is the normal one in classical Akkadian.[90] Instead of a fixed word order, however, the Akkadian-Aramaic contact seems to have resulted in a rather free word order in both languages. Thus, although the classical Akkadian word order subject-object-verb is, to be sure, a common one in Imperial Aramaic, others, such as subject-verb-object, are equally common, especially in early texts (Nerab, Teima); and although the subject-verb-object order is quite frequent in the late Akkadian dialects as well,[91] Imperial Aramaic also uses word orders rather foreign to Akkadian, such as object-verb-subject.[92]

in peripheral Akkadian texts in the second millennium, Barton's suggestion that during this early period foreign, non-Semitic influence is involved may well be correct, at least for those peripheral areas (G. A. Barton, "On the Anticipatory Pronominal Suffix in Aramaic and Akkadian," *JAOS* XLVII [1927] 260 ff.)

87. Note that, as opposed to the general use of *ša* as a genitive particle, this is a specifically Babylonian feature, hence its absence in early (Assyrian!) Mesopotamian Aramaic texts.

88. See the bibliography in Yochanan Muffs, *Studies in the Aramaic Legal Papyri from Elephantine* (Leiden, 1969) p. 23 n. and J. C. Greenfield, in *Leš.* XXXII 363 f. The exceptions are the Elephantine legal texts and the Ahiqar proverbs. Note that the Hermopolis letters, which Greenfield considers a western dialect, have the free word order.

89. Cf. Ginsberg, in *AJSL* LII 98.

90. See *GAG* § 130*b*.

91. *Ibid.*, *c*. This change is generally ascribed to Aramaic influence, but it could well be a natural development in Akkadian, which had apparently been forced into an unnatural language pattern by its borrowing of this element of Sumerian syntax; cf. J. H. Greenberg, "Some Universals of Grammar with Particular Reference to the Order of Meaningful Elements," *Universals of Language* (Cambridge, 1966) pp. 76 ff.

92. Rosenthal, *Grammar*, p. 56; H. Bauer and P. Leander, *Grammatik des Biblisch-Aramäischen* (Halle, 1927) pp. 342 ff.; *GAG* § 130*f*.

Along with this relatively free word order, a distinctive construction of Imperial Aramaic (and to a lesser extent Eastern Aramaic) is the construction object-*l*+infinitive (e.g. BA *bytʾ dnh lmbnyh*, Ezra 5:9).[93] Although Aramaists generally ascribe an Akkadian origin to this feature as well,[94] such would not seem to be the case. The Akkadian infinitive constructions have been studied by Aro, who has concluded that an Akkadian origin for this Aramaic feature is unthinkable;[95] for in the Akkadian of the first millennium, even as early as Middle Assyrian, the old constructions in which the object precedes the infinitive were no longer common. The new forms used were *ana parās* (infinitive construct form) X and *ana parāsi/u ša* X, corresponding to the older North West Semitic form *l* + infinitive construct-object.[96] Thus, an Akkadian origin for this syntactic feature must be rejected.

The construction object-infinitive is, however, standard in Old Persian, as are verb-final constructions in general.[97] It would seem, therefore, that this element of Imperial Aramaic is due to Persian influence. Similarly, since this feature is clearly non-Akkadian, and in light of the fact that in pre-Achaemenid Imperial Aramaic the normal word order is subject-verb-object whereas subject-object-verb is only found later on, the latter construction, too, is almost certainly the result of Iranian rather than Akkadian influence.[98]

The Eastern Aramaic System of States

The last of the important characteristics of the dialects of Eastern Aramaic that separate them from earlier Aramaic and

93. Found in Qumran Hebrew as well; see n. 94.

94. See above, n. 88, and most recently Jean Carmignac, "Un aramaïsme biblique et qumrânien: l'infinitif placé après son complément d'objet," *RQ* V (1966) 503-20. Add to his bibliography Brockelmann's review rejecting his previous position against Akkadian origin and agreeing now with Bauer and Leander (review of H. H. Rowley, *The Aramaic of the Old Testament, MGWJ* LXXVI [1932] 86).

95. J. Aro, *Die akkadischen Infinitivkonstruktionen* (*St.Or.* XXVI [Helsinki, 1961]).

96. *Ibid.*, p. 351. It must be said that there are many NA and NB examples of object-inifinitive, many of them actually cited by Aro for other purposes throughout his book, which he apparently has overlooked in his summary of the constructions occurring in each period, but in any case the order infinitive-object is by far the most prevalent.

97. See Roland G. Kent, *Old Persian* (2d ed., rev.; New Haven, 1953) p. 96.

98. This is hardly unexpected. Compare the clearly Iranian influence on the use of passive verbal constructions in Imperial Aramaic; cf. Kutscher, "Two 'Passive' Constructions in Aramaic in the Light of Persian," *Proceedings*, pp. 132-51.

Western Aramaic is the loss of the determining force of the definite article. Since, as E. Y. Kutscher has pointed out to me (orally), the natural course of language development is toward the development of determination, not the loss of it, this feature must be the result of external influence.

H. L. Ginsberg correctly showed that what really happens in Eastern Aramaic is that the so-called "determined" or "emphatic" state of the noun, that form with the post-positive article *-â*, becomes the normal state, while the original absolute state is preserved only in certain usages, resulting in a threefold system of nominal states strikingly similar to the Akkadian pattern of *Status rectus*, *Status constructus*, and *Status absolutus*.[99] This situation has recently been discussed at length by Moscati, who has demonstrated that the Aramaic usages of the absolute match the Akkadian usages in almost every case,[100] the two most frequent and best known of which are the predicate adjective and the distributive repetition.[101]

A difficulty with the theory that this characteristic of Eastern Aramaic is due to the influence of Akkadian syntax was also recognized by Ginsberg. He pointed out that in Neo-Babylonian final short vowels had presumably dropped and that the resulting noun forms were identical in all three states for most nouns.[102] Thus, he concluded that "We therefore cannot date the East Aramaic reorganization of the statuses too late." But if it was an early influence, why is there no significant indication of this reorganization in earlier Ara-

99. Ginsberg, in *JAOS* LXII 234, n. 26 *ad 3*.

100. S. Moscati, "Lo stato assoluto dell'Aramaico orientale," *Annali Istituto Orientale di Napoli*, Sezione Linguistica, IV (1962) 79-83. For the Akkadian see *GAG* § 62*c* ff. and G. Buccellati, "An Interpretation of the Akkadian Stative as a Nominal Sentence," *JNES* XXVII (1968) 1 ff.

101. Ginsberg, in *JAOS* LXII 234, suggests as well that the use of an enclitic pronoun with the predicative participle, so common in Eastern Aramaic, also derives, perhaps as part of the predicate usage of the absolute state, from Akkadian, where the absolute state can be conjugated with the pronominal suffixes of the permansive verb. The Akkadian suffixes involved are those corresponding to the Aramaic perfect, however, and not forms of the independent pronouns. (I have already discussed a possible influence of the Akkadian construction on the Imperial Aramaic passive perfect; see above.) Further, such enclitic pronouns occur with predicate participles or adjectives in Western Aramaic, too, though to a lesser degree (see Dalman, *Grammatik*, p. 107). It seems to have been a natural development from the common Old Aramaic practice of placing a pronominal subject after its nominal predicate (see Fitzmyer, *Sefîre*, p. 162, and also the Aššur Ostracon).

102. See most recently David B. Weisberg, *Guild Structure and Political Allegiance in Early Achaemenid Mesopotamia* (New Haven, 1967) pp. 106 ff.

maic texts from Mesopotamia, not to mention Imperial Aramaic, where Ginsberg and others find so many eastern traits? In the Aššur ostracon the three states are correctly used. In the Uruk incantantion one does find incorrect use of the states, but precisely the reverse of that in later Eastern Aramaic, for the absolute is often used when the determined sense is required.[103]

A further difficulty lies in the fact that the characteristic uses of the absolute state (predicate, distributive, and after numerals) are also found in Western Aramaic and thus would seem to have been a systematic feature of general Aramaic prior to its contact with Akkadian.

Thus, at best only the neutralization of the determined—non-determined opposition can be ascribed to the influence of Akkadian. (The Uruk incantation is representative of this first stage.) As a result of the special functions allotted to the absolute state, the emphatic form naturally developed into the unmarked form.

The Use of *kî*

Corresponding to Syriac *kaḏ*, "when," Mandaic has the written form *kḏ* and Babylonian Talmudic uses *ky*, both of which are also used for the comparative preposition "like." In Neo-Babylonian, too, *kī* and *kī ša* function in both of these ways.[104] Since such a functional similarity could hardly be coincidental, some influence must be present. There is no reason to suspect that *k* + *dy*, "when," is other than a native Aramaic development;[105] thus, NB *kī ša*, "when," is almost certainly an Aramaism. Its use as a preposition, however, probably derives from the similar double use of Akkadian *kī*, which has a long history, although it is most frequently found in NB, after the longer form *kīma* drops from common use.[106]

The BT form, which has heretofore defied explanation, could easily be regarded as a loan from NB *kī*.[107] In light of the Mandaic form *kḏ*, however, one might venture to posit a development **keḏî* > *kî*,[108] and if so, only the prepositional

103. Cf. C. Gordon, "The Aramaic Incantation in Cuneiform," *AfO* XII (1937-39) 114. Note that Gordon ascribes this to Akkadian influence as well.

104. See M. Dietrich, "Untersuchungen zur Grammatik des Neubabylonischen I. Die neubabylonischen Subjunktionen," *Lišān mitḫurti* (*AOAT*, Vol. I [Neukirchen-Vluyn, 1969]) pp. 74 ff., 88 ff.

105. Cf. BH *kaʾăšer*.

106. See *AHw.*, pp. 468 f.

107. So E. Y. Kutscher, "Studies in Galilaean Aramaic," *Tarbiz* XXIII (1953) 36, n. 47. A loan from Hebrew is certainly out of the question.

108. For the elision of intervocalic (and postvocalic) *d* in BT (under Iranian influence?), see Epstein, *Grammar*, p. 18.

use of *k^{e}*d̲î* would have been borrowed, corresponding to the NB use of *kī ša* as a preposition. Another possibility is to regard the Mandaic written form *kd̲* (a ligature) as an historical spelling for a phonetic form such as [kĭ], the same form as in BT, and borrowed from NB.[109] Such an interpretation would appear to be supported by Modern Mandaic, where the corresponding form is *ke*, which, however, could well be a borrowing from Persian.[110]

The Interrogative Particle *mî*

In Babylonian Talmudic and Mandaic, declarative sentences are made interrogative when preceded by the particle *mî* (spelled *my* in BT; *mʿ*, *myʾ* and, as a proclitic, *my-* in Mandaic). This particle may well derive from the identical Akkadian enclitic particle *-mī*, itself probably a development of the interrogative pronoun *mīnu*, "what."[111] The change from an enclitic particle in Akkadian to initial position in Babylonian Aramaic can be explained as a substitution for the earlier Aramaic interrogative *h-*, or merely as a result of the tendency to avoid enclitic and second position particles in Babylonian Aramaic.[112]

109. Cf. Michael Schlesinger, *Satzlehre der aramäischen Sprache des babylonischen Talmuds* (Leipzig, 1928) pp. 247 ff.

110. Cf. *HM*, pp. 234, 452 ff., *MD*, p. 211. The form *kidbirku* cited in *MD*, p. 211, s.v. *ki*, as a *scripta plene* is to be regarded rather as a pnonetic writing of what would in normal orthography be *kd̲d̲birku*. Note that *d* is the enclitic variant of *d̲* when used after prepositions (cf. *MD*, p. 97).

111. Cf. *AHw.*, p. 650, *GAG* § 123*b*. Note that von Soden derives the Akkadian from the similar *-mâ*, suggesting that vowel harmony is the cause of the *i* vowel. Both forms are found in OB and SB but are apparently unknown in NA or NB texts. Even if *-mi* did not occur in those dialects, however, the Aramaic form may have developed directly from the pronoun *mīnu*. Most scholars try to derive the Aramaic particle in question from Aramaic *mâ*; indeed the BT form of the latter is *mʾy*, which might easily become *my*. Schlesinger, *Satzlehre*, p. 157, n. 2, claims that *mh* is found as a rhetorical interrogative particle in YT, and *my* is apparently attested in Palestinian Midrash, but until an investigation based on good manuscripts is available, *my* must be considered a characteristic of Babylonian Aramaic alone.

112. Cf. *MG*, p. 429.

IV

ANALYSIS AND CONCLUSIONS

PHONOLOGY

As discussed in Chapter I, the Akkadian loanwords in Aramaic offer the Assyriologist an approach to the phonemic and phonetic characteristics of the late Akkadian dialects not available through the medium of the cuneiform texts alone. Similarly, one hopes for new light on Aramaic phonology, specifically on the chronology of consonantal merging and vowel reduction. The following is an attempt to assemble the evidence on such matters derivable from a study of the loanwords. In addition to this material, the evidence offered by transliterations of Akkadian names in alphabetic script and of Aramaic and other names in cuneiform as well as that of the Aramaic loans in Akkadian has also been scrutinized. The few tablets with Greek transliterations of Akkadian and Sumerian date from very late times (*ca.* 100 B.C.?) and are of little value for our purposes.[1]

Stops

Labials

The following relevant phonetic changes are apparent from the cuneiform texts themselves (cf. *GAG* § 27): *b* > *p* sometimes in the environment of *š*, *ṣ*, or *n*. Initial *b* becomes *p* in some NA words. NB has "b" where other dialects have "m" in forms of *hab/maṣīru*, "a rodent."[2]

In alphabetic transcriptions of Neo-Babylonian, Akkadian /b/ and /p/ are kept distinct and represented correctly by Aramaic "b" and "p." In Neo-Assyrian intervocalic /p/ was apparently pronounced [b].[3] In other non-word-initial posi-

1. E. Sollberger, "Graeco-Babyloniaca," *Iraq* XXIV (1962) 63-72. See also A. Ungnad, "Zur Aussprache des Spätbabylonischen," *Altorientalischen Studien, Bruno Meissner* (*MAOG*, Vol. IV [Leipzig, 1929]) 222 ff.

2. Note (*GAG Ergänz.*, p. 4**) that von Soden suggests that the b/m alternation in the script occurs only when a spirantized pronunciation of "b" is intended. This is no doubt true of the Assyrian use of "b" for [w], but in *hab/maṣīru* the spelling with "b" is NB, while the spelling with "m" does not occur in NB at all, though "m" is the standard NB way of expressing [w] (see below, Nasals). Thus, [w] is certainly not intended in the NB spelling of this word.

3. This shift is attested in alphabetic transliterations in the names *sbʾsr* < *šēpa-Aššur* (Aššur tablet 3) and *p(?)rbḥr* (Aššur tablet 6),

tions in NA, however, /b/ and /p/ are also kept distinct in the translitierations. Deller's suggestion that NA /b/ and /p/ were often confused and were pronounced almost identically must be modified accordingly.[4]

Of the loanwords, the following exhibit irregularities:

balaggu : *plaggâ*—The form *palaggu* is well attested in SB, perhaps as an Assyrianism.

haṣbu : ?—If any of the Aramaic forms aside from *ḥṣb* are indeed loans, then there are irregularities. Perhaps Syr. *ḥṣp* is a loan, with *b* > *p* because of the *ṣ*.

purkullu : *ʾrgwblʾ*—This is difficult; perhaps *p* > *b* by assimilation to the *g* and *l* in the Aramaic form. There is no certainty that the initial phoneme of the Akkadian is /p/ and not /b/, however, for all syllabic spellings are ambiguous. See below, Velars, and Chap. II, n. 268.

nabartu : *nmrtʾ* *b*>*m*—Note that the *b* is intervocalic and in the vicinity of *n*.[5]

Dentals

Alternation between *d* and *t* is rare but occurs in a few words in NA and SB. *D*, *t*, and *ṭ* are represented in transcriptions and loanwords by alphabetic *d*, *t*, and *ṭ*, respectively.[6] In NB final *mt* becomes *dd* as in *šalamtu* and **pagumtu*. Problematic loanwords are:

kutimmu : *kdm*—Syllabic spellings of this Sumerian loanword (kù-dím) are rare. It clearly has /t/ in OB but perhaps was pronounced with [d] in LB. Modern scholars are uncertain whether to transcribe the word with *t*, *ṭ* or *d*.

where the second element is clearly the Akkadian *upahhir*. Note that in names with the element *aplu* (such as Tiglathpilesar and *ʾpldr* in Aššur tablet 5) *p* is always preserved, suggesting that even in the construct form *apil* the vowel is easily elided in context and that the shift occurs only in intervocalic, not postvocalic, position. Loanwords displaying this phonetic change are *snb* < *šinipû* and *šwšbyn* < *susapinnu*.

4. Cf. *GAG Ergänz.*, p. 4**.

5. Since in NB intervocalic /m/ > [w], perhaps intervocalic /b/ was then free to vary in phonetic range toward [m]. This would explain the NB spelling of *habaṣīru* discussed above (n. 2) as a reasonable spelling for something like [*hamaṣīr*].

6. The problem of d/ṭ alternation between Sumerian and Akkadian and between Akkadian and West Semitic remains a difficult one. There is no internal Akkadian evidence to prove that Sumerian DUB becomes Akkadian *ṭuppu*, a reading based on West Semitic writings such as BH *ṭpsr* for Akk. *ṭupšarru* (cf. *dibbu*, *dappu*). Still, in light of the consistent renderings of the consonants in transcriptions and in the other loanwords, it is best to assign this change to the earlier Sumerian-Akkadian loan period. The single possible exception in the transcriptions is in O. Krückmann, *Neubabylonischen Rechts- und Verwaltungstexte* (Leipzig, 1933) No. 20, where [ ]*ḥṭn* may represent a name ending in *ah-iddin*.

natbāku, nadabāku : *ndbk*—This is the word commonly cited as an example of d/t alternation, but why is the extra vowel inserted in the form with *d*? The *d* occurs both in NA and LB examples and is certainly phonetically conditioned, assimilated to the *n* and *b*. Syllable-final *d* cannot be differentiated from *t* in cuneiform orthography, so perhaps this word always has /d/ and the form **natbāku* is only a modern, etymologically influenced but erroneous transcription.

šimtu, šindu : *šnt*—See above, p. 102.

Velars

The Babylonian phonetic change *nk* (or *mk*) > *ng* is well known and is represented in the loanwords by *tamkaru* > *t(n)gr*. The only other g/k interchange apparent from the cuneiform sources is in NA, where *g* is found for *k* very rarely in initial position;[7] yet the transcriptions consistently have "g" for NA intervocalic /k/.[8] Of the loanwords, the following have /g/ for Akkadian /k/ and may therefore be assigned an Assyrian origin: *ekurru* :*ʾgwrʾ*, *īku* : *ʾygʾ*, *šaknu* : *sgn*, *ša ekalli* : *šgl*.

Thus, one may posit the phonetic rule that in Neo-Assyrian intervocalic /k/ is pronounced approximately like West Semitic /g/.[9] It is interesting to note that the cuneiform texts give no indication of this allophone; apparently it is only the non-systematic changes which are likely to be expressed in the NA orthography.

Intervocalic doubled *kk* is preserved as unvoiced, as in *šukkallu* : *skl*.[10] The realization of /k/ in other positions is not so clear:

kimahhu—In discussing this word I suggested an Assyrian pronunciation [gimah]; however, this is one of those words which is occasionally spelled with "g" and thus offers no evidence of the normal realization of initial /k/ in NA. The

7. Cf. von Soden, "Zur Laut- und Formenlehre des Neuassyrischen," *AfO* XVIII (1957-58) 121 f., No. 2.

8. I have limited this shift to intervocalic rather than postvocalic position solely on the basis of the parallel case of the labial stops. *šaknu* : *sgn* appears to be an exception to this rule, but it may be assumed that with the dropping of final short vowels the absolute form also developed an epenthetic vowel as in the construct form *šakin*.

9. Hurrian influence may have played some part here, for it is generally agreed that in that language voicing was non-phonemic, stops being voiced in inter- (or post-)vocalic position. Cf. P. M. Purves in I. J. Gelb, P. M. Purves, and A. A. MacRae, *Nuzi Personal Names* (*OIP* LII [Chicago, 1943]) p. 184.

10. That intervocalic *kk* remained [kk] in Assyrian is demonstrated as well by the BH loan *nkt* < *nakkamtu*, "treasure," which must be from Assyrian with *mt* > *nt* > *tt* rather than Babylonian where *mt* > *nd* (> *dd*).

neighboring liquid might well be the immediate cause of the voicing in this instance.

muškēnu : *mskn*—This is a loan from Assyrian, as indicated by the altered sibilant. It is possible that /k/ in syllable-initial position always remains [k], but the unvoiced sibilant may have been of some influence here.

purkullu : *ʾrgwblʾ*—The original Akkadian consonants are uncertain. The older dictionaries list the word under *burgullu*, but from Sumerian BUR.GUL one would expect *purkullu*. Nor can one determine, if indeed *ʾrgwblʾ* is derived from this word, whether it was borrowed from NA or NB. The form to which it assimilated, *ʾrdyklʾ*, was borrowed from NB.

The problematic velars in the Aramaic forms from *gušūru* and *askuppatu* have been discussed in Chapter II, where it is suggested that they are the result of later Aramaic developments.

Sibilants

Scholars have long realized that the evidence of alphabetic transcriptions showed that in the Assyrian dialect original /š/ was pronounced [s].[11] Since most of the time the Assyrians write "š" for this sound, von Soden (*GAG* § 30*d*), however, still insists that such a pronunciation is uncertain. But precisely because of the consistent orthography it can be stated with certainty that /š/ > [s] was a systematic phonetic development in the process of which the signs for original /š/ came to be used for [s].[12]

/š/ and /s/ did not merge in Assyrian, however, for Assyrian "s" is used to write West Semitic "š" and vice versa.[13]

11. Cf. *DEA*, pp. 16 f. The few Biblical exceptions, which are cited by Delaporte, merit investigation. The place name *ʾšwr* was probably long known in the West and is not merely a transliteration (cf. L. Waterman, *Royal Correspondence of the Assyrian Empire* IV [Ann Arbor, 1936] 15 ff.). It occurs properly as *ʾšwr* in Hebrew and Old Aramaic, but as *ʾtwr* in later Aramaic. The *ś* of the name *śrʾṣr* may represent assimilation to the Hebrew cognate. The *š* of *šlmnʾsr* (Shalmanesar) is no longer to be considered an exception (see Chap. II, n. 364). To be added to the list is Hebrew *rb šqh* for the Assyrian title *rab šaqê*. Here, too, one suspects assimilation to the Hebrew root *šqh* or else a Babylonianized formation.

12. When "s" is actually written, as it is frequently in the vicinity of /b/ or /p/, does it indicate a phonetic [s]? Since this, too, is fairly systematic, it probably indicates something other than [s], that is, one of the sounds normally indicated by "s" in Assyrian orthography; see below.

13. This correspondence is generally omitted from the Akkadian grammars altogether. Nevertheless, it is certain. Well known examples are the Assyrian spellings of Jerusalem and Samaria with "s." In *DEA* we find *ú-si-ʾ* for *hwšʿ* and *ha-am-bu-su* for *ḥbš*. For the representation of

There is also a recurrent example of Akkadian *lt* > *ss*, written "š" in Aramaic.[14] Since in Old Aramaic /š/ and /ś/ are not graphically differentiated, a normal pronunciation of Assyrian "s" like Old Aramaic /ś/ is not excluded by these mutual transliterations; but if *asītu* : *ʾšytʾ*, *daltu* : *dšʾ*, *sūqu* : *šwqʾ*, *suqāqu* : *šqqʾ*, and *mesû* : *mšʾ* are indeed loans, then the Assyrian pronunciation was clearly closer to [š].

Assyrian "s" in initial position only corresponds in a few cases to Babylonian "z" (*GAG* § 30*c*). This seems to be the case as well in the word *samītu* : *zwyt*, of uncertain origin. In *simānu*, the Babylonian pronunciation was with [s], as shown by the borrowed month name, but it was apparently pronounced closer to [z] in Assyrian. Perhaps a sound [ž], the voiced form of [š], is involved, and if so, voicing can be ascribed to the subsequent nasal *m*.[15] In general, however, one can establish the regular development in Assyrian of etymological /š/ to [s] and /s/ to [š]. The following loanwords are thus loans from Assyrian: the Aramaic forms of *errēšu*, *ušallu*, *giššu*, *šinipû*, *ša rēši*, *šaknu*, *muškēnu*, *gâšu*, and *šukkallu* and, as mentioned above, *asītu*, *daltu*, *sūqu*, *suqāqu*, and *mesû*. Conversely, it may be assumed that any Aramaic word which preserves the Akkadian sibilants unchanged was borrowed from Babylonian.

Not all cases of sibilant shift in loanwords may be accounted for by the Assyrian dialect, however. Note the forms *ištānu* (*iltānu*) > *ʾstnʾ* and *ištartu* > *ʾstrtʾ*, both of which were almost certainly borrowed from Babylonian.[16] Here the spellings with *lt* for original *št* provide the clue. As indicated by the Hebrew rendering of the *l* of *Kaldu*, "Chaldea" by *ś*, this sound was heard as *śin* by the West Semites (but as *l* by the Greeks), and, like etymological *śin*, it was subsequently subject to the Aramaic sound change *ś* > *s*. Note, however, that this consonant is preserved as *l* in Aramaic when it

Assyrian "s" by alphabetic "š" cf. the names of the priests of Nerab *šnzrbn* and *šʾgbr* (see S. Kaufman, "'Siʾgabbar, Priest of Sahr in Nerab,'" *JAOS* XC [1970] 270 f.). See, too, Chap. II, n. 364.

14. This is in names with the logographically written divine element previously read as ᴰ*Ištar*, but spelled alphabetically *ʾš* (*DEA*, p. 19). This has often been assumed to be an abbreviation. As pointed out first by Stephen J. Lieberman (unpublished paper), however, the only explanation is that the ideogram ᴰ15, read ᴰ*Ištar*, in fact stands for the other word for "goddess," *iltu*, which in NA would quite normally become "issu" (cf. *GAG* § 34*d*) and, as shown by the Aramaic, was pronounced with [š].

15. The initial *ž* is in fact preserved in *ǰamanak*, the Armenian descendant of *simānu*.

16. The first is considered Babylonian because the other wind names are clearly Babylonian loans. As for *ištartu*, the Assyrian realization should have been *št* > *ss* : [šš], as in *issēn* < *ištēn*.

precedes final *-t* of the feminine affix (e.g., *manzaltu*, *marultu*) and apparently also before *ṭ* (e.g., *bulṭītu*).

The phonetic problems involving sibilants in *haṣbu*, *ša ekalli* and *paššuru* have been discussed under the respective entries.

Glottal Stop and *ḫ*

Along with the disappearance of most of the laryngeals, /ʾ/ was also lost in many positions in Akkadian; nevertheless, the phoneme /ʾ/ persisted in all of the Akkadian dialects. Words with initial vowels certainly have at least a weak glottal onset, represented by "ʾ" in alphabetic transliteration. In personal names where the second or third element begins with a vowel, "ʾ" is usually expressed in the transliterations.[17] In the two compound loanwords whose second element is *ekallu* (*arad ekalli* and *ša ekalli*), no glottal is indicated.

Akkadian words beginning with a vowel have initial /ʾ/ in their Aramaic forms. Exceptions are: the Mandaic forms from *attalû* and *ištānu*, where the loss of "ʾ" is certainly a late, Mandaic development. In *atappu*, *asumittu* and *amurriqānu* the Aramaic forms without initial " " may derive from Akkadian forms without the initial syllable *a*: Though rare among native Akkadian words, the alternation *aC-*: *C-* in initial position is not infrequent in late Akkadian (*GAG* § 14*a*). *Asumittu* is certainly of foreign origin. Although *atappu* may be from Sumerian *a-tab, and hence subject to loss of the initial *a*, the loss of the initial consonant may well have occurred later, in Aramaic, both in *tpʾ* and *mryqnʾ*. See also Chapter II, s.v. *uṣurtu*. The initial "ʾ" of *ʾštymʾ* < *šatammu* is a secondary development in Aramaic.

It should be pointed out here that there is absolutely no evidence for the preservation of *ʿayin* in first-millennium Akkadian and no firm evidence that any North West Semitic borrowing from an Akkadian word with an initial vowel has /ʿ/; see the entries *adannu*, *adê*, *arsānu*, *ebūru*, *errēšu*, *eṭēru*, *ištēn*, *izqāti*.

Akkadian /ḫ/ is borrowed as "ḥ" in Aramaic.[18] Problematic words are *kimahhu* and *nishu*. In his analysis of *kwk* : *kimahhu*, Kutscher proposes that the Eastern Syriac pronunciation of "ḥ" as [ḫ] is the origin of the form *kwk*.[19] I have argued (Chap. II, n. 160) that a Nabatean pronuciation with

17. See S. Kaufman, in *JAOS* XC 270 f.

18. In Mandaic this became "h," except in the month name *mʾšrwʾn* < *arahšamnu*. BT "h" corresponds to Akk. "ḫ" in *hurdu*.

19. E. Y. Kutscher, "*kwk (uvne mišpaḥta)*," *Eretz Israel* VIII (1967) 275 ff.

[ḫ], also discussed by Kutscher, is to be considered responsible in the case of *kwk*. Nabatean can also be used to explain the various forms of *nisḫu*. Nabatean *nsḥt* and Mandaic *nsʾ* show that this word was indeed borrowed into early Aramaic. Pronounced with [ḫ], it was borrowed into Arabic as *nusḫah* from Nabatean or a similar dialect. The later Aramaic (Syriac and Mandaic) forms with /k/ must be borrowings from Arabic. Medieval Hebrew *nusḥāh* is also from Arabic, but as it is a scholarly loanword, the representation of Arabic /ḫ/ by "ḥ" is explicable.

Nasals

It is well known that in NB/LB intervocalic "m" represents [w], both in the case of original /w/ and original /m/.[20] That is to say that [w] is the allophone of /m/ occurring in intervocalic position.[21] The following words with etymological /m/ appearing as /w/ in Aramaic were thus borrowed from Babylonian: *amāru, amurru, amuršānu,* argamannu, *himētu, lumāšu, namāru, simānu, šamallû, šamāhu, zīmu,* and perhaps *asumittu*. Of those examples where intervocalic /m/ appears in Aramaic as /m/, Palmyran *gmḥ* < *kimahhu,* Syriac *ʾmd* < *emēdu,* and *zmn* < *simānu* are certainly from Assyrian.[22] West Semitic *ʾmd, ʿmd* < *emēdu, imittu,* a Neo-Babylonian technical term, is not to be considered an exception to the rule. The well attested occurrence of *ʿayin* in the West Semitic forms indicates that this was not a full loanword but rather a loan adaptation of the cognate root to the Babylonian usage.

The only example with etymological /w/ is *amurriqānu,* which occurs as *mryqnʾ* in Syriac, almost certainly from Assyrian. Together with the evidence presented in the previous paragraph this suggests that both intervocalic /m/ and /w/ were realized as [m] in Assyrian. In light of attested cuneiform orthography, however, such a development remains uncertain. In the orthography /m/ appears either as "m" or "ʾ" (or even disappears!) and /w/ either becomes "m" or "b" (although "b" probably signifies [w]).

Doubled /m/ in Babylonian remains /m/ in the loans.[23]

20. Cf. *GAG* § 31*a*.

21. See Spirantization in Chap. III.

22. Also see s.v. *samīdu*. As mentioned above, if it is a loan, it must be very early because the preservation of both /s/ and /m/ rules out both NA and NB.

23. But in Assyrian we sometimes find "ʾʾ" for /mm/; cf. *GAG Ergänz.* § 31*d*. The Babylonian examples are *eṭemmu* (if BH *ʾṭym* is this word), *kutimmu, simmiltu, šatammu, nuhatimmu* and *ummānu*, of which only the first four are necessarily Babylonian, the first two by context and the third and fourth because of the sibilants.

The phonetic realization of final /m/ in Babylonian is not perfectly clear. *L(ʾ)m* < *līmu* is Assyrian and *ḥm* < *hāmu* also probably comes from Assyrian. In BT *nktmʾ* < *naktamu* the "m" could result from assimilation to the cognate Aramaic root *ktm*, though this is semantically unlikely. In at least one personal name, however, final /m/ is preserved.[24] Etymological /m/ in initial position is maintained in all cases.

The only problem that remains is that of initial etymological /w/. Orthographically, in MB and LB it generally drops completely, but in some cases it becomes "m." In late Assyrian it can disappear or change the following /a/ vowel to "u."[25] In the loanwords, *arittu* < *warittu* appears as *ʾrytʾ* in Aramaic, but *arahšamnu* < *warahšamnu* becomes *mrḥšwn*. The latter is certainly borrowed from Babylonian. The transliterations offer no relevant information except for the Hatran name *wrdnb*, which may be *Warad-Nabû* but might also be of Iranian origin.[26] Thus, at this stage no general rules for initial /w/ can be posited.

Liquids

Although the interchange between *n* and *l* is not unknown in Akkadian,[27] the change from /l/ to /n/ in *tarlugallu* > *trngwl* probably occurred in Aramaic, where such changes are much more common.[28] Otherwise the liquids undergo no changes in passing from Akkadian to Aramaic.[29]

Though it is not attested in any of the certain loanwords, an important NB/LB phonetic trait is the change of /r/ before /t/ or /k/ to "š," as represented in Aramaic transliteration by the spelling *ʾnšt* for the Babylonian pronunciation of the divine name *I/Enurta* (NIN.IB, usually read *Ninurta*) as op-

24. In *DEA*, No. 43, *pnbṭm* : *Pan(i)-Nabû-ṭēmu*. Aramaic spellings of *šum* as *šw* in Babylonian personal names are not decisive, for this is always followed by the vowel of the next name element. Similarly *slwʾll* in a new tablet from Nippur is *silim-Ellil*. As for *kslw* < *kislimu*, there is no evidence currently available that would demonstrate that /m/ is the original phoneme.

25. *GAG* § 21c. In *muššuru* is this actual [m] or just conditioned writing from finite forms like *umaššir* where [w] is certainly intended?

26. Cf. *KAI* II 297, No. 242, l. 1.

27. See Landsberger, *Die Fauna des alten Mesopotamian nach der 14. Tafel der Serie Ḫar-ra = ḫubullu* (Leipzig, 1934) p. 118; *GAG Ergänz.*, p. 6**; G. Dossin, "Le nom de signe '(m)ušlânu,'" *RA* LXIV (1970) 163.

28. See The *l/n* Imperfect Prefix in Chap. III.

29. In *zuruqqu* > *zrnwq* one can posit an intermediate Akkadian form **zurunqu*, as indicated by BT *zrwnqʾ*, rather than a change **zurruqqu* > *zurnuqqu*. Thus, the /r/ would not be involved in the change. Nevertheless, a dissimilation /rr/ > [rn] is certainly possible; see s.v. *aburru*.

posed to Assyrian *ʾnrt*.[30] This phonetic change, which may occur in the possible loanword *harurtu*, appears to be regular. In the cuneiform orthography it is attested for /r/ before final feminine *t* as well as internal *t*,[31] yet it does not occur in any of the loanwords with final *rt*: *egirtu*, *birtu*, *nabārtu*, and *ištartu*. Although *egirtu* is certainly Assyrian, *nabārtu*, and *ištartu* are probably Babylonian. Compare the similar treatment to final *-lt* in loanwords (above, p. 141).

Final Feminine *-t*

There is no evidence, either from cuneiform orthography, alphabetic transliteration, or loanwords, that final feminine *-t* was ever dropped in Akkadian, as it was in Hebrew, Aramaic, and Arabic.[32] In the great majority of loanwords, the Akkadian feminine *-(a)t* is taken over into Aramaic as the feminine ending and is subject to normal Aramaic morphological rules. The *-t* is neglected completely only in Mandaic *mhʾrʾ* : *mahratu*, Mandaic *mʾrwlʾ* : *marultu*, and the common form *mzl* : *mazzaltu*. The last example perhaps gives the clue for all, for Syriac also has the form *mzltʾ*, and BH has the plural *mzlwt*. This and the first two words cited might thus be masculine back-formations which developed after the borrowing. Yet final *lt* seems to present a special case (see above, p. 141), and the latter two loanwords suggest that this cluster may well have been realized as [ll].

The confusion in Imperial Aramaic over the correct absolute forms of *egirtu* and *libbatu* has already been mentioned. In Syriac, but not in Imperial Aramaic, the *-t* of *mdʾtʾ* (*maddattu*) is taken as a radical, as shown by the plural forms. The double *-tt* may be responsible here, for in the similar ending of the form *arittu* the final *-t* of the Aramaic is also taken as a radical. This suggests that the model for Aramaic *kntʾ*, pl. *knwtʾ*, was the by-form *kinātu* and not *kinattu*.

A unique case is presented by *sikkatu*, whose Aramaic forms have *-t* in the singular but form plurals with the masculine suffix on the base *sikk-* (and in Arabic, *sakk*).[33] This occurs in all of the Aramaic dialects where the word is attested.

It should be mentioned here that except for *mušarû* : Syriac *mšrtʾ* and *nishu* : Nabatean *nsḥt*, Arabic *nusḥah*, which are not without other difficulties as well, no Akkadian mascu-

30. Cf. H. Tadmor, "A Note on the Seal of Mannu-ki-Inurta," *IEJ* XV (1965) 233 f.

31. Cf. *amartu/amaštu*.

32. Also in Egyptian, and probably late Punic, transcriptions show the *-t* to have dropped.

33. *Urubātu* : *ʾwrby* may represent a parallel case.

line form is represented by a feminine *-t* form in Aramaic. (Cf. BH *dibbāh*, s.v. *bēl dabābi*.)

Vowels and Length

Although vowel length is phonemic in Akkadian, it is not always possible to determine whether a given vowel is long or short, for length is usually not indicated in cuneiform orthography. Nor can one always be certain of vowel quality, though it can often be inferred from alternate spellings that vowel gradations are involved. The late vocalization systems of Aramaic are, at best, just as unreliable. Nevertheless, the majority of the Akkadian loanwords in Aramaic have what must be considered the correct reflex of the posited Akkadian form, both as to vowel quality and quantity.

One type of noun has a systematic inconsistency in this regard, however, the bisyllabic noun with a short first syllable and a long second syllable. Although most of these nouns also have the correct Aramaic reflex, with the first short vowel reduced, such as *šaṭāru* : *šṭâr*, *šalandu* : *šladdâ*, a significant number of such nouns are subject to a lenthening of the first syllable in Aramaic, either by vowel lengthening, as in *kanūnu* : *kânônâ*, or consonant lengthening, as in *atūnu* : *ᵓattûnâ*. Some of these words, to be sure, may have previously unrecognized long first syllables in Akkadian, but the usual explanation for this change is that since pretonic short vowels are reduced in Aramaic, in order to preserve the shape of the loanword yet at the same time to make it conform to Aramaic morphophonemic patterning, it was necessary to lengthen the first syllable.[34]

Several objections must be raised to this argument. First is the problem of vowel reduction. Had it already occurred at the time of Akkadian-Aramaic contact? The Uruk incantation, dating from a period well after the period of borrowing, seems to indicate that vowel reduction was not yet complete at the time of its composition.[35] But in Uruk the short vowels are not always retained, and the spelling conventions of the scribe are not yet completely understood, primarily because of inconsistencies. Further, the composition itself might well antedate considerably the date of the tablet from which we know

34. Cf. J. Blau, "Some Difficulties in the Reconstruction of 'Proto-Hebrew' and 'Proto-Canaanite,'" *In Memoriam Paul Kahle*, ed. Matthew Black and Georg Fohrer (*BZAW*, Vol. CIII [Berlin, 1968]) p. 31, nn. 9 f. Note that his reconstruction of the Akkadian form corresponding to Syriac *Tâmûz* is incorrect. Since it was borrowed from Babylonian, the /m/ must have been doubled, as reconstructed in Chap. II s.v.

35. Cf. C. Gordon, "The Aramaic Incantation in Cuneiform," *AfO* XII (1937-39) 111.

it. Since reduction of short vowels in open syllables is a feature shared by all of the Aramaic dialects, it must have occurred at a period when all of those dialects were still in close contact, that is, during the time of Imperial Aramaic at the latest.[36] If reduction had occurred prior to the period of Akkadian and Aramaic contact, however, then one would expect to find a much greater percentage of words which have first-syllable lengthening.

Accordingly, it can quite confidently be maintained that at the time and place that a majority of the borrowings took place Aramaic vowel reduction had not yet occurred. Historical considerations lead one to suspect that this period of greatest contact was primarily the Neo-Babylonian period. In fact, of the loanwords of the bisyllabic shape under discussion which are properly transferred and whose original Akkadian dialect can be determined, all except *suqāqu* and *ša rēši* are Babylonian.[37] Babylonian words which are subject to the change may thus be assumed to have been borrowed later, after vowel reduction.

Other considerations must be taken into account, however. Of the Babylonian month names, which one can safely assume were all borrowed from Babylonian at the same time, *nisannu* and *simānu* show lengthening in the first syllable in Aramaic, while in *šabāṭu* the vowel is reduced.[38] This evidence suggests that at the time of the borrowing of the month names /i/ (and perhaps /u/) were subject to reduction while, as in Geʾez, /a/ was still preserved.[39] Such an historical reconstruction agrees well with the evidence of Syriac, which generally has no spirantization of *bdgkpt* following a (reduced)

36. K. Beyer, "Der reichsaramäische Einschlag in der ältesten syrischen Literatur," *ZDMG* CXVI (1966) 198, 201, claims that Aramaic vowel reduction only occurred "erst n. Chr.," although he offers no proof for this assertion. E. Y. Kutscher has demonstrated the presence of vowel reduction in the Genesis Apocryphon and probably in earlier texts as well (review of Fitzmyer, *Genesis Apocryphon*, *Or.* n.s. XXXIX [1970] 178 f.)

37. To be sure, BH *sārîs* preserves the *qamatz* in the plural form *sārîsîm*. H. Tadmor (orally) notes the spelling *ša-a rēši* in *PRU* IV 17.25 l. 22 and suggests that Hebrew preserves here an old western pronunciation of this term.

38. The situation is unclear with *ṭebētu*, whose vocalization is known only from Hebrew, where pretonic vowels are lengthened, and with *elūlu*, where Syriac and Hebrew differ in the length of the vowel.

39. Does the pretonic lengthening of /a/ in Hebrew as opposed to the usual reduction of /i/ or /u/ (or lengthening of the following consonant) reflect a similar stage? If this reconstruction of the chronology of Aramaic vowel reduction is correct, then those Babylonian loans which preserve the vowel /a/ in the first syllable can be dated latest of all. This seems to work: The only relevant forms are *asuppu*, *šatammu*, and

original /i/ but does have spirantization after reduced /a/, demonstrating that spirantization was introduced after the reduction of the former but before the reduction of the latter.[40]

But what of the words borrowed from Assyrian that show first-syllable lengthening? If vowel reduction had not yet taken place in the Neo-Babylonian period, it certainly had not yet occurred during the time of the major Assyrian contact. Since the number of such words is small, one must reckon first of all with simple error in the correct Akkadian form.[41] Another explanation is that of stress. First-syllable stress has been suggested for the Assyrian dialect.[42] If this theory is correct, first-syllable lengthening in the Aramaic loans can be explained as the result of an attempt to reproduce the foreign stress pattern of the Assyrian. In such a situation, uniformity in the shapes of the borrowed words is especially unlikely, and thus normal forms like *suqāqu* are to be expected.[43] In *ša rēši*, of course, the stress is on the second syllable of the compound, and *srîsâ* is thus the only possible Aramaic form.[44]

Although when borrowing words from case-inflecting languages Aramaic is likely to take such words over without the case endings,[45] if the final short-vowel case endings had

maruš/ltu, and the latter two are known only from Mandaic. Note especially that the Mandaic form *šʾtʾmʾ* is thus shown to be a later borrowing than BT and Syriac *ʾštymʾ*, where the vowel was reduced and a prothetic ʾ added. Words such as *malāhu* and *pahāru* should not be considered necessarily late on these grounds, for one might expect their assimilation to the *qattâl nomen professionis* formation, regardless of whether vowel reduction had already occurred or not.

40. Cf. T. Nöldeke, *Compendious Syriac Grammar*, J. A. Chrichton, trans. (London, 1904) § 23 D; W. Fischer, "Zur Chronologie morphophonematischer Gesetzmässigkeiten im Aramäischen," in *Festgabe für Hans Wehr*, ed. W. Fischer (Wiesbaden, 1969) p. 177. The Syriac evidence thus confirms the general contemporaneousness of vowel reduction and spirantization, which I have posited on the basis of Akkadian and Aramaic comparisons.

41. The Assyrian loans are *asītu, egirtu, kanūnu,* and *ušallu,* and probably *hi/erītu, lilītu,* and *māhāzu.*

42. Cf. E. Reiner, *A Linguistic Analysis of Akkadian* (The Hague, 1966) pp. 38 f.

43. Assyrian stress might also have had other effects on loanwords. The Aramaic form of *simānu,* with two short vowels, is quite different from that of the Babylonian month name with two long vowels. Rather than posit the Akkadian form *simanu* (as in Landsberger, "Jahreszeiten im Sumerisch-akkadischen," *JNES* VIII [1949] 256, nn. 44 f.) perhaps one should think in terms of an Assyrian form such as *[zímān], with the initial stress producing in the Aramaic ear the effect of two short vowels. In Aramaic itself, the Syriac form *zab̲nâ* must be a back-formation from *zb̲an,* although the JAr. dialects preserve correctly *zimnâ*.

44. See n. 37.

45. H. Schaeder, *Iranische Beiträge* I (Halle, 1930) 261 f.

still been in use in late Akkadian, one might expect at least some clue to their existence in the Aramaic forms of the loanwords; but no Aramaic forms of Akkadian loanwords whose absolute forms end in a consonant give any indication of any case ending (see below for *hubullu* and *amurru*). Thus, the evidence supports the generally accepted belief that the case endings had disappeared in the colloquial late Akkadian dialects.

Akkadian nouns ending in a final long vowel usually appear in Aramaic with final *-ê*, which becomes *-yâ* in the emphatic state. Included here are *asû, attalû, burû, manû, nudunnû, pattû, rabû, šadû, šamallû,* and *tubalû*. The Aramaic forms clearly derive either from the genitive singular ending in *-ê*, or, more likely, from the construct form ending either in *-î* or *-ê*.[46] This fact supports the view that final long (circumflexed) vowels were still pronounced in NB, though short vowels had dropped.[47] Indeed *-ê* may have been the ending for all cases, at least in NB. If the nominative-accusative ending were actually *-û* (as the grammars claim), one might expect more traces of *-w* in Aramaic; but *-w* occurs only in the rare Aramaic forms derived from *edû* and *gagû* (and see *nagû*). No final vowel at all occurs in the Aramaic forms of *šinepû* and *bārānû*. Note that these two are loans from Assyrian, whereas those that have *-y*, whenever origin can be determined, are from Babylonian. Two words which end in a final *-y* in Aramaic but appear to derive from Akkadian words without a final vowel are *ʾwryʾ* : *amurru* and the JAr. and Mandaic *ḥbwlyʾ* : *ḥubullu*.[48]

Vowel quality is almost always preserved in the Aramaic forms of Akkadian loanwords, with the following exceptions:

Akkadian *ā* becomes Aramaic *ō* in *bārānû, diqāru,* and *māhāzu,* all Eastern Aramaic forms and thus difficult to explain, though before *n* this vowel change is not unknown in Aramaic.[49] As suggested earlier (s.v. *māhāzu*), the *ô* in *mâḥôz* may be due to Canaanite influence. The change in *diqāru*

46. Cf. *GAG* § 64*i*. By analogy with forms ending in a consonant, the construct or absolute state would certainly have been considered the basic form of the word and would be the one most likely to have been borrowed.

47. Cf. J. P. Hyatt, *The Treatment of Final Vowels in Early Neo-Babylonian* (New Haven, 1941) pp. 56 f. and David B. Weisberg, *Guild Structure and Political Allegiance in Early Achaemenid Mesopotamia* (New Haven, 1967) p. 106.

48. The usual explanation of *ḥbwlyʾ* as a *qtulyâ* abstract form (cf. *HM*, p. 201, Noldeke, *Compendious Syriac Grammar* § 137) may be correct, but it hardly applies to *amurru*; but see above, s.v., for a possible explanation. An alternative explanation is to regard this *y* as a development of a schwa vowel after the doubled consonant in the construct state; cf. *GAG* § 64*c*, *h*.

49. Nöldeke, *Compendious Syriac Grammar* § 44.

may be considered an Akkadian development.[50] From *maškanu* Syriac has *meškânâ*,[51] while in Nabatean and JAr. the form is *maškôn*. In a western form *ā* > *ō* is not unusual, but how is one to explain the long vowel? Apparently the Akkadian form is to be transcribed as *maškānu*, as the Syriac forms suggests as well.[52]

In *muškēnu* Aramaic has *is* for Assyrian /us/, and the West Semitic form corresponding to Babylonian *nishu* has *us*. This probably results from an Akkadian tendency to centralize high short vowels before sibilants.[53]

Mandaic has *nʾndbyʾ* from *nindabû* and *tʾtwrʾ* from *titurru*. Syriac also has *a* in the first syllable of the latter, but BT preserves the *i*. The change *u* > *a* occurs in the Aramaic forms of *(mul)lumāšu* and *nuhatimmu*, and, with a long vowel, in the BT and Mandaic form *gnânâ* < *ganūnu*.[54] I am unable to explain the third case, but I have suggested explanations for the others in Chapter II. Isolated phonetic difficulties are presented by *sawkânâ* < *sikkānu*, the various Aramaic forms of *muterru*, and Hatran, Mandaic *prykʾ* < *parakku*.

The diphthong of Syriac *šawtâp̄â* (Akk. *šutappu*) is problematic. A possible explanation is to ascribe its origin to analogy with the verbal form *šawtep̄*. See also s.v. *hūqu*.

Akkadian consonantal length is generally preserved in Aramaic, but its preservation apparently depends on the shape of the word. In monosyllablic forms, for example, *dappu*, *giššu*, *giṭṭu*, consonantal length is always preserved. In final position in words of more than one syllable, consonantal length may be preserved, as in *asuppu* (BH *ăsuppîm*) and *balaggu* > *plaggâ*, or the vowel may be lengthened instead, for example, *šuttâp̄â* < *šutappu*. Whenever the vowel is lengthened, it probably derives from an Akkadian by-form rather than a secondary Aramaic development.[55] In some words, however, no length is preserved at all, and the vowel is subject to reduction: *arad ekalli*, *nikassu*, and dialectal forms of *tarlugallu*,

50. Cf. *GAG* and *GAG Ergänz.* § 9*c*.

51. For the *e* vowel see Nöldeke, *Compendious Syriac Grammar*, p. 32 and n. 2.

52. Cf. the OA *maškānum* (*AHw.*, p. 627).

53. Cf. *GAG* § 9*g*, and W. von Soden and W. Röllig, *Das akkadische Syllabar* (2d ed.) p. xxiv.

54. All JAr. forms of this word, even those spelled *gynwn*, are to be vocalized with mobile schwa in the first syllable and not *i* followed by doubled *n* (as in Jastrow, *Dictionary*, p. 258).

55. For the "free variation" between vowel and consonantal length in Akkadian, cf. Reiner, *A Linguistic Analysis of Akkadian*, pp. 45 f. Since it seems fairly systematic, at least in the late Akkadian dialects, while "compensatory lengthening" is less frequent in Aramaic (cf. Noldeke, *Compendious Syriac Grammar* § 43 B), the source seems to be Akkadian.

hubullu, kimahhu, and BA *šēglāṯā* < *ša ekalli*. The process involved is probably one of back-formation from absolute forms where the doubling is not expressed, e.g. *ardēkal* : *ardēḵlā*; *ḥḇul* : *ḥuḇlā*. Thus, this reduction never occurs where the Akkadian has a long vowel in the final syllable which would always be expressed.

The more significant aspects of our phonological findings may be summarized as follows.

In late Akkadian, in both the Babylonian and Assyrian dialects, final case vowels had dropped. Internal short vowels were preserved and were, with some exceptions, pronounced as written. The final feminine *-t* was preserved in all forms.

In Neo-Babylonian, intervocalic /m/ had become [w]. Accordingly [w] is written "m." Internal *št/lt* was pronounced *śt*. Otherwise, except for final vowels and regular sound changes expressed in the orthography only some of the time, for example, /rt/ > [št], NB was pronounced as written.

In Neo-Assyrian, the main stress was probably fixed on the first syllable. Intervocalic /k/ became [g], though written "k," and intervocalic /p/ was likewise pronounced [b]. Etymological /š/ became [s], usually written "š," and etymological /s/ became [š], written "s," though in initial position "s" can indicate [z] or [ž] as well.

In Aramaic the reduction of pretonic short vowels appears to have begun in the Imperial Aramaic period, perhaps during the time of the Neo-Babylonian period or slightly later; *u* and *i* were reduced prior to the reduction of *a*.

Spirantization

Although it has not been pointed out in each of the relevant consonant categories, the evidence for spirantization can be reviewed here. On the one hand the Aramaic evidence, of loanwords and transcriptions, proves that it is not the case that Akkadian had spirantization of stops while Aramaic did not (during the period of contact). Nowhere in the transcriptions is Akkadian *d* represented by alphabetic *z*, *t* by *š*, *k* by *ḥ*, or *g* by ʿ; nor is any systematic problem encountered in the spirantization of any of the stops in the loanwords.[56]

On the other hand, of the bisyllabic forms mentioned above which have a short first syllable in Akkadian but a long one in Aramaic, instead of vowel lengthening the second consonant is lengthened only in *egirtu, igaru, šutappu, atūnu,*

56. The only possible example is /k/ for /ḫ/ in the Syr. form *nwskʾ* from *nishu*, but since this is unique, the explanation of the development of this word proposed above (p. 142) seems much more probable than a direct loan.

and *titurru*. This is some, though admittedly far from strong, evidence that at least as regards *t/ṯ* and *g/ḡ* the phonemic merger and subsequent spirantization might already have begun in Aramaic at the time of these loans, since the doubling was then necessary to maintain the non-spirantized pronounciation and preserve the foreign shape of the word. But in many other examples no doubling occurs, so it remains uncertain whether spirantization can be cited as the cause of such doubling. its limitation to *g* and *t* is certainly suggestive, however.

One might argue that if both Akkadian and Aramaic had spirantization, no differences could be expressed or detected through the orthography. Yet it has already been demonstrated that Old Aramaic could not have had spirantization.[57] We must thus conclude on the basis of the evidence above that spirantization was either a native Aramaic development or a borrowing from a language other than Akkadian and that it started to become systematized sometime during the period of Akkadian and Aramaic contact.

THE DEVELOPMENT OF THE ARAMAIC DIALECTS

Old Aramaic

The only loanwords occurring in Old Aramaic are *snb* : *šinepû*, *srs* : *ša rēši*, and *mṣr* : *miṣru*. From a much earlier borrowing are *skn* : *šaknu* at Hama and the possible early loan *spr* at Sefire. No grammatical influences occur. Elsewhere in this study I have shown that the following Aramaic words which occur in Old Aramaic are not to be considered loans from Akkadian: Zakir *ḥrṣ*; Samalian *prs*, *šql*; Samalian (and Sefire) *ršy*; BR RKB *krsʾ* and the dissimilation in *kyṣʾ*; and Sefire *ʿdy* and *tl*.[58]

It remains to discuss some of the more uncertain interpretations of Old Aramaic forms based on Akkadian etymologies:

gb (Zakir B:8, *KAI*, No. 202)—Hardly Akk. *gabbu*, "all." Most scholars interpret it as the common Aramaic word for "side" or read *gb[l]*, "border."

ʾpš (Zakir B:11)—Though understood by early scholars to be Akk. *apsû*,[59] *ʾpš* is almost certainly to be taken as the proper name still surviving today in the name of the site where the stele was found.[60]

smr (Kilammuwa II, *KAI*, No. 25)—A relationship with late

57. Chap. III, n. 6.

58. Chap. II, s.v. *adê*, *harīṣu*, *parsu*, *rašû*, *tillu*; Chap. I, s.v. *kussû*, *šiqlu*; and see Dissimilation of Emphatics in Chap. III.

59. M. Lidzbarski, *Ephemeris für semitische Epigraphik* III (Giessen, 1915) 9.

60. Cf. *KAI* II 210.

Akk. *asmarû*, "lance" (in *CAD*, s.v. *azmarû*) is not inconceivable, but the Akkadian itself is a foreign word, and phonetic considerations (sibilant and final vowel) as well as semantic difficulties preclude a loan.

wšnm (Hadad, l. 4, *KAI*, No. 214)—The context is broken. Perhaps the word is similar to Akk. *šanûma*, "again," but, if so, the similarity is almost certainly coincidental. Adverbs are rarely borrowed; see below, p. 168.

⌜*n*⌝*šh* (Hadad, ll. 28, 29)—Although the context and readings are uncertain, Montgomery's interpretation "oath," from Akk. *nīšu*, makes good sense semantically,[61] but in the light of the sibilant difficulty if the word were borrowed from Assyrian as we would expect, and the infrequent use of *nīšu* in late Akkadian, this must remain highly uncertain.[62]

htnʾbw (BR RKB, l. 14, *KAI*, No. 216)—This is hardly to be considered a "*tan*" form "unter ostsemit. Einfluss gebildet."[63] I agree with Cross and Freedman and with Poebel that it is a reflexive of a by-form **nʾb* of a root which occurs in two other well known by-forms, *ʾbh* and *yʾb*.[64]

ʿll byt (Sefire I A-6)—The comparison offered by Fitzmyer with *ērib bīti* is scarcely correct, for the latter is a temple official (*CAD*, Vol. E, p. 290).[65] A comparison with *ērib ekalli*, a palace official, would be more reasonable on semantic grounds, but this is a rare compound and is not attested as a NA official term. Thus, Tadmor's interpretation, "legitimate successor," is almost certainly the correct one.[66]

ʾš⌜*r*⌝*th*⌜*m*⌝ (Sefire I B 11)—The reading and context are uncertain. If correctly read, it could be "their Asherahs" but hardly Akk. *ašīrtu*, "sanctuary."[67]

61. J. A. Montgomery, "Babylonian *niš* 'oath' in West-Semitic," *JAOS* XXXVII (1917) 329 f.

62. It should be noted that in Akkadian one swears a *nīš šarri* or *nīš īli*, the oath of the king or god, whereas in Hadad ⌜*n*⌝*sh* would appear to mean "his oath."

63. *KAI* II 233.

64. F. M. Cross and D. N. Freedman, *Early Hebrew Orthography* (New Haven, 1952) p. 30; A. Poebel, *Das appositionell bestimmte Pronomen der 1. Pers. Sing. in den westsemitischen Inschriften und im alten Testament* (*AS*, No. 3 [Chicago, 1932]) p. 51, n. 5. Z. Ben-Hayyim, "Comments on the Inscriptions of Sfire," *Leš*. XXXV (1971) 250, makes the reasonable suggestion that the correct cognate is Hebrew *nʾp*.

65. J. A. Fitzmyer, *The Aramaic Inscriptions of Sefîre* (Rome, 1967) p. 32.

66. H. Tadmor, "Notes to the Opening Lines of the Aramaic Treaty from Sefire," *Sefer Shmuel Yeivin* (Jerusalem, 1970) pp. 401 ff. Although Tadmor's conclusion is based on the Akkadian parallel *ana bīt abīšu ērub*, this expression is found primarily in Mari and Amarna and thus would seem to be a native North West Semitic construction. See n. 73, below.

67. Cf. E. Lipiński, "The Goddess Aṯirat in Ancient Arabia, in Babylon, and in Ugarit," *Orientalia Lovaniensia Periodica* III (1972) 115.

kym (Sefire III 1)—Dupont-Sommer's interpretation "likewise" is certainly best. None of the scholars go so far as to suggest an actual loan here, rather just a formation similar to Akk. *kīam* or *kīma*.[68] In fact neither of those Akkadian words provides the exact meaning required here.

šr/gbwh (Sefire III 13-14)—Read "his family," Syr. *šarbṯâ*.[69]

From the area of flora and fauna come the words *šrn*, "wild cat," and *šhlyn*, "cress" (Sefire I A 33, 36). There is nothing particularly Akkadian about either word, but both occur in that language.[70] A loanword relationship is prohibited for *šhlyn* since, as shown by Syr. *taḥlê*, the original initial consonant is /ṯ/. Sumerian ZA(G).HI.LI indicates that this is an old culture word for a very common vegetable.[71]

Thus, Old Aramaic contains only the political-cultural borrowings *srs*, *snb*, and *mṣr*, to which one might add at best only *nš*. These loans occur only at Samʾal and Sefire and are expected evidence of the cultural and political contact with and domination by the Neo-Assyrian Empire known from the historical sources. No non-political loanwords occur. On this basis and since Old Aramaic also has none of the non-lexical Akkadian influences characteristic of Mesopotamian Aramaic and Imperial Aramaic[72] one may conclude that the Old Aramaic of Syria gives no indication of any intimate contact with spoken Akkadian.[73] This renders highly improbable that

68. Fitzmyer, *Sefîre*, pp. 163 f.

69. Franz Rosenthal, "Notes on the Third Aramaic Inscription from Sefîre-Sûjîn," *BASOR*, No. 158 (1960) p. 29, n. 8.

70. Cf. J. C. Greenfield, "Three Notes on the Sefire Inscriptions," *JSS* XI (1966) 100.

71. Cf. R. Campbell-Thompson, *A Dictionary of Assyrian Botany* (London, 1949) pp. 55 f.

72. For the problem of genitive *zy* in Sefire, see above, Chap. III, n. 74.

73. It must be re-emphasized here that similar or even identical phraseology in political documents and commemorative and memorial stelae cannot be considered evidence of interlinguistic contact, nor can the references to or worship of divinities whose origins may be in Mesopotamia. Such problems must always be approached with great hesitancy and care. For example, it is true that there are "Akkadian" parallels to the phrase in Sefire III 11, "seek my head to kill me" (J. C. Greenfield, "Bḥinot Leshoniyot biKtovet Sfire," *Leš*. XXVII/XXVIII [1964] 306; cf. Fitzmyer, *Sefîre*, p. 113), but these all occur in Hittite treaties. Thus, this phrase is hardly of Akkadian origin but is rather to be assigned to the Hittite political-cultural sphere. Tadmor (see n. 6) suggests that the scribes of the Sefire treaty actually knew Akkadian and were translating directly from Akkadian prototypes. I find his position extreme, but even if true it would only confirm my argument about the nature of Old Aramaic, for, as shown above, there are very few actual loanwords. It is clear that the scribes were attempting to compose in pure Aramaic and that this Aramaic was not eastern!

position which considers Old Aramaic to be official, Assyrian Aramaic.

The available material does not allow any significant positive conclusions about the nature of Old Aramaic, however. The corpus of Standard Old Aramaic is too small to present any observable major dialectal differentiations, except for the imperfect consecutive of the Zakir inscription.[74] Since this is in an isogloss with South Canaanite,[75] one might expect the Aramaic of Damascus, an intermediate point, to be within the isogloss as well. If this argument is correct, it suggests that the Standard Old Aramaic of Samʾal and Sefire, which are the only two text groups of any length but which do not have the imperfect consecutive, was not Damascene Aramaic either. There are, however, only a few examples of historical narrative in Standard Old Aramaic outside of Zakir (which itself uses the perfect after *w*- more often than the prefixed form), and Degen may be correct in suggesting (p. 115 n.) that the construction was more widespread than our limited evidence would indicate. In such a case the possibility of a Damascene origin remains open.[76] Given the evidence available, however, there is no reason to suppose that Standard Old Aramaic, whether in fact it was "standardized" or not, was anything other than the native Aramaic of northern Syria.[77]

74. The differences cited by G. Garbini, *L'Aramaico antico* (*AANL*, "Memorie," Scienze Morali, Series VIII, Vol. VII [Rome, 1956]) p. 275, are mostly the result of incorrect analysis. The dialectal connections posited by Greenfield between Samalian and Sefire, as opposed to the remaining "Standard Aramaic," do not seem to me to be proven. Cf. R. Degen, *Altaramäische Grammatik* (*AbKM*, Vol. XXXVIII, 3 [Wiesbaden, 1969]) p. 137.

75. This is the prime example used by many to show that the Syrian Aramaeans borrowed more than just the alphabet from the Phoenicians. But the imperfect consecutive does not conclusively occur in Phoenician, so the language of Zakir could hardly be said to be an artificial Aramaic-Phoenician jargon on the evidence of this verbal construction. Cf. Degen, *Altaramäische Grammatik*, p. 114, n. 21.

76. The paleographical evidence would appear to be compatible with this position; cf. B. L. Haines, "A Paleographical Study of Aramaic Inscriptions Antedating 500 B.C.," *Harvard Theological Review* LX (1967) 489.

77. The conclusions of this study can be applied to the problems of Akkadian (and Aramaic) loanwords in Biblical Hebrew as well. Suffice it to point out here that especially in matters of chronology and phonology these conclusions should be quite useful. To give just one example, aside from a few very early loans such as *hykl* and *skn*, one would expect pre-Exilic Biblical Hebrew to have only the same type of loans as are found in Old Aramaic, for if anything the contact between Hebrew and Akkadian during that period must have been less extensive than that between Old Aramaic and Akkadian. Further, such loans must be from Assyrian. Loanwords whose phonology shows them to be from Babylonian, such as *nksym* : *nikassu*, must be fairly late.

Mesopotamian Aramaic

There are differences between the early Aramaic of Mesopotamia and Old Aramaic, but in general these are not the obvious differences which characterize later Eastern Aramaic. As expected, there is a large number of loanwords, especially on the dockets, but one cannot be sure that all of the Aramaic forms represent actual Aramaic words and are not, in some cases, just transliterations of Akkadian forms.[78] Thus, the "loanwords" *skl, lʾm, kdm,* and perhaps *dnh/t* are unique to Mesopotamian Aramaic.

As discussed in Chapter III, Mesopotamian Aramaic makes frequent use of *zy* as a genitive particle, and the word order is characteristically free. None of the other characteristics of Eastern Aramaic occurs except for final *-ê* of the determined plural in the Uruk incantation. As yet there is very little material to analyze, but is clear that *y-* is the imperfect prefix in early Mesopotamian Aramaic, though *l-* is used for the jussive, and that the noun states are properly used. There is no evident weakening of the laryngeals, and, at least in the Aššur ostracon, nasalization does not occur, as shown by the form *ʾt,* "you."

Imperial Aramaic

Although the Akkadian loanwords attested to date in Old Aramaic are limited to the political sphere, there can be little doubt that other loans also occurred in Old Aramaic but are not yet attested in our small corpus of texts; the evidence suggests that the number of other types of loans must have been small. If one makes the almost certain assumption that Akkadian ceased to be a significant spoken language sometime during the Imperial Aramaic period, it may be concluded that, except for political loanwords and those few unknown Old Aramaic loanwords from Akkadian, all the Akkadian loanwords in Western Aramaic must have reached the West through Imperial Aramaic.[79] We are thus provided with a vocabulary of Imperial Aramaic extending beyond that actually attested in the Aramaic texts from the Imperial Aramaic period, including those few words attested only in late Biblical Hebrew which may be suspected of being of Imperial Aramaic origin.[80]

78. Might the dockets not have functioned as written records to be used by bilinguals who were literate only in the simpler alphabetic writing system? If so, perhaps one should not even grant these words the status of "foreign word" in Aramaic.

79. Excepting those few Hebraisms in JAr. which might have entered Hebrew directly from Akkadian; see n. 80.

80. The great majority of Hebrew words of Akkadian origin reached Hebrew through Aramaic and are actually attested in Aramaic. As such

In spite of the large Imperial Aramaic vocabulary which can be assembled in this fashion, the lexical borrowings provide very little guidance in the attempt to differentiate among the various dialects of Imperial Aramaic. Aside from one possible exception, no matter how one may wish to group the texts, Akkadian loanwords are found in all groups and all genres, perhaps not equally, but at least in sufficient quantity and variety to prevent the determination of dialectal divisions solely on lexical grounds. One might suggest, of course, that Eg. *dbb* would not have been used in Babylonian Imperial Aramaic, that *AD nšy byt* was not ordinarily understood in Egyptian Aramaic, or that Teima *swt* would not have been used in Elephantine; but except for these and perhaps a few others, one would not be surprised to find any of the Imperial Aramaic loanwords in a new-found exemplar of a group in which it had not previously been attested.[81]

The possible exception is the text of the proverbs of Ahiqar. Greenfield, in discussing Kutscher's valuable observation that the Ahiqar proverbs, as opposed to the narrative framework, are of western origin, claims that the proverbs contain no Akkadian loanwords.[82] Presumably he takes *knh*, "colleague," "comrade" (ll. 90, 163), to be cognate with and not a loan from *kinattu*. This seems to be quite unlikely. At the

they have been treated in Chap. II. But because of the historical contact between Hebrew and Babylonian during the exile, it cannot be determined with certainty whether or not any of the few definite Akkadianisms in BH which do not occur in Aramaic were actually found in Imperial Aramaic (and the same for Mishnaic Hebrew). Similarly, a word like BH *ṭpsr* < Ass. *ṭupšarru* could be borrowed through Old Aramaic, Imperial Aramaic, or even a direct loan from Assyrian, since it is from the political-cultural sphere.

81. Great care must be used here, however. For example, the word *šṭâr* < *šaṭāru* does not occur in Eg. (except for one late administrative text) though it is very common in later Aramaic. For "document" the word *spr* is used. One might conclude that the word was not yet known in the fifth century at Elephantine and that on these grounds the Elephantine dialect could be separated from that of contemporary Babylonia or even earlier Nerab, where *šṭr* occurs. More likely, however, it was known, but only in the meaning "cuneiform document," and hence the opportunity for its use did not arise in the preserved texts. Later, as the meaning became generalized to "contract," "document," the attestations of *šṭr* become understandably more frequent. The earliest such use apparently is in the papyri from Samaria (see n. 88, below). The use of *hnṣl* in the meaning "to save" in Adon l. 7 probably means that the loanword *šyzb* was not yet widespread. Note that the two words are used together in Dan. 3 and 6, but the latter is much more frequent.

82. J. C. Greenfield, in *Leš*. XXVII/XXVIII (1964) 312; *idem*, "Dialect Traits in Early Aramaic," *Leš*. XXXII (1968) 364, n. 33.

very least, however, loanwords are quite rare in the proverbs.[83] More important than quantity is the fact that in the proverbs one finds good Aramaic words such as *hnṣl* and *rpʾ* rather than the equivalent Akkadian loans *šyzb* and *ʾsy*.

The non-lexical characteristics studied in Chapter III are distributed as follows in Imperial Aramaic:

Nasalization occurs in almost all of the Imperial Aramaic texts, including both the narrative and proverbs of Ahiqar. The exceptions are the inscriptions of Nerab, the short Gözne inscription,[84] and, from Egypt, the Bauer-Meissner papyrus, the Hermopolis letters, the undated, fragmentary *AP*, No. 49 and the very late papyrus *AP*, No. 81. It is important to note that assimilation and non-assimilation or nasalization are not mutually exclusive in a given text. In Bauer-Meissner the form *ʾntn* (meaning?) occurs once; in the Sabbath Ostracon *ʾnpy* and *ʾpyky* are found in the same line; and though *mdʿm* is the normal Hermopolis form, *mndʿm* does occur once.[85]

The genitive use of *zy* is frequent in all of Imperial Aramaic except for the Ahiqar proverbs. Kaddari has compiled the ratio of construct state to *zī*-phrases for many of the Imperial Aramaic texts; they rank as follows in order of increasing frequency of *zī*-phrases: Aḥiqar's proverbs (17.33), (Genesis Apocryphon [12.00]), Elephantine papyri (7.85), Ezra (7.35), Ahiqar's Tale (5.00), Daniel (4.52), Behistun inscription (0.23).[86]

Free word order is found in all the Imperial Aramaic texts except for the legal texts from Elephantine and the Ahiqar proverbs.[87] The order subject-object-verb, however, is a characteristically Achaemenid feature.

The different distribution of each of these features makes analysis difficult. While nasalization, *zy* genitive,

83. Other troublesome words in the proverbs are *wynyqnhy* (l. 92; Chap. II, s.v. *niqû*) and *ʾrḥ*, "fetter" (ll. 80, 196). Ginsberg is almost certainly correct in finding the latter word in Second Isaiah (*ANET*, p. 428, n. 2). This could hardly be a loan from Akk. *arhu*, "half-brick" (cf. Chap. II, s.v.), though that loan may develop the meaning "lath" in later JAr. (cf. G. Hoffmann, "Lexikalisches," *ZAW* II [1882] 70 ff.) and even possibly "pole"; but could this development have occurred as early as Second Isaiah? One might suggest a connection with Akk. *werû*, "copper." Compare Akk. *siparru*, "bronze," used in the meaning "fetters" (see *CAD*, Vol. E, p. 323*a*). Cf. also SB, NB *eru*, "headband."

84. *KAI*, No. 259.

85. Cf. J. C. Greenfield, in *Leš*. XXVII/XXVIII 366, nn. 41-44.

86. M. Z. Kaddari, "Construct State and dī-Phrases in Imperial Aramaic," *Proceedings*, p. 103.

87. Of couse isolated examples of the order object-verb do occur (e.g., Ahiqar, l. 91), but as in Old Aramaic, these are infrequent and seem to be used only for emphasis or for poetic reasons.

and free word order can be considered new features of Imperial Aramaic as opposed to Old Aramaic, it is clear that each feature has its own history. Free word order and *zy* genitive are well attested in early Mesopotamian Aramaic, but nasalization does not occur there. Imperial Aramaic before the fifth century presents precisely the same pattern, except that the change from "Semitic" word order is not so severe. Nasalization (and non-assimilation), whose first traces are to be found in Bauer-Meissner and Hermopolis, becomes widespread only during the fifth century, but when it does, since it is purely a phonetic trait, if affects all of the dialects equally for a time. We may be quite confident that if we had a copy of the Ahiqar proverbs dating from the sixth century instead of the fifth, the language of the great majority of the proverbs would be identical except for the nasalization, which is almost certainly a secondarily introduced phenomenon in the text as we know it. Sometime after the period of the bulk of the Elephantine texts nasalization became limited, in Egypt at least, to Imperial Aramaic used for official, literary, or monumental purposes and hence does not appear in *AP,* Nos. 49 and 81. Unfortunately, there are few texts from the late Achaemenid or early Seleucid periods, so for now this explanation must go untested.[88]

What then is Imperial Aramaic? Since, as I have shown, the jussive *l-* was probably commonly used in Mesopotamian Aramaic, it cannot be true that Imperial Aramaic was ever nothing more than contemporary Mesopotamian Aramaic, for *l-* occurs only in BA and there only in a special case. In the later periods, when Mesopotamian Aramaic had already developed some of the other characteristics of Eastern Aramaic, such as *-ê,* the difference between it and Imperial Aramaic was even more distinct. Yet, it is also quite obvious that Imperial Aramaic, in all of its forms, is different from Old Aramaic and is different as well from the later Western Aramaic dialects which can be considered, to some degree, to be derived from a language similar to or the same as Old Aramaic. Thus, while the characteristic traits of Imperial Aramaic are eastern, it is not Eastern or Mesopotamian Aramaic; nor is it Western or Syrian Aramaic. It must be something in-between. Nor is it necessarily artificial in origin. That is to say, it is reasonable that this dialect mixture arose in the process of normal intercourse between dialect groups and quite possibly even became a native

88. It is hoped that the fourth-century texts from Samaria will soon be published and shed further light on these problems; see F. M. Cross, "Papyri of the Fourth Century B.C. from Dâliyeh," in D. N. Freedman and J. C. Greenfield, eds., *New Directions in Biblical Archaeology* (Garden City, 1966) pp. 41 ff.

language for some. Certainly at Elephantine it is difficult to imagine that the private letters on ostraca, which have free word order, were written in a dialect whose syntax was significantly different from the writer's native speech. Thus, quite naturally, each of the characteristics of Imperial Aramaic spread differently through the Aramaic speech community. The genitive use of *zy/dy/d* was most widespread and longest lasting. Free word order was also widespread, affecting local dialects such as that of Hermopolis, but in the West at least, such dialects gradually disappeared. Nasalization and an Iranian word order were the latest and most limited traits. In this picture, the Ahiqar proverbs are to be viewed as survivals from earlier times, orthographically modernized, as is the formulaic legal phraseology of the Elephantine papyri.

Although one can posit the existence of "colloquial" Imperial Aramaic dialects, differing at different times and in different places, it is also evident that at any given time there was a literary standard, a model to be followed in literary composition or inscriptions. Biblical Aramaic, the official letters of the Jews of Elephantine (*AP,* Nos. 30-34), and the various inscriptions can be viewed as efforts to achieve this standard. The chief lasting characteristics of this dialect appear to be excessive use of the object-verb word order, the use of the *zy* genitive construction, frequent nasalization, and perhaps the passive perfect construction. Although, as will be shown below, there is reason to suggest that Imperial Aramaic had its origin in the dialects of the Aramaic population centers of the Balīḫ and Ḫābūr valleys during the final stages of the Assyrian Empire,[89] the major formative period of what may be called Standard Imperial Aramaic, as demonstrated by the Iranian origin of its characteristic word order, must be ascribed to the era of Persian dominance. The Nerab inscriptions may be considered representatives of the first, Assyrian, stage of Imperial Aramaic. With the increasing importance of Babylonia under the Chaldeans and the Persians, first Babylonian features, notably nasalization, and then Iranian word order became fundamental elements of this standard. Characteristically Mesopotamian grammatical features, such as *l-* jussive and the *-ê* determined plural, which no doubt had already developed in Mesopotamian Aramaic, were not accepted into Imperial Aramaic, perhaps because they were too foreign to non-eastern speakers of Aramaic. But in time the Mesopotamian grammatical traits did manage to make their way into the area of Syriac speech.

89. See the discussion of Syriac, below.

Monumental Dialects

Our material provides little new information on the monumental dialects. Except for the two new words occurring only in Hatran, *parakku* and *aškāpu*, and the unusual word *ʾpkl*, the Akkadian loanwords making their first appearance in these dialects may be assumed to have formed part of the Imperial Aramaic vocabulary.[90]

Jewish Aramaic

The Targums

In Targums Onkelos and Jonathan (Prophets) the following Akkadian loanwords, which occur otherwise only in Eastern Aramaic, can be found:

ʾrgwblʾ : *purkullu*, also in Syriac;

ʾrytʾ : *arittu*, also BT and Targum Psalms;

ʾškrʾ : *iškaru*, only in Syriac and Arabic in the meaning "field";

gyssyn : *giššu*, also Syriac, BT, Mandaic, but only in the Peshitta is it used for "loins," as here;

ḥ(y)bwlyʾ : *hubullu*, also Syriac, BT, Mandaic, Targum Hagiographa;

ršy : *rāšû*, also BT and Mandaic;

šybbʾ : *šē bābi*, also Palm., BT, Mandaic, Syriac (and in Pseudo-Jonathan but not Neofiti).

The following vocabulary items are characteristic of these two Targums and Imperial Aramaic as well.

dš : *daltu*, well known from Imperial Aramaic but not used in JPA at all; occurs in Samaritan and in Eastern Aramaic;

zypʾ : *zīpu*, "mold"; since the denominative verb "falsify" occurs in MH, it seems safe to say that this was an Imperial Aramaic word, but in this, the original meaning, it occurs nowhere else;

ʾgwrʾ : *ekurru*, outside of Imperial Aramaic (Eg.) this

90. These words are the Aramaic forms of *asû*, *kanūnu*, *kimahhu*, *māhāzu*, *nishu*, *šē bābi*, *šutappu*, and *tamkaru*. I know of no Imperial Aramaic texts whose content would have required the use of any of these, though *asu* might occur in a broken text. As has been pointed out above (p. 157), *rpʾ* is used in the Ahiqar proverbs, but these proverbs are not really to be considered Imperial Aramaic. Since Palmyran does have connections with Eastern Aramaic (cf. F. Rosenthal, *Die Sprache der palmyrenischen Inschriften und ihre Stellung innerhalb des Aramäischen* [*MVAG*, Vol. XLI (Leipzig, 1936)] *passim*), *mḥwz*, which later is found only in Eastern Aramaic, might have been a borrowing from the East and not an Imperial Aramaic term, but Canaanite influence on the vowel (see Chap. II, s.v.) could only have occurred in Imperial Aramaic.

word occurs only in Targum Jonathan, for Mandaic *ᶜkwrᵓ* must be a separate borrowing of the Babylonian form.
Other specifically eastern (and Imperial Aramaic) words used in Onkelos and Jonathan can be found in Chapter II, s.v. *nagû*, *paruššû*, *šusuppu* (*twtbᵓ*) and *ziqtu*. There is no certain loanword which Onkelos and Jonathan share only with Western Aramaic.

This lexical data, linking the two targums with Imperial Aramaic and Eastern Aramaic, lends itself to two rather different interpretations. At first glance the evidence seems to be indicative of an eastern origin for these targums; and, solely on the basis of the lexical material presented here, such an interpretation cannot be excluded. The preservation of the form *ᵓgwrᵓ* and of the original meanings of *gyssyn* and *zypᵓ*, however, points to a very early origin for these targums. Given this early origin, one must consider the possibility that the targums were in fact produced in the West but were written in a literary dialect strongly influenced by Imperial Aramaic and its eastern elements. In light of the groundbreaking studies of Kutscher, Kaddari, and Tal,[91] there can no longer be any doubt that this second interpretation is the correct one.[92]

Although the time of origin of the Palestinian targums to the Pentateuch and the nature of their development remain uncertain,[93] it is generally agreed that the Pseudo-Jonathan Targum is the latest of all and is dependent on the other Palestinian targum(s) as well as on Targum Onkelos and, in language, on the Babylonian Talmud.[94] Further evidence of this

91. E. Y. Kutscher, "Das zur Zeit Jesu gesprochene Aramäisch," *ZNW* LI (1960) 46-56; *idem*, "The Language of the 'Genesis Apocryphon': A Preliminary Study," *Scripta Hierosolymitana* IV (1965) 10 f.; M. Z. Kaddari, "Studies in the Syntax of Targum Onkelos," *Tarbiz* XXXII (1963) 232 ff.; A. Tal, "The Language of the Targum of the Former Prophets and Its Position within the Aramaic Dialects" (Diss.; Hebrew University, 1971).

92. See my discussion of this issue in "The Job Targum from Qumran," *JAOS* XCIII (1973) 326 f.

93. As I have argued elsewhere (*ibid.*), the fact that the Palestinian targum tradition does not share in the tradition of what may be called Standard Literary Aramaic would seem to indicate that it dates from a later time, after the demise of that tradition. In light of the undoubtedly early character of much of the midrashic and halakhic material reflected in that targum, however (see the various introductions to the several volumes of A. Diez Macho's edition of Targum Neofiti I [*Neophyti I* (3 vols.; Madrid and Barcelona, 1968-71)]), it can be argued that in origin the Palestinian targum was a non-written (i.e., non-"literary"), probably northern work.

94. Cf. Kutscher, in *Scripta Hierosolymitana* IV 10, n. 45. In a recent monograph, G. J. Kuiper (*The Pseudo-Jonathan Targum and Its Relationship to Targum Onkelos* [Rome, 1972]) has attempted to demonstrate that Pseudo-Jonathan is anterior to Onkelos. His arguments for such a

is offered by the otherwise solely Babylonian Talmudic words *ʾšl* (*ašlu*), *ʾbwlʾ* (*abullu*), *prqd* (*purqidam*), and *kwwr* (*kamāru*)[95] (see also *kkʾ*, s.v. *kakku*), for in the same passages in the Fragment Targum and Neofiti, representing the legitimate Palestinian tradition, these words are not used. Similarly *dš* (*daltu*) and *šybb* (*šē bābi*) are found only in Onkelos and Pseudo-Jonathan, but not in Neofiti or the Fragment Targum.

Babylonian Talmudic

The language of the Babylonian Talmud is not monolithic. There are a few tractates written in a dialect which in appearance is much closer to Targumic Aramaic: Nedarim, Nazir, Meilah, Kritot, Tamid, and part of Temurah.[96] All scholars agree that these are the latest tractates of the Talmud, but there is uncertainty about whether the language is archaizing or late, spoken, Gaonic Aramaic.[97] An analysis of the Akkadian loanwords in BT shows that, except for common Aramaic terms (e.g., *ʾsy*), no Akkadian loanwords appear in these tractates, though one might have expected a few if indeed the tractates had their origin in the colloquial Aramaic of Gaonic Babylonia. Thus, archaization should be suspected.

Mandaic

All of the lexical and grammatical traits studied above point only to the East as the home of the Mandaic dialect of Aramaic. There are no words or features of this group which Mandaic has in common only with Western Aramaic, and the Eastern Aramaic features are numerous.

Not surprisingly, the Akkadian loanwords unique to Mandaic are composed of names of objects of the material culture and religious and astrological terminology.[98] Where it can be de-

tionship to Targum Onkelos [Rome, 1972]) has attempted to demonstrate that Pseud-Jonathan is anterior to Onkelos. His arguments for such a position are generally fallacious, as demonstrated by the linguistic evidence assembled below.

95. The single occurrence in YT is almost certainly due to contamination as well.

96. Cf. J. N. Epstein, *Grammar of Babylonian Aramaic* (Tel Aviv, 1960) pp. 14 ff.

97. *Ibid.*, p. 16.

98. For the religious terms see *ekurru*, *ginû*, *ištaru*, *maruš/ltu*, *munambû*, *sāhiru*, and *šatammu*. In astrological terminology, *zyqpʾ* : *ziqpu* and *šʾrʾ* : *šāru* are unique to Mandaic, but reflexes of *attalû* and *lumāšu* occur in Syriac as well, and *mazzaltu* is widespread. Many of the planet names, which as divine names have not been studied here, are also from Babylonian.

termined, all of these unique terms are loans (or better, survivals?) from Babylonian. It must be noted that the two most important of these loanwords in the religious sphere, *ʿkwrʾ* and *gynyʾ*, refer specifically in Mandaic to pagan practices, as does *prykʾ*, which Mandaic shares with Hatran (and Syriac). The disparaging connotations attached to these words suggest that at one time they were part of the vocabulary of a competitive cult but do not necessarily prove that the Mandean religion had its origins elsewhere than in Babylonia.[99] Mandaic borrowed freely and apparently without prejudice from the astrological and magical terminology and traditions of the Babylonians.

Syriac

Syriac has many Akkadian loanwords in common with Imperial Aramaic and Western Aramaic, but the great majority of the loans in Syriac are those it shares with the other dialects of Eastern Aramaic.[100] The latter are almost all loanwords from Babylonian.[101] Fourteen loanwords are exclusive to Syriac, of which nine are probably from Assyrian;[102] but six of the nine are architectural or topographical terms.

In light of the special situation of Syriac as a widespread literary and religious language and the extensive lexicon provided by the Syriac texts, these statistics, which demonstrate very little lasting Assyrian influence in the Aramaic-

99. To be sure, the other religious terms do not indicate any strong connections with Babylonian religion either. *Nʾndbyʾ* is rare and of uncertain usage, as is *šʾtʾmʾ*, though the latter, in the passage cited in *MD*, is associated with demons and very probably has evil connotations. I suspect that the *MD* translation "temple functionary" is based solely on the Akkadian meaning for want of anything better (cf. G. Widengren, *Iranisch-semitische Kulturbegegnung in parthischer Zeit* [Colgne and Opladen, 1970] p. 34, n. 115). *Šāhiru* and *marultu* are merely lexical items, without religious connotations. The Akkadian divine names in Mandaic would all seem to belong to the realm of astrology.

100. Lexical considerations do not allow a determination of the relationship of the three Eastern dialects. Although Babylonian Talmudic and Mandaic are certainly closer to each other than either is to Syriac, each actually has more loanwords in common with Syriac than they have in common with each other. There are only a few different words involved, however, and the cause is certainly one of chance, due to the different semantic areas treated in the various literatures rather than any genetic relationship.

101. The only certain exception is *giššu*, which, as shown above, must have been in Imperial Aramaic as well.

102. Cf. *amurriqānu, balaggu, agurru, ediltu, atappu, hīrītu, īku, kāru,* and *nabārtu*. *Šup̄lâ* (*šuplu*) and *rap̄šâ* (*rapšu*) are certainly from Babylonian, and the history of *ggwyʾ* (*gagû*) is uncertain. *ʾMd* (*emēdu*) could be from either, but *šwḥ* (*šamāhu*) is from Babylonian.

speaking areas previously inhabited or controlled by the Assyrians, are rather unexpected. Syriac, as the language of Edessa, was the heir to a long Aramaic tradition extending, in the area of Harran, back to the beginnings of the history of the Arameans. But no later than the early ninth century the Balīḫ region was under Assyrian political control and remained an important Assyrian provincial center. In fact Harran was the final stronghold of the Assyrian Empire.[103] One might have expected a great deal of Assyrian influence during this period, but most of the influences that did occur are already found in Imperial Aramaic and are thus widespread in Aramaic and not limited to Syriac. The only reasonable explanation for this distribution would seem to be that Imperial Aramaic itself had its original home in the Aramaic of the Balīḫ and Ḫābūr valleys and thus shares much in common with Syriac. The great influence of Babylonian Aramaic in grammar and lexicon, which probably began as early as the Neo-Babylonian period, when Haraan held such an important position,[104] also may have obliterated earlier Assyrianisms. Farther east, in the region of Assyria itself, however, one might have expected more Assyrian traits to reveal themselves through the veneer of literary Syriac, but it is not impossible that the Assyrian dialect was short-lived after the demise of the Assyrian Empire, and that the shifting of population groups eliminated both Assyrian and strongly Assyrianized Aramaic.[105] Perhaps further study of the Eastern Neo-Aramaic dialects can illuminate this issue.[106]

A QUANTITATIVE ANALYSIS OF THE LEXICAL DATA

When divided into semantic categories (see Table 1), the Akkadian loanwords group themselves into fairly predictable patterns.[107] In Imperial Aramaic[108] the largest percentage

103. Cf. W. W. Hallo, "Haran, Harran," in C. F. Pfeiffer, ed., *The Biblical World* (Grand Rapids, 1966) pp. 280 ff.

104. Cf. *ibid.*, and J. Lewy, "The Late Assyro-Babylonian Cult of the Moon and Its Culmination at the Time of Nabonidus," *HUCA* XIX (1946) 405 ff.

105. Cf. J. M. Frey, "Assyriens ou Araméens?" *L'Orient Syrien* X (1965) 141-60, who treats some of these points in his discussion of the inaccuracy of the term "Assyrian" for the speakers of Eastern Neo-Aramaic.

106. Note, however, that the two preserved loanwords in Eastern Neo-Aramaic, *sitta* (*esittu*) and *semmilta* (*simmiltu*) are from Babylonian as well.

107. The semantic categories were chosen rather arbitrarily as suggested by the nature of the lexical material. Excluded from consideration are those loans which already appear in Old Aramaic and forms found exclusively in Mesopotamian Aramaic. The classification used is as follows:

Political-Legal: *bēl dabābi, dabābu, bēl dīni, bēl piqitti, biltu,*

TABLE 1

The Types of Loanwords in Aramaic Dialects

	Imperial Aramaic	Western Aramaic	Eastern Aramaic	
			Syriac	Other
Political-Legal Terminology	27	12	13	3
Names of Professions	19	16	18	2
Architecture	16	13	15	6
Religion	4	2	3	7
Astronomy	1	1	3	1
Topographical Features	5	4	15	7
Scribal Terminology	5	3	3	2
Tools and Utensils	6	4	15	8
Other Items from the Material Culture	7	4	20	10
General Vocabulary	17	12	23	10
	107	71	128	56

of loanwords (25%) are from the realm of politics and law, but since many of these are unique to Imperial Aramaic, they might better be considered foreign words rather than loanwords. Next in frequency are the names of professions (18%). This group of words is fairly stable, occurring in later Eastern and Western Aramaic with only a few additions in Eastern Aramaic. It has long been recognized that architectural terms are frequent among Akkadian loanwords. In Imperial Aramaic they make up about one-sixth of the total loanwords, and these, too, are generally preserved in both Eastern and Western Aramaic, again with a few additions in the East. Imperial Aramaic also has a significant percentage (16%) of loans which may be classed as general vocabulary, words whose borrowing is an indication of strong linguistic, rather than just cultural, contact.

emēdu, gerû, hāmū, hubullu, ilku, iškaru, kurru, maddattu, manû, maškanu, miksu, miṣru, nikassu, nudunnû, paqāru, pīhatu, pilku, rabû, rašû, susapinnu, ṣītu, ṭēmu, zūzu;

Professions: *arad ekalli, asû, āšipu, aškāpu, errēšu, gagû, hazannu, ikkaru, išparu, lahhinu, malāhu, naggāru, nappahu, nuhatimmu, pahāru, purkullu, ša ekalli, šamallû, šatammu, šutappu, talmīdu, tamkaru, ummānu;*

Architecture: *abullu, agurru, amāru, arhu, asītu, askuppu, asuppu, bābu, birtu, daltu, ediltu, gāmiru, ganūnu, gišru, gušūru, hittu, igāru, kimahhu, natbāku, tarbaṣu, titurru, urubātu, uššu;*

Religion: *ekurru, ginû, ištaru, lilītu, maqlūtu, nindabû, nubbû, parakku, šēdu, sāhiru, maruštu;*

Astronomy: *attalû, lumāšu, mazzaltu, ziqpu;*

Topography: *amurru, appāru, arittu, atappu, birītu, hirītu, īku, iškaru, ištānu, kāru, māhāzu, mātu, midru, mušannītu, mušarû, nērebu, suqāqu, sūqu, šadû, šāru, šūtu, ušallu;*

Scribal: *asumittu, egirtu, giṭṭu, nishu, šaṭāru, šiptu;*

Tools and Utensils: *ašlu, bukānu, diqāru, esittu, haṣbu, kannu, kanūnu, marru, muterru, nabārtu, naktamu, nāmaru, nazzītu, pagulu, pattû, rapšu, sikkatu, simmiltu, tubalû, zabbilu, zibanītu, zuruqqu;*

Others: *argamannu, arru, arsānu, ašāšu, balaggu, burû, hurdu, itannu, kalakku* (1), *kalakku* (2), *kišādu, kukku, kuspu, kutallu, mahrat elippi, makkītu, pagumtu, pūru, qudāšu, quppu, qurqurru, rapāqu, riqītu, sikkanu, ṣumbu, šuplu, zīpu, zaqīpu, kiššu, amuršānu, bulṭītu, kamāru, šambaliltu, tarlugallu;*

General: *abbūtu, amurriqānu, bārānû, edû, gāšu, giššu, himētu, himṣu, immāti, inbu, karṣu, kinattu, kutallu, libbatu, mesû, muškēnu, napharu, nišû, pīqu, puhru, purqidam, pūtu, simānu, sunqu, ša la, šalamtu, šamāhu, šanû, šē bābi, šiknu, šillatu, šuššu, šūzubu, tibûtu, uṣurtu, zīmu, tajjāru.*

108. As used here Imperial Aramaic includes the vocabulary hypothesized for Imperial Aramaic on the basis of its occurrence in Western Aramaic, Palmyran, and Nabatean.

Except for the political and legal terminology which might be considered foreign in Imperial Aramaic, Western Aramaic preserves approximately the same percentages in the semantic distribution of the loanwords as are found in Imperial Aramaic. This is to be expected if the Western Aramaic loans derive from Imperial Aramaic, since the effects of time and chance should be semantically impartial.

The most important new types of loanwords found in Eastern Aramaic are also predictable: topographic terms and items of the material culture, both of which are semantic areas with their basis in geography. As such, some of these words are better termed "survivals."

About one-fourth (52) of the certain Akkadian loanwords in Aramaic are of Sumerian or pre-Sumerian origin. This is as expected, for those terms foreign to the Semitic-speaking Akkadians and borrowed by them were also foreign to the Arameans. Similarly, many of these old words were further borrowed from Aramaic into Arabic. (The attested percentage is necessarily greater than the actual proportion of Sumerian words. Since Sumerian origin is one of the best clues available for determining a loan and many actual loans may give the impression of being common Semitic, our sample must be biased in favor of Sumerian and substrate words.)

If the loanwords are divided into parts of speech, the following approximate distribution obtains:

	Imperial Aramaic	Eastern Aramaic
nouns	91 %	90 %
verb-noun complexes[109]	4	2
verbs	3	6
adjectives	1	1
adverbs	1	1
prepositions	1	.5
interjections	—	—
pronouns	—	—

Compare this distribution with that of the Aramaic loanwords in Akkadian in the provisional list collected by W. von Soden:[110]

nouns	66 %
verbs	24
adjectives	2.4
adverbs	3.6
prepositions	1.8
interjections	—
pronouns	1.2

Though no modern statistical analyses of such distributions for a large number of languages are available, based on what is known, the latter distribution approximates rather well the expected pattern from an "upper" language to a "lower" language.[111] Combined with the striking paucity of verbs among the Akkadian loanwords in Aramaic,[112] it seems to indicate quite clearly that though in the areas of politics and culture Akkadian may have been dominant, during the period of closest linguistic contact between Akkadian and Aramaic the latter was the dominant language. One might suggest as well that the period of actual close contact (i.e., bilingualism) was short and that the replacement of Akkadian by Aramaic proceeded at a fairly rapid pace. It is quite probable that in the LB period, and perhaps even earlier, the great majority of those writing Akkadian documents were native Aramaic speakers. The high proportion of Aramaic verbs in their Akkadian would be natural in an imperfectly learned, dying language.

This conclusion, formed solely on the basis of the lexical influences, gives one cause to reconsider the likelihood of finding phonological and grammatical influences of Akkadian in Aramaic. Such influences have been known to occur even without actual dominance, however, especially in phonology.[113] The only non-lexical influence which can without question be ascribed to late Akkadian is the loss of laryngeals. Such Mesopotamian Aramaic traits as nasalization, free word order, and *zy* genitive might go back to a much earlier period, while the general uncertainty expressed in Chapter III on the other traits studied therein must be reemphasized and given added weight in light of the lexical distribution.

Though the relationship between Akkadian and Aramaic during the first millennium remains somewhat elusive, it should now be fairly clear that the major period of contact

109. I.e., *abbūtu ṣabātu, karṣu akālu, libbatu malû, ṭēmu šanû*.

110. W. von Soden, "Aramäische Wörter in neuassyrischen und neu- und spätbabylonischen Texten. Ein Vorbericht," *Or.* n.s. XXXV (1966) 1 ff., and *Or.* n.s. XXXVII (1968) 261 ff. I have omitted from the calculations those few words which I have taken as Akkadian loans (e.g., *egirtu*). Although future work should greatly increase the total number of Aramaisms, his corpus is large enough to insure a fairly accurate sample of the distribution.

111. See L. Deroy, *L'Emprunt linguistique* (Paris, 1956) p. 67, and E. Haugen, "The Analysis of Linguistic Borrowing," *Language* XXVI (1950) 221.

112. Even if one were to add all the possible verbs mentioned in Chap. II, the percentage would not increase significantly. Since the two languages involved are very similar and the Aramaisms in Akkadian show that verbs could easily be borrowed in that direction, it cannot be argued that verbs could not be borrowed because of the differences in the verbal systems, as may be the case with Arabic and Spanish, for example (cf. Deroy, *L'Emprunt*, pp. 70 f.).

113. See L. Bloomfield, *Language* (London, 1935) pp. 470 f.

starts later, lasts for a shorter period of time, and is of a different nature from that which scholars have previously surmised. Most of the Akkadian loanwords in Aramaic may be termed "cultural borrowings," for the Aramaeans owed much to Mesopotamian society in the areas of science, the arts, religion, and law; but Aramaic was the dominant language, and the demise of Akkadian followed soon after the loss of native Mesopotamian rule.

BIBLIOGRAPHY

Aisleitner, Joseph. *Wörterbuch der ugaritischen Sprache*. Berlin, 1967.

Albeck, Hanoch. *Introduction to the Mishna*. Jerusalem, 1959 (Heb.).

Albright, William F. "An Archaic Hebrew Proverb in an Amarna Letter from Central Palestine," *BASOR*, No. 89 (1943) pp. 29-32.

______. "Notes on Assyrian Lexicography and Etymology," *RA* XVI (1919) 173-94.

______. "Notes on Egypto-Semitic Etymology II," *AJSL* XXXIV (1917-18) 215-55.

______. "Syria, the Philistines and Phoenicia," *CAH*, fasc. 51. Rev. ed; Cambridge.

Alt, Albrecht. "Hohe Beamte in Ugarit," *Studia Orientalia Ioanni Pedersen Dicata*. Havniae, 1953. Pp. 1-11.

Altheim, F., and R. Stiehl. *Die Araber in der alten Welt*, Vols. I, II. Berlin, 1964-65.

Aro, Jussi. *Die akkadischen Infinitivkonstruktionen* (*St.Or.*, Vol. XXVI). Helsinki, 1961.

______. *Glossar zu den mittelbabylonischen Briefen* (*St.Or.*, Vol. XXII). Helsinki, 1957.

______. "Die semitischen Zischlaute (ṯ) š, ś und s und ihre Vertretung im Akkadischen," *Or.* n.s. XXVIII (1959) 321-35.

______. *Studien zur mittelbabylonischen Grammatik* (*St.Or.*, Vol. XX). Helsinki, 1955.

Baillet, M., J. T. Milik, and R. de Vaux. *Les 'petites grottes' de Qumrân*, Vol. III of *DJD*. Oxford, 1962.

Barr, James. "St. Jerome and the Sounds of Hebrew," *JSS* XII (1967) 1-36.

Barth, J. *Etymologische Studien*. Leipzig, 1893.

______. *Die Nominalbildung in den semitischen Sprachen*. Leipzig, 1894.

Barton, G. A. "On the Anticipatory Pronominal Suffix before the Genitive in Aramaic and Akkadian," *JAOS* XLVII (1927) 260-62.

Batto, B. "DINGIR.IŠ.ḪI and Spirantization in Hebrew," *JSS* XVI (1971) 33-34.

Bauer, H., and P. Leander. *Grammatik des Biblisch-Aramäischen*. Halle, 1927.

Bauer, H., and B. Meissner. "Ein Aramäischer Pactvertrag aus dem 7. Jahre Darius' I," *Sitzungsberichte der Preussischen*

Akademie der Wissenschaften, Philos.-Hist. Klasse. Berlin, 1936. Pp. 414-24.

Baumgartner, Walter. "Zur Mandäerfrage," *HUCA* XXIII (1950-51) 41-71. Published with additional notes in *Zum alten Testament und seiner Umwelt*. Leiden, 1959. Pp. 332-57.

Bendavid, Abba. *Biblical Hebrew and Mishnaic Hebrew*, Vol. I. Tel-Aviv, 1967 (Heb.).

Ben-Hayyim, Z. *The Literary and Oral Traditions of Hebrew and Aramaic amongst the Samaritans*, Vols. II and III, 2. Jerusalem, 1957, 1967 (Heb.).

______. "Samaritan," in Franz Rosenthal, ed., *An Aramaic Handbook*, Part II. Wiesbaden, 1967.

Benoit, P., J. T. Milik, and R. de Vaux. *Les grottes de Murabbaᶜat*, Vol. II of *DJD*. Oxford, 1961.

Beyer, Klaus. "Der reichsaramäische Einschlag in der ältesten syrischen Literatur," *ZDMG* CXVI (1966) 242-54.

Bezold, Carl. "Aus der Antwort auf diesen Brief," *ZA* XXV (1911) 357-58.

______. *Babylonisch-assyrisches Glossar*. Heidelberg, 1926.

Black, Matthew. "Aramaic Studies and the Language of Jesus," *In Memoriam Paul Kahle*, ed. Matthew Black and Georg Fohrer (*BZAW*, Vol. CIII). Berlin, 1968. Pp. 17-28.

Blau, Joshua. *On Pseudo-Corrections in Some Semitic Languages*. Jerusalem, 1970.

______. "The Origins of Open and Closed e in Proto-Syriac," *BSOAS* (1969) 1-9.

______. "Some Difficulties in the Reconstruction of 'Proto-Hebrew' and 'Proto-Canaanite,'" *In Memoriam Paul Kahle*, ed. Matthew Black and Georg Fohrer (*BZAW*, Vol. CIII). Berlin, 1968. Pp. 29-43.

Bloomfield, Leonard. *Language*. London, 1935.

Borger, R. "Assyriologische und altarabische Miszellen," *Or.* n.s. XXVI (1957) 1-11.

______. Review of *CAD* E, *Bi.Or.* XVIII (1961) 151-54.

Bowman, R. A. *Aramaic Ritual Texts from Persepolis* (*OIP*, Vol. XCI). Chicago, 1970.

______. "Arameans, Aramaic, and the Bible," *JNES* VII (1948) 65-90.

______. "An Interpretation of the Assur Ostracon," in L. Waterman, *Royal Correspondence of the Assyrian Empire*, Vol. IV. Ann Arbor, 1936. Pp. 275-82.

Brand, Yehoshua. *Klei HaHeres BeSifrut HaTalmud*. Jerusalem, 1953.

Bresciani, E., and M. Kamil. *Le lettere aramaiche di Hermopoli*, *AANL*, "Memorie," Scienze Morali, Series VIII, Vol. XII. Rome, 1966. Pp. 357-428.

Brinkman, J. A. *A Political History of Post-Kassite Babylonia, 1158-722 B.C.* (*An.Or.*, Vol. XLIII). Rome, 1968.

Brockelmann, Carl. *Grundriss der vergleichenden Grammatik der semitischen Sprachen*, Vols. I, II. Berlin, 1908, 1913.

______. *Lexicon Syriacum*. 2d ed. Halle, 1928.

______. Review of H. H. Rowley, *The Aramaic of the Old Testament*, *MGWJ* LXXVI (1932) 84-87.

Brønno, E. "Samaritan Hebrew and Origen's Secunda," *JSS* XIII (1968) 192-201.

Buccellati, Giorgio. *The Amorites of the Ur III Period*. Naples, 1966.

______. "An Interpretation of the Akkadian Stative as a Nominal Sentence," *JNES* XXVII (1968) 1-12.

Buxtorf, J. *Lexicon Chaldaicum, Talmudicum et Rabbinicum*, ed. B. Fischer. Leipzig, 1875.

Cantineau, J. *Grammaire du Palmyrénien épigraphique*. Cairo, 1935.

______. *Le Nabatéen*, Vols. I, II. Paris, 1930, 1932.

Caquot, André. "Une inscription araméenne d'époque assyrienne," in *Hommages a André Dupont-Sommer*. Paris, 1971. Pp. 9-16.

Carmignac, Jean. "Un aramaîsme biblique et qumrânien: l'infinitif placé après son complément d'object," *RQ* V (1966) 503-20.

Cowley, A. E. *Aramaic Papyri of the Fifth Century B.C.* Oxford, 1923.

______. *The Samaritan Liturgy*. Oxford, 1909.

Cross, F. M., and D. N. Freedman. *Early Hebrew Orthography*. New Haven, 1952.

Cross, F. M., and R. J. Saley. "Phoenician Incantations on a Plaque of the Seventh Century B.C. from Arslan Tash in Upper Syria," *BASOR*, No. 197 (1970) pp. 42-49.

Dalman, Gustaf H. *Aramäisch-neuhebräisches Handwörterbuch zu Targum, Talmud und Midrasch*. Göttingen, 1938; reprint Hildesheim, 1967.

______. *Grammatik des jüdisch-palästinischen Aramäisch*. Leipzig, 1905; reprint Darmstadt, 1960.

Degen, Rainer. *Altaramäische Grammatik der Inschriften des 10.-8. Jh. v. Chr.* (*AbKM*, Vol. XXXVIII, 3). Wiesbaden, 1969.

Delaporte, Louis. *Épigraphes Araméens*. Paris, 1912.

Deller, K. "Zur Syntax des Infinitivs im Neuassyrischen," *Or.* n.s. XXXI (1962) 225-35.

______, and M. Dahood. Review of Moscati, *Comparative Grammar*, *Or.* n.s. XXXIV (1965) 35-44.

Deroy, Louis. *L'Emprunt linguistique*. Paris, 1956.

Diakonoff, I. M. *Semito-Hamitic Languages*. Moscow, 1965.

Dietrich, Manfried. *Die Aramäer Südbabyloniens in der Sargonidenzeit* (*AOAT*, Vol. VII). Neukirchen-Vluyn, 1970.

______. "Untersuchungen zur Grammatik des Neubabylonischen I.

Die neubabylonischen Sudjunktionen," *Lišān mithurti* (*AOAT*, Vol. I). Neukirchen-Vluyn, 1969. Pp. 65-97.

Diez Macho, Alejandro. *Neophyti I*: Vol. I, *Genesis*; Vol. II, *Exodo*; Vol. III, *Levitico*. Madrid and Barcelona, 1968, 1970, 1971.

Donner, H., and W. Röllig. *Kanaanäische und aramäische Inschriften*: Vol. I, *Texte* (1962; rev. ed., 1966); II, *Kommentar* (1964; rev. ed. 1968); Vol. III, *Glossare, Indizes, Tafeln* (1964). Wiesbaden.

Doubles, Malcolm C. "Indications of Antiquity in the Orthography and Morphology of the Fragment Targum," *In Memoriam Paul Kahle*, ed. Matthew Black and Georg Fohrer (*BZAW*, Vol. CIII). Berlin, 1968. Pp. 79-89.

Driver, G. R. *Aramaic Documents of the Fifth Century B.C.* Oxford, 1954; abridged ed., Oxford, 1957.

______. "The Aramaic Papyri from Egypt; Notes on Obscure Passages," *JRAS*, 1932, pp. 77-90.

______. "A Babylonian Tablet with an Aramaic Endorsement," *Iraq* IV (1937) 16-18.

______. "Brief Notes," *PEQ*, 1945, pp. 5-14.

______. "Problems in Aramaic and Hebrew Texts," *An.Or.* XII (1935) 46-70.

Drower, E. S. *The Book of the Zodiac*. London, 1949.

______, and R. Macuch. *A Mandaic Dictionary*. Oxford, 1963.

Dupont-Sommer, André. *Les Araméens*. Paris, 1949.

______. "Sur les débuts de l'histoire araméenne," (Suppl. *VT* I. Leiden, 1953. Pp. 40-49.

Ebeling, Erich. *Das aramäisch-mittelpersische Glossar Frahang-i-Pahlavik im Lichte der assyriologischen Forschung* (*MAOG*, Vol. XIV, 1). Leipzig, 1941.

Edzard, D. O. "Mari und Aramäer?" *ZA* n.f. XXII (1964) 142-49.

______. Review of *MAD*, No. 3, *ZA* n.f. XX (1961) 259-64.

Eilers, W. *Iranische Beamtennamen in der keilschriftlichen Überlieferung*, Vol. I (*AbKM*, Vol. XXV, 5). Leipzig, 1940.

______. "Neue aramäische Urkunden aus Ägypten," *AfO* XVII (1954-56) 322-35.

Ellenbogen, Maximilian. *Foreign Words in the Old Testament: Their Origin and Etymology*. London, 1962.

Epstein, J. N. "Biblisch-Talmudisches," *OLZ* XX (1917) 274-78.

______. "Gloses babylo-araméennes," *REJ* LXXIII (1921) 27-58.

______. *Grammar of Babylonian Aramaic*. Tel Aviv, 1960 (Heb.).

______. "Notes on Post-Talmudic-Aramaic Lexicography," *The Jewish Quarterly Review* XII (1922) 299-390.

______. *Prolegomena ad letteras amoraiticas*. Jerusalem, 1962 (Heb.).

______. "Zum magischen Texte," *JAOS* XXXIII (1913) 279-80.

Falk, Zeev W. "Neo-Babylonian Law in the Halakhah," *Tarbiz* XXXVII (1967) 39-47 (Heb.).

Falkenstein, A. *Das Sumerische*, in *Handbuch der Orientalistik*, Vol. II. Leiden, 1959.
______. "Sumerische Bauausdrücke," *Or*. n.s. XXXV (1966) 229-46.
Fitzmyer, Joseph A. *The Aramaic Inscriptions of Sefire* ("Biblica et Orientalia," Vol. XIX). Rome, 1967.
______. *The Genesis Apocryphon of Qumran Cave I*. 2d ed., rev.; Rome, 1971.
Fraenkel, S. *Die aramäischen Fremdwörter im Arabischen*. Leiden, 1886; reprint, Hildesheim, 1962.
Frayha, A. *A Dictionary of the Non-Classical Vocables in the Spoken Arabic of Lebanon Collected and Annotated*. Beirut, 1947 (Arab.).
Friedrich, Johannes. "Die aramäischen Tonurkunden," in *Die Inschriften vom Tell Halaf* (*AfO* Beiheft VI). Berlin, 1940. Pp. 70 ff.
______. *Phönizisch-punische Grammatik* (*An.Or.*, Vol. XXXII). Rome, 1951. 2d ed., with W. Röllig (*An.Or.*, Vol. XLVI). Rome, 1970.
______. "Zur Stellung des Jaudischen innerhalb der nordwest-semitischen sprachgeschichte," *AS*, No. 16 (1965) pp. 425-29.
Furlani, G. "Tre trattati astrologici siriaci sulle eclissi solare e lunare," *AANL, Rendiconti*, Series VIII, Vol. II (1947) pp. 576-606.
Garbini, Giovanni. *L'Aramaico antico* (*AANL*, "Memorie," Scienzi Morali, Series VIII, Vol. VII). Rome, 1956. Pp. 235-85.
Geers, Frederick W. "The Treatment of Emphatics in Akkadian," *JNES* IV (1945) 65-67.
Gelb, I. J. *Glossary of Old Akkadian* (*MAD*, No. 3). Chicago, 1957.
______. "La lingua degli Amoriti," *AANL, Rendiconti*, Classe. . . Morali, Series VIII, Vol. XIII (1958) pp. 143-64.
______. *Old Akkadian Writing and Grammar* (*MAD*, No. 2). 2d ed., Chicago, 1961.
______. "The Word for Dragoman in the Ancient Near East," *Glossa* II (1968) 93-104.
Ginsberg, H. L. "An Aramaic Contemporary of the Lachish Letters," *BASOR*, No. 111 (1948) pp. 24-27.
______. "Aramaic Dialect Problems," *AJSL* L (1933) 1-9.
______. "Aramaic Dialect Problems. II," *AJSL* LII (1936) 95-103.
______. "Aramaic Letters," *ANET*, ed. James B. Pritchard. 3d ed., Princeton, 1969. Pp. 491-92, 633.
______. "Aramaic Studies Today," *JAOS* LXII (1942) 229-38.
______. *The Legend of King Keret* (*BASOR* "Supplementary Studies," Nos. 2-3). New Haven, 1946.
______. "The North-West Semitic Languages," in B. Mazar, ed.,

World History of the Jewish People, Vol. II. Tel Aviv, 1967. Pp. 62-75 (Heb.).
______. *Studies in Koheleth*. New York, 1950.
______. "Ugaritic Myths, Epics and Legends," *ANET*, ed. James B. Pritchard. 2d ed., Princeton, 1955. Pp. 129-55.
Ginzberg, Louis. "Beiträge zur Lexikographie des Jüdisch-Aramäischen. II," *MGWJ* LXXVIII (1934) 9-33.
Goetze, A. "The Akkadian Masculine Plural in -anu/i and Its Semitic Background," *Language* XXII (1946) 121-30.
______. "An Old Babylonian Prayer of the Divination Priest," *JCS* XXII (1968) 25-29.
______. Review of Ravn, *Relative Clauses, JCS* I (1947) 73-80.
Gordon, cyrus H. "The Aramaic Incantation in Cuneiform," *AfO* XII (1937-39) 105-17.
______. "The Cuneiform Aramaic Incantation," *Or.* n.s. IX (1940) 29-38.
______. *Ugaritic Textbook* (*An.Or.*, Vol. XXXVIII). Rome, 1965; with Supplement, 1967.
Greenberg, Joseph H. "The Patterning of Root Morphemes in Semitic," *Word* VI (1950) 162-81.
______. "Some Universals of Grammar with Particular Reference to the Order of Meaningful Elements," in J. Greenberg, ed., *Universals of Language*. Cambridge, 1966. Pp. 73-113.
Greenfield, Jonas C. "Amurrite, Ugaritic and Canaanite," *Proceedings*. Jerusalem, 1969. Pp. 92-101.
______. "Bḥinot Leshoniyot biKtovet Sfire," *Leš*. XXVII-XXVIII (1963-64) 303-13.
______. "Dialect Traits in Early Aramaic," *Leš*. XXXII (1968) 359-68 (Heb.).
______. "The Etymology of *ʾmtḥt*," *ZAW* LXXVII (1965) 90-92.
______. "The Lexical Status of Mishnaic Hebrew." Ph.D. diss., Yale University, 1956.
______. "Lexicographical Notes I," *HUCA* XXIX (1958) 203-28.
______. "Lexicographical Notes II," *HUCA* XXX (1959) 141-51.
______. "Samaritan Hebrew and Aramaic in the Work of Prof. Zev Ben-Ḥayyim," *Biblica* XLV (1964) 261-68.
______. "The Small Caves of Qumran," *JAOS* LXXXIX (1969) 128-41.
______. "Studies in Aramaic Lexicography I," *JAOS* LXXXII (1962) 290-99.
______. "Three Notes on the Sefire Inscriptions," *JSS* XI (1966) 98-105.
______. Review of Ben-Hayyim, *Literary and Oral Traditions*, Vol. III, 2, *Biblica* L (1969) 98-102.
Grondahl, Frauke. *Die Personennamen der Texte aus Ugarit*. Rome, 1967.
Hallo, W. W. *Early Mesopotamian Royal Titles*. New Haven, 1957.
______. "The Road to Emar," *JCS* XVIII (1964) 57-88.

Happ, Heinz. "Zu ásgándēs, áskandēs, ástandēs = 'Bote,'" *Glotta* XL (1962) 198-201.
Haugen, Einar. "The Analysis of Linguistic Borrowing," *Language* XXVI (1950) 210-31.
Held, Moshe. "A Faithful Lover in an Old Babylonian Dialogue," *JCS* XV (1961) 1-26.
______. "The Root *ZBL/SBL* in Akkadian, Ugaritic and Biblical Hebrew," *JAOS* LXXXVIII (1968) 90-96.
Henning, W. "Arabisch *ḫarağ*," *Or.* n.s. IV (1935) 291-93.
Henshaw, Richard A. "The Office of *šaknu* in Neo-Assyrian Times. I, II," *JAOS* LXXXVII (1967) 517-25, LXXXVIII (1968) 461-83.
Hillers, Delbert T. "Ugaritic šnpt 'Wave-Offering,'" *BASOR*, No. 198 (1970) pp. 42.
Hoffmann, G. "Lexikalisches," *ZAW* II (1882) 53-72.
Holma, H. *Die Namen der Körperteile im Assyrisch-Babylonischen, eine lexikalisch-etymologische Studie*. Helsinki, 1911.
______. *Die assyrisch-babylonischen Personennamen der Form quttulu*. Helsinki, 1914.
Hope, T. E. "Loan-Words as Cultural and Lexical Symbols," *Archivum Linguisticum* XIV (1962) 111-21, XV (1963) 29-42.
Hrozný, Fr. *Das Getreide im alten Babylonien*. Wien, 1913.
Huffmon, H. B. *Amorite Personal Names in the Mari Texts: A Structural and Lexical Study*. Baltimore, 1965.
Hyatt, J. P. *The Treatment of Final Vowels in Early Neo-Babylonian*. New Haven, 1941.
Jacobovitz, J. "LeInyan 'prqd,'" *Leš.* XXXI (1967) 240.
Jastrow, Marcus. *A Dictionary of the Targumim, the Talmud Babli and Yerushalmi, and the Midrashic Literature*. 2 vols.; reprint, New York, 1950.
Jean, Charles-F., and Jacob Hoftijzer. *Dictionnaire des inscriptions sémitiques de l'ouest*. Leiden, 1965.
Jouon. P. "Notes grammaticales, lexicographiques et philologiques sur les papyrus araméens d'Egypte," *Mélanges de l'Université Saint-Joseph* XVIII (1934) 1-90.
Kaddari, M. Z. "Construct State and *dī-* Phrases in Imperial Aramaic," *Proceedings*. Jerusalem, 1969. Pp. 102-15.
______. "Studies in the Syntax of Targum Onkelos," *Tarbiz* XXXII (1963) 232-51 (Heb.).
Kaufman, Stephen A. "Akkadian and Babylonian Aramaic—New Examples of Mutual Elucidation," *Leš.* XXXVI (1972) 28-33; XXXVII (1973) 102-4 (Heb., with English summary).
______. "The Job Targum from Qumran," *JAOS* XCIII (1973) 317-27.
______. "'Siʾgabbar, Priest of Sahr in Nerab,'" *JAOS* XC (1970) 270-71.
Kent, Roland G. *Old Persian*. 2d ed., rev.; New Haven, 1953.
Knudsen, E. E. "Spirantization of Velars in Akkadian," *Lišān*

mitḫurti (*AOAT*, Vol. I). Neukirchen-Vluyn, 1969. Pp. 147-55.

Köbert, R. "Gedanken zum semitischen Wort- und Satzbau, 1-7," *Or.* n.s. XIV (1945) 273-83.

Koehler, L., and W. Baumgartner. *Lexicon in Veteris Testamenti Libros*, with *Supplementum ad Lexicon* . . . . Leiden, 1958; 3d ed., rev., 1967.

Kohut, A. *Aruch Completum*. 8 vols.; reprint, New York, 1955.

Koopmans, J. J. *Aramäische Chrestomathie*. Leiden, 1962.

Koskinen, K. "Kompatibilität in den dreikonsonantigen hebräischen Wurzeln," *ZDMG* CXIV (1964) 16-58.

Kraeling, Emil G. *The Brooklyn Museum Aramaic Papyri*. New Haven, 1953.

Krauss, S. *Griechische und lateinische Lehnwörter im Talmud, Midrasch und Targum*. 2 vols.; Berlin, 1898-99.

______. *Qadmoniyot HaTalmud*. 2 vols.; Berlin and Wien, 1924, 1929; Tel Aviv, 1929.

______, B. Geiger *et al.* *Additamenta ad librum Aruch Completum*. Reprint, New York, 1955.

Kuiper, Gerard J. *The Pseudo-Jonathan Targum and Its Relationship to Targum Onkelos*. Rome, 1972.

______. "A Study of the Relationship between *A Genesis Apocryphon* and the Pentateuchal Targumim in Genesis 14_{1-12}," *In Memoriam Paul Kahle*, ed. Matthew Black and Georg Fohrer (*BZAW*, Vol. CIII). Berlin, 1968. Pp. 149-61.

Kutscher, Eduard Yechezkel. "Aramaic," in *Encyclopedia Judaica* III 259-87. Jerusalem, 1971.

______. "Aramaic Calque in Hebrew," *Tarbiz* XXXIII (1963) 118-30 (Heb.).

______. "Aramit," *Enṣiqlopedya Miqrait* I 383-93. Jerusalem, 1950.

______. "HaAramait HaMiqrait—Aramit Mizrahit hi o Maaravit?" *First World Congress of Jewish Studies* I 123-27. Jerusalem, 1952.

______. *A History of Aramaic*, Part I. Hebrew University, Jerusalem, 1972-73.

______. "Contemporary Studies in North-Western Semitic," *JSS* X (1965) 21-51.

______. "kwk (uvne mišpaḥta)," *Eretz Israel* VIII (1967) 273-79.

______. *The Language and Linguistic Background of the Isaiah Scroll*. Jerusalem, 1959 (Heb.).

______. "The Language of the 'Genesis Apocryphon': A Preliminary study," *Scripta Hierosolymitana* IV (1965) 1-35.

______. "The Language of the Hebrew and Aramaic Letters of Bar-Koseva and his Contemporaries. A. The Aramaic Letters," *Leš.* XXV (1960-61) 117-33 (Heb.).

______. "LeSheelot Milloniyot Maḥoz = Namal," *Leš.* VIII (1937) 136-45.
______. "Marginal Notes to the Biblical Lexicon," *Leš.* XXVII-XXVIII (1963-64) 183-88, XXX (1966) 18-24 (Heb.).
______. "Marginal Notes to the Mishnaic Lexicon and a Grammatical Note," *Leš.* XXXI (1967) 107-17 (Heb.).
______. "Mittelhebräisch und Jüdisch-Aramäisch im neuen Köhler-Baumgartner," Suppl. *VT* XVI (1967) 158-75.
______. "New Aramaic Texts," *JAOS* LXXIV (1954) 233-48.
______. "On the Terminology of Documents in Talmudic and Gaonic Literature," *Tarbiz* XVII (1946) 125-27, XIX (1947) 53-59, 125-28 (Heb.).
______. "pḥw and Its Cognates," *Tarbiz* XXX (1961) 112-19 (Heb.).
______. "Studies in Galilean Aramaic," *Tarbiz* XXI (1951) 192-205; XXII (1952) 53-63, 185-92; XXIII (1953) 36-60; reprint, Jerusalem, 1969 (Heb.).
______. "Two 'Passive' Constructions in Aramaic in the Light of Persian," *Proceedings*. Pp. 132-151.
______. "Ugaritica Marginalia," *Les.* XXXIV (1969-70) 5-19 (Heb., with English summary).
______. *Words and Their History*. Jerusalem, 1961 (Heb.).
______. "Das zur Zeit Jesu gesprochene Aramäisch," *ZNW* LI (1960) 46-54.
______. Review of Fitzmyer, *Genesis Apocryphon*, *Or.* n.s. XXXIX (1970) 178-83.
______. Review of Rosenthal, *Die aramaistische Forschung*, *Kiryat Sepher* XIX (1942-43) 177-81.
Lambert, W. G. *Babylonian Wisdom Literature*. Oxford, 1960.
Landsberger, Benno. "Akkadisch-hebräische Wortgleichungen," Suppl. *VT* XVI (1967) 176-204.
______. "Bemerkungen zur altbabylonischen Briefliteratur," *ZDMG* LXIX (1915) 491-528.
______. *The Date Palm and Its By-products according to the Cuneiform Sources* (*AfO* Beiheft XVII). Graz, 1967.
______. *Die Fauna des alten Mesopotamien nach der 14. Tafel der Serie Ḫar-ra = ḫubullu*. Leipzig, 1934.
______. *The Fauna of Ancient Mesopotamia* (*MSL*, Vol. VIII). Rome, 1962.
______. "Jahreszeiten im Sumerisch-akkadischen," *JNES* VIII (1949) 248-97.
______. *Der kultische-Kalender der Babylonier und Assyrer* ("Leipziger semitistische Studien, Vol. VI, 1-2). Leipzig, 1915.
______. *Samʾal*. Ankara, 1948.
______. "Über Farben im Sumerisch-akkadischen," *JCS* XXI (1967) 139-73.

______. "Zu den aramäischen Beschwörungen in Keilschrift," *AfO* XII (1937-39) 246-57.
______. "Zur Mehlbereitung im Altertum," *OLZ* XXV (1922) 337-44.
______, and O. R. Gurney, "Practical Vocabulary of Assur," *AfO* XVIII (1958) 328-41.
Leander, P. *Laut- und Formenlehre des Ägyptisch-Aramäischen.* Göteborg, 1928.
______. *Ueber die sumerischen Lehnwörter im Assyrischen.* Uppsala, 1903.
Leslau, Wolf. *Ethiopic and South Arabic Contributions to the Hebrew Lexicon* (University of California "Publications in Semitic Philology," Vol. XX). Berkeley and Los Angeles, 1958.
Levine, Baruch A. "The Language of the Magical Bowls," in Jacob Neusner, *A History of the Jews in Babylonia*, Vol. V. Leiden, 1970. Pp. 343-75.
______. "*Mulūgu/Melûg*: The Origins of a Talmudic Legal Institution," *JAOS* LXXXVIII (1968) 271-85.
______. "Notes on an Aramaic Dream Text from Egypt," *JAOS* LXXXIV (1964) 18-22.
Levy, Jacob. *Chaldäisches Wörterbuch über die Targumim.* 2 vols.; Leipzig, 1881.
______. *Neuhebräisches und chaldäisches Wörterbuch über die Talmudim und Midraschim.* 4 vols.; Leipzig, 1876-89.
Lewy, H. *Die semitischen Fremdwörter im Griechischen.* Berlin, 1895.
Lewy, Julius. "Amurritica," *HUCA* XXXII (1961) 31-74.
______. "Apropos of the Akkadian Numerals *iš-ti-a-na* and *iš-tí-na*," *Ar.Or.* XVII (1949) 110-23.
______. "Old Assyrian *puruʾum* and *pūrum*," *RHA*, fasc. 36 (1938) pp. 117-24.
______. "The Old Assyrian Surface Measure *šubtum*," *Analecta Biblica* XII (1959) 216-26.
______. "Zur Amoriterfrage," *ZA* n.f. IV (1928-29) 243-72.
Lidzbarski, Mark. *Altaramäische Urkunden aus Assur* (*Wissenschaftliche Veröffentlichungen der Deutschen Orient-Gesellschaft*, Vol. XXXVIII). Leipzig, 1921.
______. *Ginzā, der Schatz oder das grosse Buch der Mandäer* ("Quellen der Religionsgeschichte," Vol. XIII). Göttingen, 1925.
______. *Handbuch der nordsemitischen Epigraphik.* Weimar, 1898.
______. *Das Johannesbuch der Mandäer.* Giessen, 1915.
______. *Mandäische Liturgien.* Berlin, 1920; reprint Hildesheim, 1962.
Liverani, Mario. "Antecedenti dell'onomastica Aramaica antica," *RSO* XXXVII (1962) 65-76.
______. "Elementi innovativi nell'Ugaritico non-letterario,"

AANL, Rendiconti, Series VIII, Vol. XIX (1964) pp. 173-91.

Löw, Immanuel. "Lexikalische Miszellen," in *Festschrift zum siebzigsten Geburtstage David Hoffman's.* Berlin, 1914. Pp. 119-38.

Macuch, Rudolf. "Anfänge der Mandäer," in F. Altheim and R. Stiehl, *Die Araber in der alten Welt* II 76-190.

______. *Handbook of Classical and Modern Mandaic.* Berlin, 1965.

Mannes, S. *Über den Einfluss des Aramäischen auf den Wortschatz der Mišnah an Nominal- und Verbalstämmen.* Berlin, 1899.

Margoliouth, J. P. Supplement to the *Thesaurus Syriacus.* Oxford, 1927.

Masson, Émilia. *Recherches sur les plus anciens emprunts sémitiques en Grec.* Paris, 1967.

Mazar, B. "The Aramean Empire and Its Relations with Israel," *BA* XXV (1962) 97-120.

Meissner, B. "Lexikographische Studien," *OLZ* XXV (1922) 241-47.

______. Review of Zimmern, *Beiträge zur Kenntnis, ZA* XV (1900) 412-21.

Milik, J. T. "Les papyrus araméens d'Hermoupolis et les cultes syro-phéniciens en Égypte perse," *Biblica* XLVIII (1967) 546-623.

______. "Parchemin judéo-araméen de Doura-Europos, an 200 AP. J.-C.," *Syria* XLV (1968) 97-104.

Mitchell, T. C. "A South Arabian Tripod Offering Saucer Said to Be from Ur," *Iraq* XXXI (1969) 112-14.

Montgomery, James A. *Aramaic Incantation Texts from Nippur* (*PBS*, Vol. III). Philadelphia, 1913.

______. "Babylonian *niš* 'oath' in West-Semitic," *JAOS* XXXVII (1917) 329-30.

Morag, S. Review of Kutscher, *Language and Linguistic Background, Kiryat Sepher* XXXVI (1961) 24-32 (Heb.).

Moran, William S. "A New Fragment of DIN.TIR.KI = *Bābilu* and *Enūma Eliš* vi 61-66," *Analecta Biblica* XII (1959) 257-65.

______. "Some Akkadian Names of the Stomachs of Ruminants," *JCS* XXI (1967) 178-82.

Moscati, Sabatino. "Lo stato assoluto dell'Aramaico orientale," Instituto Orientale di Napoli, *Annali,* Sezione Linguistica, IV (1962) 79-83.

______, *et al. An Introduction to the Comparative Grammar of the Semitic Languages.* Wiesbaden, 1964.

Muffs, Yochanan. *Studies in the Aramaic Legal Papyri from Elephantine.* Leiden, 1969.

Nathan, N. M. "Aus talmudischen Kontrakten," *OLZ* VI (1903) 182-83.

Naveh, Joseph. *The Development of the Aramaic Script.* Jerusalem, 1970.

______. "The Origin of the Mandaic Script," *BASOR*, No. 198 (1970) pp. 32-37.

Nöldeke, Theodor. "Aus einem Briefe des Herrn Prof. Th. Nöldeke an C. Bezold," *ZA* XXV (1911) 355-57.

______. *Compendious Syriac Grammar*, J. A. Chrichton, trans. London, 1904; a translation of *Kurzgefasste syrische Grammatik*, reprint, Darmstadt, 1966.

______. *Mandäische Grammatik*. Halle, 1875; reprint, Darmstadt, 1964.

______. *Neue Beiträge zur semitischen Sprachwissenschaft.* Strassburg, 1910.

Nyberg, H. S. *Hilfsbuch des Pehlevi*. 2 vols.; Uppsala, 1928, 1931; 2d ed., *A Manual of Pahlavi*, Vol. I; Wiesbaden, 1964.

Oksaar, Els. "Bilingualism," in T. A. Sebeok, ed., *Current Trends in Linguistics*, Vol. IX. The Hague, 1972. Pp. 476-511.

Oppenheim, A. Leo. "Akk. *arad ekalli* = 'Builder,'" *Ar.Or.* XVIII (1949) 227-35.

______. ed. *The Assyrian Dictionary of the Oriental Institute of the University of Chicago*. 12 vols. to date; Chicago and Glückstadt, 1956--.

______. "Essay on Overland Trade in the First Millennium B.C.," *JCS* XXI (1967) 236-54.

______. "A Fiscal Practice of the Ancient Near East," *JNES* VI (1947) 116-20.

______. *The Interpretation of Dreams in the Ancient Near East* ("Transactions of the American Philosophical Society, Vol. XLVI, 3). Philadelphia, 1956.

______, and L. F. Hartman. *On Beer and Brewing Techniques in Ancient Mesopotamia* (*JAOS* Suppl. X). New Haven, 1950.

Payne, Smith, R. *Thesaurus Syriacus*. 2 vols.; Oxford, 1879, 1901.

Pennacchietti, F. A. *Studi sui pronomi determinative semitici* ("Pubblicazioni del Seminario di Seministica, Richerche," Vol. IV). Napoli, 1968.

Perles, Felix. "Babylonisch-talmudische Glossen," *OLZ* VIII (1905) 335-39, 381-85. "Nachträge," IX (1906) 227-28.

______. "Ergänzungen zu den 'Akkadischen Fremdwörtern,'" *OLZ* XXI (1918) 65-72.

______. "Lexikalisches Allerlei," *MGWJ* LXXVI (1932) 285-99.

Petschow, Herbert. *Neubabylonisches Pfandrecht*. Berlin, 1956.

Polotsky, H. J. "Aramaic, Syriac, and Geʾez," *JSS* IX (1964) 1-10.

Porten, Bezalel. *Archives from Elephantine*. Berkeley and Los Angeles, 1968.

______, and J. C. Greenfield. "The Aramaic Papyri from Hermopolis," *ZAW* LXXX (1968) 216-31.

Rabin, C. "Hittite Words in Hebrew," *Or.* n.s. XXXII (1963) 113-39.

______. "Milim BeIvrit HaMiqrait MiLašon HaIndo-Aryim SeBeMizraḥ HaQarov," in *Sefer Shmuel Yeivin*. Jerusalem, 1970.

______. "The Nature and Origin of the Šafʾel in Hebrew and Aramaic," *Eretz Israel* IX (1969) 148-58 (Heb.).

Ravn, O. E. *The So-Called Relative Clauses in Accadian or the Accadian Particle ša*. Copenhagen, 1941.

Reiner, Erica. *A Linguistic Analysis of Akkadian*. The Hague, 1966.

Renger, Johannes. "Überlegungen zum akkadischen Syllabar," *ZA* LXI (1971) 23-43.

Rimalt, E. S. "Wechselbeziehungen zwischen dem Aramäischen und dem Neubabylonischen," *WZKM* XXXIX (1932) 100-122.

Röllig, W. Review of Salonen, *Türen*, *WZKM* LXII (1969) 298-301.

Rosenthal, Franz, ed. *An Aramaic Handbook*. 2 vols.; Wiesbaden, 1967.

______. *Die aramaistische Forschung seit Theodor Nöldeke's Veröffentlichungen*. Leiden, 1939.

______. *A Grammar of Biblical Aramaic*. Wiesbaden, 1963.

______. "Notes on the Third Aramaic Inscription from Sefîre-Sûjîn," *BASOR*, No. 158 (1960) pp. 28-31.

______. *Die Sprache der palmyrenischen Inschriften und ihre Stellung innerhalb des Aramäischen* (*MVAG*, Vol. XLI, 1). Leipzig, 1936.

Rundgren, Fr. "Parallelen zu Akk. *šinēpūm* '2/3,'" *JCS* IX (1955) 29-30.

______. "Semitische Wortstudien," *Orientalia Suecana* X (1961) 99-136.

______. *Über Bildungen mit* (ʾ)*š- und n-t- Demonstrativen im Semitischen*. Uppsala, 1955.

Salonen, Armas. *Agricultura Mesopotamica*. Helsinki, 1968.

______. "Akkad. *mušannītu* = Arab. *musannāh*," *Or.* n.s. XXXII (1963) 449-51.

______. *Die Fussbekleidung der alten Mesopotamier*. Helsinki, 1969.

______. *Die Hausgeräte der alten Mesopotamier*, Vols. I, II. Helsinki, 1965, 1966.

______. *Hippologica Accadica*. Helsinki, 1955.

______. *Die Landfahrzeuge des alten Mesopotamien*. Helsinki, 1951.

______. *Die Möbel des alten Mesopotamien*. Helsinki, 1963.

______. "Die Öfen der alten Mesopotamier," *Baghdader Mitteilungen* III (1964) 100-124.

______. *Die Türen des alten Mesopotamien.* Helsinki, 1963.
______. *Die Wasserfahrzeuge in Babylonien* (*St.Or.*, Vol. VIII, 4). Helsinki, 1939.
______. *Zum Aufbau der Substrate im Sumerischen* (*St.Or.*, Vol. XXXVII, 3). Helsinki, 1968.
Salonen, E. *Glossar zu den altbabylonische Urkunden aus Susa* (*St.Or.*, Vol. XXXVI). Helsinki, 1967.
______. *Die Waffen der alten Mesopotamier* (*St.Or.*, Vol. XXXIII). Helsinki, 1965.
______. Review of *AHw.* 9, *Or.* n.s. XXXIX (1970) 441-45.
Sarfatti, G. "ʾsp = 'portico,'" *Les.* XXXI (1966) 79.
Schaeder, Hans H. *Iranische Beiträge*: Vol. I, *Schriften der Königsberger Gelehrten Gesellschaft.* Halle, 1930.
Schall, Anton. *Studien über griechische Fremdwörter im Syrischen.* Darmstadt, 1960.
Schlesinger, Michael. *Satzlehre der aramäischen Sprache des babylonischen Talmuds.* Leipzig, 1928.
Schulthess, F. "Aramäisches IV," *ZA* XXVII (1912) 230-41.
______. *Lexicon Syropalaestinum.* Berlin, 1903.
Soden, Wolfram von. *Akkadisches Handwörterbuch.* 11 fascs., *a-s*; Wiesbaden, 1959--.
______. "Aramäisches *ḥ* erscheint im Spätbabylonischen vor *m* auch als *g*," *AfO* XIX (1959-60) 149.
______. "Aramäische Worter in neuassyrischen und neu- und spätbabylonischen Texten. Ein Vorbericht. I (*agâ-*mūš*)," *Or.* n.s. XXXV (1966) 1-20; "II (*n*-z und Nachträge)," *Or.* n.s. XXXVII (1968) 261-71.
______. *Grundriss der akkadischen Grammatik* (*An.Or.*, Vol. XXXIII). Rome, 1952. Reissued together with *Ergänzungsheft zum Grundriss der akkadischen Grammatik* (*An.Or,.* Vol. XLVII). Rome, 1969.
______. "Der hymnisch-epische Dialekt des Akkadischen," *ZA* n.f. VII (1933) 90-183.
______. "izqātu, išqātu 'Kettenringe', ein aramäisches Lehnwort," *AfO* XX (1963) 155.
______. "Die Spirantisierung von Verschlusslauten im Akkadischen: ein Vorbericht," *JNES* XXVII (1968) 214-20.
______. "Vedisch *magham*, 'Geschenk'—neuarabisch maǧǧānīja, 'Gebührenfreiheit,'" *JEOL* XVIII (1964) 339-44.
______. "Vokalfärbungen im Akkadischen," *JCS* II (1948) 291-303.
______. "Zum akkadischen Wörterbuch. 1-5," *Or.* n.s. XV (1946) 423-31; "15-30," XVI (1947) 437-58.
______. "Zum akkadischen Wörterbuch," *Or.* n.s. XX (1951) 162-64.
______. "Zur Einteilung der semitischen Sprachen," *WZKM* LVI (1960) 177-91.
______. "Zur Laut- und Formenlehre des Neuassyrischen," *AfO* XVIII (1957) 121-22.

______, and W. Röllig. *Das akkadische Syllabar* (*An.Or.*, Vol. XLII). 2d ed., rev; Rome, 1967.

Sollberger, E. "Graeco-Babyloniaca," *Iraq* XXIV (1962) 63-72.

Speiser, E. A. *Oriental and Biblical Studies, Collected Writings of E. A. Speiser,* J. J. Finkelstein and M. Greenberg, eds., Philadelphia, 1967.

Starcky, J. "Un Contrat nabatéen sur papyrus," *RB* LXI (1954) 161-81.

______. "Un Texte messianique araméen de la grotte 4 de Qumran," *Travaux de l'Institut Catholique de Paris* X 51-66.

Tadmor, Hayyim. "A Note on the Seal of Mannu-ki-Inurta," *IEJ* XV (1965) 233-34.

______. "Notes to the Opening Lines of the Aramaic Treaty from Sefire," in *Sefer Shmuel Yeivin*. Jerusalem, 1970. Pp. 397-405 (Heb.).

Tal, Abraham. "The Language of the Targum of the Former Prophets and its Position within the Aramaic Dialects." Diss.; Hebrew University, 1971.

Tallqvist, Knut L. *Assyrian Personal Names*. Helsingfors, 1914.

______. "Himmelsgegenden und Winde," in *St.Or.* II (Helsinki, 1928) 105-166.

______. *Neubabylonisches Namenbuch zu den Geschäftsurkunden aus der Zeit des Šamaššumukîn bis Xerxes*. Helsingfors, 1905.

Teixidor, Javier. "Notes hatréennes," *Syria* XLIII (1966) 91-97.

Telegdi, S. "Essai sur la phonétique des emprunts Iraniens en Araméen talmudique," *JA* CCXXVI (1935) 177-256.

Thompson, R. Campbell-. *A Dictionary of Assyrian Botany*. London, 1949.

______. *A Dictionary of Assyrian Chemistry and Geology*. Oxford, 1936.

Tsereteli, K. "Über die Reflexivstämme in den modernen aramäischen Dialekten," *RSO* XXXIX (1964) 125-32.

Tur-Sinai, N. *The Language and the Book*, Vol. II. Jerusalem, 1950 (Heb.).

Ungnad, A. "Lexikalisches," *ZA* XXXI (1918) 248-76.

______. *Neubabylonische Rects- und Verwaltungsurkunden, Glossar*. Leipzig, 1937.

______. "Zur Aussprache des Spätbabylonischen," *Altorientalischen Studien, Bruno Meissner* (*MAOG*, Vol. IV). Leipzig, 1929. Pp. 222-25.

van der Ploeg, J. P. M., *et al. Le Targum de Job de la grotte XI de Qumrân*. Leiden, 1971.

van Selms, A. "Akkadian *dullu(m)* as a Loan-Word in West Semitic Languages," *JNWSL* I (1971) 51-58.

______. "The Best Man and Bride—From Sumer to St. John," *JNES* IX (1950) 65-75.

Vattioni, Francesco. "Epigrafia aramaica," *Augustinianum* X (1970) 493-532.

______. "Preliminari alle iscrizioni aramaiche," *Augustinianum* IX (1969) 305-61.

Vinnikov, I. N. "Slovar'aramejskich nadpisej (Dictionary of the Aramaic Inscriptions)," *Palestinskij Sbornik*, Vols. III (1958)-XIII (1968).

Wagner, Max. "Beiträge zur Aramaismenfrage im alttestamentlichen Hebräisch," Suppl. *VT* XVI (1967) 355-71.

______. *Die lexikalischen und grammatikalischen Aramaismen im alttestamentlichen Hebräisch* (*BZAW*, Vol. XCVI). Berlin, 1966.

Weinreich, Uriel. *Languages in Contact*. New York, 1953.

Weisberg, David B. *Guild Structure and Political Allegiance in Early Achaemenid Mesopotamia*. New Haven, 1967.

______. "Some Observations on Late Babylonian Texts and Rabbinic Literature," *HUCA* XXXIX (1968) 71-80.

Widengren, G. *Iranisch-semitische Kulturbegegnung in parthischer Zeit*. Köln and Opladen, 1960.

Wilcke, C. "ku-li," *ZA* XXV (1969) 65-99.

Yamauchi, Edwin M. *Mandaic Incantation Texts*. New Haven, 1967.

Yaron, R. "'ksp zwz' in the Elephantine Documents," *Leš*. XXXI (1967) 287-88 (Heb.).

______. "Minutiae Aramaicae," *JSS* XIII (1968) 202-11.

Zimmern, Heinrich. *Akkadische Fremdwörter als Beweis fur babylonischen Kultureinfluss*. 2d ed.; Leipzig, 1917.

______. *Babylonische Busspsalmen*. Leipzig, 1885.

______. "Nazoräer (Nazarener)," *ZDMG* LXXIV (1920) 429-38.

INDEX OF NORTH WEST SEMITIC WORDS